Rethinking
MADAM PRESIDENT

Rethinking MADAM PRESIDENT

Are We Ready for a Woman in the White House?

EDITED BY
Lori Cox Han
Caroline Heldman

BOULDER
LONDON

Published in the United States of America in 2007 by
Lynne Rienner Publishers, Inc.
1800 30th Street, Boulder, Colorado 80301
www.rienner.com

and in the United Kingdom by
Lynne Rienner Publishers, Inc.
3 Henrietta Street, Covent Garden, London WC2E 8LU

Library of Congress Cataloging-in-Publication Data
Rethinking madam president: are we ready for a woman in the White House? /
edited by Lori Cox Han and Caroline Heldman.
p. cm.
Includes bibliographical references and index.
ISBN 978-1-58826-543-2 (hardcover : alk. paper)—ISBN 978-1-58826-519-7
(pbk. : alk. paper)
1. Women presidents—United States. 2. Women political candidates—
United States. 3. Women in politics—United States. 4. United States—Politics
and government—2001– I. Han, Lori Cox. II. Heldman, Caroline, 1972–
JK516.R373 2007
324.7082'0973—dc22
2007003133

British Cataloguing in Publication Data
A Cataloguing in Publication record for this book
is available from the British Library.

Printed and bound in the United States of America

The paper used in this publication meets the requirements
of the American National Standard for Permanence of
Paper for Printed Library Materials Z39.48-1992.

5 4 3 2 1

To the first woman president
of the United States,
whoever she may be

Contents

Preface ix

1 Is the United States *Really* Ready for a Woman President?
Lori Cox Han 1

2 Cultural Barriers to a Female President in the United States
Caroline Heldman 17

3 The Significance of Social and Institutional Expectations
Sue Thomas and Jean Reith Schroedel 43

4 Shaping Women's Chances: Stereotypes and the Media
Gina Serignese Woodall and Kim L. Fridkin 69

5 Masculinity on the Campaign Trail
Georgia Duerst-Lahti 87

6 Money and the Art and Science of Candidate Viability
Victoria Farrar-Myers 113

7 Political Parties: Advancing a Masculine Ideal
Meredith Conroy 133

8 Women as Executive Branch Leaders
Karen M. Hult 147

9 Leadership Challenges in National Security
Meena Bose 169

10 A Woman in the White House? Never Say Never
Ann Gordon 185

Bibliography 193
The Contributors 217
Index 221
About the Book 229

Preface

The idea for this book first arose following a panel at the 2005 meeting of the Western Political Science Association discussing the state of women as officeholders and political appointees. By the fall of 2005, as media speculation continued to grow about 2008 being "the year" for a woman to get elected to the White House, and amid the hype over the now-cancelled but much heralded ABC drama *Commander in Chief*, we knew that it was the perfect time to bring together scholars of both the presidency and women in politics to assess what chance a woman had of being elected president in 2008. We believed that all the talk about potential candidacies and early frontrunners for both parties lacked a realistic analysis of the current political environment and the many obstacles that have always faced a woman candidate seeking the presidency. Our instincts kept telling us that despite the many news stories and public opinion polls devoted to the topic of electing a woman president (and we certainly acknowledge that the topic makes a great news story), too many issues were being glossed over. We remain optimistic that it is a question of when, not if, a woman will reach the White House, yet our knowledge of the subject suggests that it might not be as soon as some would hope. Thus, we aimed to bring together in this book the scholarship and perspectives of several political scientists to more accurately assess where the United States really is in terms of electing a woman president. We hope that the work collected here will contribute to the expanding literature devoted to this topic and provide a better understanding of the many factors affecting the unique process of electing a president in the United States.

* * *

There are many people to acknowledge for their help in guiding this project from an initial idea to its finished form. First and foremost, we want to thank all our contributors for sharing their expertise and their time; we will be eternally grateful to them. We are also indebted to our editor, Leanne Anderson, for her excitement about, enthusiasm for, and support of this project right from the start. Her knowledge and experience have proved invaluable.

Lori Cox Han would also like to thank Nadia Arriaga, for always keeping the department organized and running smoothly; Roberta Lessor, dean of Wilkinson College of Letters and Sciences, for her continued enthusiasm for this project; and Tom, Taylor, and Davis, for all their patience and support.

Caroline Heldman would like to thank her able research assistants, Georgia Faye Hirsty, Sarah Oliver, and Vanessa Belongia, for their labor. She would also like to thank her fellow faculty members at Occidental College for their support during the writing process; her former colleagues at Whittier College; Tony Barnstone for his very thoughtful comments; and Fred Bergerson, Deborah Norden, John Neu, and Mike McBride for their support and enthusiasm.

—Lori Cox Han and Caroline Heldman

1

Is the United States *Really* Ready for a Woman President?

Lori Cox Han

By the end of the 2005–2006 television season, Americans had witnessed some groundbreaking and historic—albeit fictional—events: the first woman, the first African American, and the first Hispanic American to serve as president of the United States. On ABC's *Commander in Chief*, the American television audience was introduced to President Mackenzie Allen, an Independent vice president to a Republican president who dies in office. Portrayed by Oscar-winner Geena Davis, President Allen faces many domestic and international crises during her accidental presidency, all the while juggling the demands of a husband, three children, and a widowed mother who all live together in the White House. However, despite the media hype, early high ratings, and Davis's Emmy nomination and Golden Globe win for Best Actress in a Drama Series in 2006, the show was cancelled after just one season due to low ratings. On NBC's *The West Wing*, the Emmy-award-winning series ended its seven-year run with the election and inauguration of President Matt Santos, a Hispanic congressman from Texas played by veteran television actor Jimmy Smits (previously of *LA Law* and *NYPD Blue* fame). However, loyal viewers of *The West Wing* will never know how the new president would fare in office, since the series' final episode ends with Santos's inauguration. And on the Fox action series *24*, actor Dennis Haysbert portrayed President David Palmer, an African American who was a popular and strong leader in the White House, particularly in his handling of national security issues. Unfortunately for fans of President Palmer, his character was assassinated at the start of the show's fifth season.

Although the portrayal of diversity in the White House was prominent yet somewhat fleeting during the 2005–2006 television season, it did show that at least in Hollywood, candidates pursuing the Oval Office can overcome gender and racial barriers. But can life really imitate art? Is the United States *really* ready to elect its first female, African American, or Hispanic president? Such portrayals on television or in the movies may be helpful in at least introducing the notion of "difference" to American citizens when considering images of presidential leadership that move beyond the white male club that has always dominated the Oval Office. This rethinking of the presidency, especially in regard to gender, may be contributing to the current attention paid by many political observers to whether the United States is ready to elect its first female president. According to Eleanor Clift and Tom Brazaitis in their book *Madam President: Women Blazing the Leadership Trail*, "cultural symbols prepare the way for real-life women to pursue the highest office in the land."[1]

Yet many of the fictionalized portrayals of a woman running for or serving as president seem to be out of touch with political reality, what one reporter called "the gulf between fact and fiction [that] makes the Grand Canyon look like a pothole."[2] For example, many of the plots and subplots depicted on *Commander in Chief* were inaccurate or unbelievable enough to make any political scientist cringe. To be fair, the producers of the show were likely more concerned with the entertainment value of their product than factual accuracy. This may explain why the new president (an Independent elected on a Republican ticket) selected her former Democratic rival for the vice presidency as *her* new vice president; why the Speaker of the House, who had presidential aspirations of his own, would resign his powerful leadership position and seat in Congress to serve as president for twenty-four hours while President Allen had emergency gallbladder surgery (her Democratic vice president had already resigned due to family issues); and how President Allen almost single-handedly added the Equal Rights Amendment (ERA) to the Constitution by pushing both Illinois and Florida to approve the amendment (never mind the fact that the real ERA had an extended expiration date of 1982 written into the proposed amendment and that many of the original thirty-five states that did approve the original amendment might not approve it again today). Perhaps a more realistic portrayal of the first woman president would have fared even worse in the ratings, although for those of us who study the presidency and/or women in politics, it is hard to imagine the first woman president breaking protocol to dance with the Russian president at her first state dinner while wearing an off-the-shoulder royal blue evening gown more appropriate for one of Geena Davis's red-carpet strolls at an awards show than attire for the "leader of the free world."

Nonetheless, the timing of *Commander in Chief*'s run (although limited) on the small screen was no coincidence, as it aired during a time when intense media attention was being focused on the prospects for a serious woman presidential candidate in the real world. Following the 2004 presidential election, political pundits and pollsters repeatedly asked whether the United States is ready for a woman president, and news coverage suggested that the time might be right to elect a woman to the White House. Two of the most talked-about potential candidates leading up to the 2008 presidential election have been Democratic senator Hillary Rodham Clinton of New York and Republican secretary of state Condoleezza Rice. Both women have been at the top of public opinion polls in recent years for candidates voters would like to see running for president. By the end of 2006, most news organizations had all but given the Democratic nomination to Clinton, regularly labeling her as the clear Democratic frontrunner even before she declared her candidacy (although the potential candidacy of Senator Barack Obama also began to capture much media attention by year's end). And despite Rice's pronouncements to the contrary, she is regularly questioned by the news media about her possible candidacy in 2008 or beyond. The allure of Hillary for president, Condi for president, or even Hillary versus Condi for president, seemed to be just too much for the news media to ignore. But is either of these potential candidacies as viable as news coverage would make them seem, or do these political projections resemble another Grand Canyon–sized pothole that separates fact from fiction about the first woman president?

The Real Political Environment

Several polls suggest that Americans would overwhelmingly support a woman candidate for president. For example, three separate polls in early 2006 showed a large majority of respondents saying they would vote for a woman for president. A CBS News poll found 92 percent of respondents saying they would vote for a qualified woman, a Hearst/Siena College Research Institute poll found 79 percent of respondents willing to vote for a woman, and 69 percent of respondents in the California Field Poll stated that the United States is ready for a woman president.[3] A February 2005 poll by the Siena College Research Institute found that six out of ten voters are ready for a woman president and that 81 percent of those surveyed would vote for a woman president. Potential candidates for 2008 that topped the survey included Clinton, Rice, and Senator Elizabeth Dole (R-NC).[4] These types of poll results have been common in recent years. A Gallup Poll in May 2003 found that 87 percent of Americans were willing to vote for a qualified woman for president. Similarly, a Roper Poll in February 2003 found that 76 percent of "influential Americans" think that a woman will be elected president within the next twenty years. Other polls also suggest a "desire for women's leadership at the pinnacle of government."[5]

Popular narratives of the 2008 election also revolve around the possibility of a female president, with the topic discussed frequently in both the print and broadcast press. A quick search on the Internet will also produce numerous web pages devoted to the Clinton and possible Rice candidacies. Political strategists Dick Morris and Eileen McGann's book *Condi vs. Hillary: The Next Great Presidential Race* has been widely discussed by political pundits, as has Susan Estrich's book, *The Case for Hillary Clinton.* In fact, even before she declared to run, the potential candidacy of the former First Lady spawned its own cottage industry of books devoted to whether she would run, how she could win, how she could be stopped, and/or what a second Clinton presidency would be like.[6]

Clearly, there are abundant signs in popular culture that the United States may be ready for a woman in the White House, but can that translate into electoral success for a woman candidate in 2008? What most of the media coverage and hype surrounding this issue does not take into account is the reality of the harsh political environment that a woman presidential candidate will face in 2008 and beyond. What voters say to pollsters "in theory" may represent a tremendous disconnect from what they would actually do in the voting booth if given the chance to support a woman candidate. Likewise, gains in media coverage and party treatment of female candidates do not necessarily apply to the presidency, an office that continues to be viewed as a male prerogative, and the prevailing dominance of foreign policy issues on the national agenda (including national security and the war on terrorism) may not bode well for a successful female candidacy. These issues are traditionally viewed as "male" issues, whereas domestic issues such as health care, education, and the environment continue to be viewed as softer, "female" issues.[7]

Despite the presence of polls that show readiness for a woman president in the United States, other surveys have shown a decrease in support for electing a woman president in the aftermath of the 9/11 terrorist attacks. In some polls, respondents show a preference for male leadership traits and characteristics over those of female leaders, and a belief that men are more competent to handle issues related to national security and terrorism in the post-9/11 world.[8] Those responses show that there may be some disconnect between the results of some polls suggesting the election of a woman president is imminent and the reality of how voters will actually respond. A closer look at the CBS Poll from February 2006 shows another interesting disconnect among the views of the respondents—although 92 percent said they would vote for a qualified woman for president, only 55 percent said they believe that the United States is ready for a woman president. And it is important to note that the 92 percent said they would vote for a woman *if she were qualified.*

What exactly does it mean to be qualified for president? Understanding this aspect of a presidential election is quite important, even if it does not include hard and fast rules for who can and cannot run. Technically speaking, the only constitutional requirements for a president include that he or she be at least thirty-five years of age, a natural-born citizen, and a fourteen-year resident of the United States. However, many other unofficial requirements exist, and there the prospect becomes trickier for a woman candidate. In general, viable presidential candidates must have any number of things, which can but do not always include prior political experience, name recognition, party support, adequate funding and fundraising abilities, strong appeal for the base of the party (particularly in the primaries) and appeal to independent or swing voters (particularly during the general election), and strong leadership and communication skills. As a result, "a number of informal qualifications have limited the pool of potential nominees," with factors such as religion, race, and gender making the pool of viable candidates for both president and vice president almost exclusively Protestant, white, and male.[9] The health and age of the candidate, as well as family ties and personal relationships (particularly marital status and fidelity) are also important characteristics for candidates.[10]

Although party affiliation and policy preferences are still important factors, the decline of partisan loyalty among voters in recent decades has placed more emphasis on the candidate as an individual, on character, personality, and campaigning style. In addition, political news reporting has become more cynical, sensationalized, and hypercritical, leading to an increased focus on the "cult of personality" during presidential campaigns.[11] Soft news, defined as news having no real connection to substantive policy issues, has also steadily increased since the early 1980s in response to competition within the marketplace.[12] As a result, character issues for presidential candidates often take precedence in the daily news cycle over more substantive policy issues. Americans look for honesty, integrity, intelligence, strong communication skills, flexibility, compassion, open-mindedness, and a commitment to both the public good and a democratic process in their presidential candidates.[13] For women candidates, developing an effective image based on these character traits is crucial to combating negative stereotypes in the news media; it requires emphasizing her "perceived image and issue strengths—honesty and trustworthiness and dealing with social concerns—as well as [establishing] her credibility as a tough and decisive leader able to handle such issues as crime, foreign policy, and the economy."[14]

The Post-Ferraro Drought

More than twenty years have now passed since Geraldine Ferraro's historic bid for the vice presidency as Democrat Walter Mondale's running mate in 1984, and public anticipation for the second female running mate has remained high in recent years. Yet in the five presidential elections that have come and gone since then, no major party candidate has selected a female running mate. Why has there been no progress on this front?

Perhaps most importantly, despite all the progress made in women gaining elective office since the 1980s, few women have achieved the types of positions that would place them in the pool of potential presidential candidates. State governors (particularly from large states), current or former vice presidents, and prominent US senators and members of the House of Representatives (particularly those in high-profile leadership positions) top the news media's lists of potential candidates for the next election. These "lists" are sometimes generated prior to the completion of the presidential election at hand, because political pundits want to start handicapping future presidential races; for example, Hillary Clinton's presidential ambitions were discussed long before she even ran for the US Senate in 2000. Four of the five most recent presidents, all former state governors, have also benefited from the status of being a Washington outsider (Governors Jimmy Carter of Georgia, Ronald Reagan of California, Bill Clinton of Arkansas, and George W. Bush of Texas).

Unfortunately, women candidates do not often find their way into this group of potential presidential candidates. No woman has ever served as vice president, and in Congress, no woman held a top leadership position until Nancy Pelosi became the House Democratic minority leader in 2003; the final leadership barrier was broken in the House of Representatives when Pelosi became Speaker of the House in January 2007. However, as of 2007, she still remains the only woman to hold a top congressional leadership position. Given the recent preference among US voters for executive leadership experience at the state level, women have been especially disadvantaged. As of 2007, only twenty-nine women have ever served as governor (and three succeeded their husbands in the job), and even though being governor of a large state is one of the most likely stepping stones to being considered a viable candidate for the White House, only one of the six largest electoral states (California, New York, Texas, Florida, Illinois, and Pennsylvania) has ever elected a woman as governor. (In Texas, Democrat Ann Richards served one term as governor from 1991–1995; Miriam Amanda "Ma" Ferguson, a Democrat, served as governor from 1925–1927 and 1933–1935.)

Many other factors limit the number of women in such positions. Among them is the traditional view still espoused by some Americans that men should hold public leadership roles while women remain at home tending to domestic responsibilities and childrearing. The US political system is also biased in favor of incumbents, which means that fewer women in elected office leave inadequate numbers of role models for younger women who might aspire to political careers.[15] The structural impediment of incumbency should not be overlooked: in 2004, 98 percent of House incumbents and 96 percent of Senate incumbents were reelected. Even in 2006, a midterm election year that saw Republicans lose their control of both the House and the Senate, the incumbency reelection rate in Congress was 94.3 percent. The redistricting to create safe seats at both the federal and state levels has also contributed to the incumbency glut, which may help those women currently in office but makes it harder for even more women candidates to break through that barrier. Women also tend to run for political office later in life than men due to the "double burden" of work and family responsibilities from which many professional women suffer.[16] In addition, the candidate emergence phase of a campaign—when a person moves from being a potential to an actual candidate—is still one of the biggest hurdles for women to overcome, particularly in seeking the presidency. Women are significantly less likely than men to receive encouragement (either from a current or former politician or from a financial supporter) to run for office or to deem themselves qualified to run for office.[17]

The tone and content of news media coverage of potential women candidates for the presidency also matters. Even though the news media are usually quick to herald the fact that American voters seem ready to elect a woman president, recent studies on media coverage of women candidates at all levels of government show that women are still viewed as a political anomaly, that a disproportionate amount of coverage is devoted to clothing and hairstyles, and that the mass media in general still often rely on negative stereotyping of women.[18] For example, on the election of Michelle Bachelet as president of Chile, the *Los Angeles Times* shared with its readers that Bachelet was "wearing a two-piece, cream-colored suit featuring an Asian-style jacket," as she "waved from her standing perch in an official Ford Galaxy convertible as the heavily guarded motorcade made its way toward the presidential palace."[19] It is hard to imagine news coverage of the election of a male leader in any country, including the United States, that would include a similar description of his attire.

As I have argued in an earlier volume on electing a woman president, getting elected, as opposed to governing, may be the biggest hurdle that a potential women president will face. The constitutional and institutional parameters of the office of the presidency itself will not change if a woman is elected to it.[20] Yet the male notion of leadership that is expected of presidents from the American electorate is still a major hurdle for women candidates to overcome. The executive branch is seen as "the most masculine of the three branches of government, due mostly to its hierarchical structure, the unity of command, and the ability for a president to act decisively when the need arises."[21] The presidency also "operates on the great man model of leadership," which leaves women defined as the "other" in the executive branch.[22] The expectation of "presidential machismo" also plays a role, which is "the heroic image desired by many Americans to have their president exhibit tough and aggressive behavior on the international stage."[23] This idealized and heroic vision of the presidency is often portrayed in the mass media, and perhaps no better example exists than the movie

Air Force One, in which Harrison Ford plays a president who both single-handedly and literally throws a terrorist hijacker off Air Force One while delivering the line, "Get off my plane."

Why Hillary (Probably) Won't Win and Condi (Probably) Won't Run in 2008

It is the combination of all the above-mentioned factors that contribute to the current political environment facing any potential woman candidate for president. Yet despite the fact that the task is somewhat daunting, optimism abounds among those determined to elect the first woman president sooner rather than later. For example, the White House Project, a nonpartisan organization dedicated to placing more women in top leadership positions within government and business, promoted its list of "8 for '08," which included Hillary Clinton, Condoleezza Rice, Senator Olympia Snowe (R-ME), Senator Susan Collins (R-ME), Senator Kay Bailey Hutchison (R-TX), Governor Janet Napolitano (D-AZ), Governor Kathleen Sebelius (D-KS), and Mayor Shirley Franklin (D-Atlanta). Senators Elizabeth Dole (R-NC) and Dianne Feinstein (D-CA), once touted as possible presidential or vice presidential contenders, were noticeably absent from that list (although age may have played a factor, since both Dole and Feinstein would be over seventy in 2008).[24]

Yet only two women on that list—Clinton and Rice—garnered any serious discussion of a possible run for the presidency in 2008. Clinton, of course, dominated such speculation for years, and following her declared candidacy in January 2007, she was considered possibly the strongest candidate and probable frontrunner among the Democratic candidates for the upcoming primary season. According to Dick Morris, a one-time strategist to her husband Bill, "Hillary Clinton is on a virtually uncontested trajectory to win the Democratic nomination and, very likely, the 2008 presidential election."[25] Morris adds: "The entire Democratic Party base loves her."[26] Similarly, Susan Estrich, a law professor and campaign manager to Democratic nominee Michael Dukakis in 1988, states: "Not only does [Hillary Clinton] have the most money, the best organization, and the most loyal staff among all the potential players—she's also young enough, old enough, smart enough, bold enough, and for all those reasons beloved enough by the voters of the Democratic Party."[27] But, how accurate is this assessment?

Beyond the media spin and political punditry is a candidate that perhaps has too many labels to live down and too much political baggage. For example, is she too liberal, based on her early years as First Lady and the failed campaign for health care reform, or too conservative, based on her Senate voting record in support of the war in Iraq? Although name recognition can do wonders for a presidential candidate, particularly during the invisible primary period (which consists of campaigning well before any primaries or caucuses are held), perhaps too much is known about Clinton to maintain the necessary momentum throughout the primaries. Many successful party nominees in recent years gained much of their recognition much later in the process and were not well known on the national stage (like Jimmy Carter, Bill Clinton, or George W. Bush, although the latter certainly benefited from his father's name recognition). That means that most other Democratic hopefuls have more of a clean slate going into the primaries, whereas Clinton already has many recognized detractors.[28] For all of Clinton's star power, she may be too divisive within the Democratic Party because of her support for the war in Iraq. She has been an ardent supporter of homeland security issues and sought out a seat on the Armed Services Committee. Her recent, more hawkish views on military and defense issues have already lost her support among some within the Democratic base (she has been booed by antiwar activists in public appearances), which would harm her chances in the primaries (where support from the party base is crucial).[29] Certainly, Clinton's ability to raise funds and attract big donors is a major factor in determining whether she is a viable candidate, and at least in this regard, her husband is a tremendous asset (that, and the fact that few candidates, if any, can top Bill Clinton on the campaign trail). Yet money and name recognition alone will not win a presidential election, and although the pundits who contend that Clinton is the one to beat may be right, she faces not only the same hurdles as other women candidates but some of her own unique hurdles as well. As a recent *Washington Post* article points out, "Never has a politician stepped onto a presidential stage before an audience of voters who already have so many strong and personal opinions about her . . . there is evidence of unease—about her personal history, demeanor and motives—among the very Democratic and independent voters she would need to win the presidency."[30]

The "Obama factor" should not be overlooked either. Media hype about Senator Barack Obama's (D-IL) decision to run for president highlights the desire within the Democratic Party for a strong "anyone but Hillary" candidate. A presidential run by Obama—whose father is black and mother is white—not only adds racial diversity to the Democratic field in 2008, but also the excitement over his candidacy given his relative inexperience at the national political level (having just been elected to the US Senate in 2004) suggests that voters are still looking for that Washington outsider to clean up the perceived mess inside the beltway. Obama stands in stark contrast to Clinton among Democratic voters—each represents an underrepresented demographic within American politics, yet one seemingly offers a breath of fresh air to voters, while it is hard to imagine much that we have not already learned in great detail about the other.

Similarly, although not as much attention has been focused on a potential Rice candidacy, many of the predictions in the press and among political pundits that the secretary of state would be a formidable rival not only to Clinton in the general election but to members of the Republican Party in the wide-open 2008 primaries seem somewhat overblown. Take, for example, Morris's assessment that Rice posed a "mortal threat" to Clinton: "With her broad-based appeal to voters outside the traditional Republican base, Condi has the potential to cause enough major defections from the Democratic Party to create serious erosion among Hillary's core voters. She attracts the same female, African American, and Hispanic voters who embrace Hillary, while still maintaining the support of conventional Republicans."[31] Little, if any, evidence exists to back up the claim that Rice would have that level of broad-based appeal with a national electorate or even within the Republican Party. Yet the publication of Morris's book in 2005, along with the endorsement of First Lady Laura Bush in early 2006, seemed to help catapult Rice as a serious presidential contender, even as she has continued to deny any interest in running for the office.[32] (However, it is interesting to note that Laura Bush qualified her statement a bit in December 2006 by stating that Rice, as a single woman, would have a difficult time winning the presidential election.) Although the possibility of a Rice candidacy continues to draw speculation, especially with her foreign policy experience (a positive attribute for any presidential candidate), it seems unlikely because of her lack of electoral experience, her close ties to President George W. Bush and the war in Iraq (both are now viewed as unpopular with a majority of Americans, particularly following the Republican Party's defeat in the 2006 midterm elections), and the fact that all constituencies of the Republican Party may not be ready to take the historic step of embracing an African American woman as its presidential nominee.

The Plan of the Book

The topic of electing a woman president is both timely and important. Although this is not the first book in recent years to raise the issue and probably will not be the last, we attempt to bring a more realistic perspective, based on our training as political scientists, to this much-talked-about and critical question. From a scholarly perspective, much of the popular commentary of late about electing a woman president seems to lack substantive analysis beyond the latest public opinion polls. Although it may make for interesting news coverage, the disproportionate focus on Clinton and Rice has skewed the overall and necessary debate about electing a woman president. As such, we attempt to move beyond the previous superficial talk of Hillary v. Condi to consider the real issues facing any potential woman candidate as the nation gears up for the 2008 presidential campaign.

In his book *Can She Be Stopped?* John Podhoretz writes:

> It is perhaps the least politically correct question imaginable: Can a woman win the presidency of the United States? At first blush, the question itself seems very nearly illegal, the sort of thing that could result in the denial of tenure, or an Equal Employment Opportunity Commission investigation into views so unenlightened that they surely violate some equal-rights statute. ... Still, you can be sure that an honest public discussion of the positive and negative aspects of having a woman president will never be conducted.[33]

With no disrespect to Mr. Podhoretz intended, I have been asking those very questions of my students in a variety of political science courses during the past several years (as do many of my colleagues). And to my knowledge, no one's tenure decision (including my own) has ever been affected by asking the question of if or when the United States will elect a woman president, and whether it is in the best interests of the United States to do so. However, although I never shy away from encouraging students to think critically about this issue, I also truly believe that America should and will eventually elect a woman president. Unfortunately, that reality may be further away than 2008, and that is the question addressed throughout this book.

The issues considered in the chapters that follow provide a scholarly assessment of the political environment in 2008 and beyond and how those factors will either benefit or inhibit women presidential candidates. The first few chapters of the book consider the social aspects of gender and how that affects women politicians seeking the presidency. In Chapter 2, Caroline Heldman considers the many cultural beliefs about the presidency, and how pop culture portrayals of the presidency contribute to Americans' gendered views of the office. In Chapter 3, Sue Thomas and Jean Reith Schroedel provide an analysis of sociocultural expectations about the roles of men and women in society and how the "masculine" image of the US presidency may mean that only an occasional "exceptional" woman will have a chance to break through that image and become president.

The next two chapters look at the context of gender on the campaign trail, not only through the many emphases on masculinity during the presidential campaign, but also through news media coverage and the stereotyping that often occurs of women candidates. In Chapter 4, Gina Serignese Woodall and Kim L. Fridkin analyze current research on media stereotypes of women candidates and the impact that stereotyping in media coverage has on women candidates for the presidency. In Chapter 5, Georgia Duerst-Lahti considers the dominance of masculinity on the presidential campaign trail, not only in media coverage of candidates but in expected behaviors of the candidates, and how that emphasis on masculinity hinders women candidates.

The institutional aspects of both campaigning and governing are considered in the next four chapters. Money and issues of campaign finance are critical factors for potential presidential candidates, and in Chapter 6, Victoria Farrar-Myers assesses the state of fundraising for women candidates seeking the presidency, based on recent fundraising data from women congressional candidates. In Chapter 7, Meredith Conroy analyzes the impact that political parties can have on the selection of presidential candidates and what role parties may play for electing a woman president in the near future. Karen M. Hult addresses the status of women as executive branch leaders in Chapter 8 and how that enlarges or shrinks the pool of potential presidential candidates. In Chapter 9, Meena Bose considers the challenges that a woman presidential candidate will face in convincing voters that she can handle national security issues involving terrorism and military action. Finally, the concluding chapter by Ann Gordon points out that we should "never say never" regarding the election of a woman to the presidency, even amid the many obstacles in place for female contenders in 2008 and beyond.

Notes

1. Clift and Brazaitis, *Madam President,* p. vii.
2. Rowat, "There's a Female President on TV."
3. See CBS News, "Ready for a Woman President?"; Powell, "Poll Finds Readiness for Female President"; and Smith, "Voters Think US Ready for Woman as President."
4. "Poll: Majority Ready for Woman President."
5. Wilson, *Closing the Leadership Gap*, p. 17.
6. For example, see Morris and McGann, *Condi vs. Hillary;* Estrich, *The Case for Hillary Clinton*; Podhoretz, *Can She Be Stopped?*; Morris and McGann, *Rewriting History*; Tyrrell, *Madame Hillary*; and Bowen, *Hillary!*
7. For a discussion on how "women's" issues are viewed differently than "men's" issues, see Dolan, *Voting for Women.*
8. See Lawless, "Women, War, and Winning Elections."
9. Wayne, *The Road to the White House 2004*, pp. 182–183.
10. Ibid., p. 183.
11. For a discussion on this trend in news coverage, see Patterson, *Out of Order*; and Sabato, *Feeding Frenzy.*
12. See Patterson, "Doing Well and Doing Good."
13. Cronin and Genovese, *The Paradoxes of the American Presidency*, pp. 32–37.
14. Bystrom, "On the Way to the White House," p. 104.
15. Falk and Jamieson, "Changing the Climate of Expectations," pp. 45–47.
16. Ibid.
17. See Fox and Lawless, "Entering the Arena?"
18. Many studies on this topic have been conducted in recent years. For example, see Paletz, *The Media in American Politics,* pp. 135–139; Kahn, *The Political Consequences of Being a Woman*, pp. 134–136; Kropf and Boiney, "The Electoral Glass Ceiling?"; Bystrom et al., *Gender and Candidate Communication,* p. 21; Heith, "The Lipstick Watch," pp. 124–126; and Heldman, Carroll, and Olson, "'She Brought Only a Skirt.'"
19. McDonnell and Vergara, "Chile's First Female President Sworn In."
20. See Han, "Presidential Leadership: Governance from a Woman's Perspective."
21. Han, *Women and American Politics*, p. 106.
22. Duerst-Lahti, "Reconceiving Theories of Power," p. 18.
23. DeConde, *Presidential Machismo*, p. 5.
24. "8 for '08: The White House Project and Parade Announce."
25. Morris and McGann, *Condi vs. Hillary*, p. 1.
26. Ibid., p. 30.
27. Estrich, *The Case for Hillary Clinton,* p. 4.
28. See "The Ceiling of Political Ambition."
29. For example, see Bevan, "Hillary's Eye on the White House"; and Farrell, "Hillary Sticking to Guns."

30. Romano, "Beyond the Poll Numbers."

31. Morris and McGann, *Condi vs. Hillary*, p. 2.

32. Rice ruled out a possible run for the presidency during an appearance on NBC's *Meet the Press* on Sunday, March 13, 2005.

33. Podhoretz, *Can She Be Stopped?* pp. 54–55.

2

Cultural Barriers to a Female President in the United States

Caroline Heldman

> In Europe and Asia and elsewhere, women have ruled over millions. It's not an abstract concept. But in America, men are still afraid, and I don't think women are too comfortable with the idea of a female being in charge.
>
> —*Madonna*[1]

Is Hillary Clinton or Condoleezza Rice "man enough" to be president of the United States? This politically incorrect question cuts to the heart of why Americans have yet to elect a female president.[2] Women have broken through glass ceilings in American politics in state houses, where they currently hold 23.5 percent of the seats, and have even made inroads in Congress, where they comprise 16.3 percent of the House and Senate.[3] Beyond US borders, female heads of state are fast losing their novelty. Women currently lead Germany, Ireland, Latvia, Finland, the Philippines, Liberia, and Chile. But despite emergent gains for women in US and world politics, the US presidency remains a male bastion. Political pundits and laypeople alike understand that being male is a basic requirement for the presidency, but few seem alarmed that this prerequisite denies a majority of American citizens the privilege of serving their country in this capacity.[4] This chapter is premised on the normative assertion that nonmeritorious limitations on who can hold the presidency are not desirable in a democratic republic where equality of representation is a prized goal. Fair representation in this office is more symbolically important than in other offices; equitable presidential elections are a basic requirement for a functioning democratic republic. The widely held cultural beliefs examined in this chapter act as a barrier to both women and true democratic representation.

Two primary questions are addressed in this chapter: What cultural beliefs about the presidency hinder women, and how do popular culture portrayals of the presidency promote these beliefs? This chapter begins with a critical assessment of public support for a female commander in chief. The next section focuses on cultural beliefs about gender that translate into biased beliefs about the presidency. The last part of this chapter examines the influence of popular culture in shaping beliefs about a presidency. Through analysis of the first television program to feature a female president, *Commander in Chief,* I conclude that popular culture furthers stereotypes that act as barriers for women seeking the White House.

Public Support for a Female President

The lack of female presidents in the United States to date is not due to a lack of candidates. Twenty women have declared their candidacy for president of the United States since the nation's inception, starting with New York publisher Victoria Woodhull in 1872. More notable candidates include attorney Belva Lockwood, who ran under the Equal Rights Party label in 1884; Senator Margaret Chase Smith, who entered several Republican primaries in 1964; Shirley Chisholm, a congresswoman from New York who won 151 delegates at the 1972 Democratic Convention; and Elizabeth Dole, who made a strong initial showing in the 2000 Republican primary season. Geraldine Ferraro was nominated as vice president on the losing Democratic Mondale-Ferraro ticket against popular incumbent President Ronald Reagan in 1984. These attempts to break through the ultimate glass ceiling of the White House have failed to leave even a scratch on the tempered barrier, although public opinion polling might seem to suggest otherwise.

Public opinion polls indicate strong support for a female president. According to some polls, over 90 percent of Americans say they will vote for a qualified female presidential candidate.[5] This number has increased steadily from 52 percent in 1955 to 73 percent in 1975 and 82 percent in 1987.[6] However, support drops dramatically to around 50 percent when respondents are asked whether the country is ready for a female president, or if they think their friends and family would vote for a female presidential candidate.[7] This lower level of support is a better indicator of the actual level, given the social desirability implicit in questions involving gender. The problem of social desirability in surveys is best illustrated with surveys involving race. For example, David Sears and his colleagues found that respondents exhibited less overt racism in responding to survey questions but continued to hold underlying (symbolic) racist beliefs.[8] Carole Kennedy finds polling on support for a woman president to be suspicious as well, noting that social desirability "might lead individuals to provide the socially acceptable response rather than their true predilections."[9]

Another shortcoming of polling research on support for a female president is the way the question is typically asked: "Would you vote for a woman for president, *if she were qualified*" (emphasis added),[10] or "If your party nominated a women for president, would you vote for her *if she were qualified for the job*" (emphasis added).[11] I propose that in the minds of many voters, being a woman makes one inherently not qualified for the job of the presidency. Questions that include the word "qualified" are actually measuring voter support for a female president who has magically transcended her gender. This proposition is upheld by the fact that support for a "qualified" female president drops from over 90 percent to 72 percent when respondents are asked, "Would you be personally willing to vote for a woman president?"[12] Support drops even lower, to around 50 percent, when respondents are asked more directly, "If the Democratic/Republican party nominates a woman for president in 2008, are you very likely, likely, not very likely, or not at all likely to vote for her?"[13] Furthermore, a recent national poll found that 30 percent of Americans do not support a female presidential candidate, regardless of her party affiliation, a handicap that would have cost a female candidate *every* presidential contest to date. To put this figure into context, the biggest popular margin in history (the 1968 Nixon/McGovern race) was 23 percent. The primary reason given for opposition to a female president is that "women are not up to the job,"[14] and 11 percent of respondents who oppose a female presidency stated, "It's a man's job." A more nuanced look at public opinion polls uncovers significant opposition to a female presidency.

Existing scholarship has exposed both attitudinal and structural barriers for female presidential contenders. Attitudinal barriers that work against women getting to the White House include gendered evaluations of competency for executive positions;[15] the discounting of women's qualifications by both men and women;[16] and the norm of masculinist ideology politics, defined as an ideology that revolves around men being the norm when it comes to human nature, placing greater value on traditionally male pursuits (androcentrism).[17]

Structural barriers include party bias in disproportionately recruiting and grooming men;[18] biases in the amount and type of media coverage that favors male candidates;[19] incumbency advantage, which tends to benefit male candidates;[20] the establishment of institutions and practices that allow men to disproportionately accumulate power;[21] and presidential elections that center around stereotypically "male issues," such as security, crime, and the economy.[22] Attitudinal and structural barriers work together in recursive relationships that enforce the idea and reality of an exclusively male presidency.

Election of a female president is seen by some as inevitable given the economic, political, and social progress of women as a result of the second wave of feminism. Rosy claims that it will happen in the near future, however, fail to account for deep-seated cultural beliefs about gender that translate into beliefs about the presidency as rightfully male in the minds of many American women and men. The next section explicates persistent societal ideas about gender that affect the electoral prospects of female presidential candidates, including hypermasculinity and candidate feminization, citizen-soldiers, the separate spheres ideology, and female objectification.

Masculinity and the Presidency

The first cultural belief that works against female presidential candidates is the marriage of masculinity and the presidency. The masculine bias of the presidency is such a normalized part of American politics and culture that it is virtually invisible. As Georgia Duerst-Lahti points out, "Executive political power is arguably the most manly of all areas."[23] This emphasis on masculinity distinguishes the position of the presidency from other political offices and limits the applicability of existing scholarship based on female candidates running for lower offices. However, current research is a good starting point for understanding the unique aspects of the presidency that hinder female candidates.

Cheryl King writes that political institutions suffer from compulsory masculinist ideology that serves as the standard for both men and women.[24] "Patterns of domination, subordination, and the exclusion of women are core elements to the historical development of our most basic institutions," including political institutions.[25] Successful leaders have been constructed as masculinist leaders, a position that benefits men and serves to generally exclude women from the highest echelons of power, and the presidency stands apart from lower offices in its hypermasculinity. Both men and women must adopt masculine characteristics to be successful in political office, but women are naturally disadvantaged in this pursuit because "it is difficult for women to prove their allegiance to and mastery of the masculinist ideology."[26] The "traditionally masculine schema" involves being tough, competitive, incisive, and displaying initiative and intellectual acuity.[27] The "traditional feminine schema" traits are conscientiousness, consideration, flexibility, enthusiasm, and dedication—characteristics that facilitate efficient leadership but do not fit with expectations of hypermasculine presidential leadership. Women who do manage to jump the hurdles and gain a position of significant power in American politics likely have less power than men in the same position because the legitimacy of their authority is questioned.[28] Women may wear masculinist ideology, but they cannot embody it because masculinity is an exclusively male prerogative. The prevailing ideology of the presidency discourages the rational voter from electing a woman as commander in chief. The marriage of masculinity and the presidency lays the groundwork for both irrational opinion about exclusively male leadership and rationalization for this opinion.

Popular culture, including erudite political punditry, solidifies the presidency as a masculine domain through persistent use of gendered use of language. One of the more insidious ways American minds are raised to think of presidents as only men, and the office of the presidency as rightfully male, is the pervasive use of the male pronoun when referring to the office in general.[29] A quick perusal of the presidential literature, television news, and water cooler conversations show that scholars, pundits, and laypeople alike almost exclusively use the male pronoun when referring to the office of the presidency. Despite the claim that using the universal "man," "mankind," or "he" does not bias the listener, compelling research finds that men and women imagine a male actor when a male pronoun is used. Pervasive use of "he" to refer to an office that can technically be occupied by both men and women limits our collective imagination of the possibility of a female president.

The idea of female candidates as interlopers in the masculine domain of politics is also apparent in the informal use of the first name to refer to high-ranking female officials who are presidential contenders. Senator Clinton is typically referred to as "Hillary" in popular culture, an infantilizing term that lacks power and legitimacy. Likewise, Dr. Rice is frequently referred to as "Condi." Gendered language of this sort is not consciously disrespectful, perhaps, but the gender difference is not random and has the "real world" consequence of delegitimizing knowledge, experience, and ultimately, leadership.

The importance of masculine ideology in American politics is apparent in the important role gender plays in presidential elections, even when both candidates are male. Meredith Conroy examines whether male presidential candidate association with feminine or masculine traits is tied to electoral success.[30] She analyzes media coverage as a measure of traits and finds that in all but one of the last five elections, the candidate more associated with masculine traits won the election. The exception was the 1996 Clinton-Dole election in the wake of sexual allegations that saw President Clinton positioning himself as a virtuous man, running from the "manly" label. The office of the presidency has been entwined with masculinity to such a great extent that gender is a major factor in presidential elections, whether or not a woman is running, as seen in an attempt to feminize the opposition.

"Feminization" of the opponent is frequently used to discredit the opponent in presidential elections. The effectiveness of such a campaign can be linked to modes of gender socialization whereby little boys learn what it means to be a man by rejecting everything that is feminine (e.g., anything pink, dolls), thus creating their identity through the rejection, "othering," and subjugation of the feminine/female. Girls and boys learn their relative value in American culture during acquisition of gender role identity. The gender hierarchy is supported and passed on by men who disproportionately occupy positions of power involved in social value creation (political offices, mass media production, positions of authority), and by women who comprise the vast majority of primary caretakers. As in childhood when a boy is mocked for wearing nail polish, the "feminization" of a male candidate immediately puts him in the category of female/other/lesser.

One high-profile example of feminizing one's opponent is when Michael Dukakis became a national laughingstock during his 1988 bid against George H.W. Bush for wearing an oversized military helmet while driving a tank. The image projected a candidate who literally and figuratively could not fill the hat. Opponents used this picture to feminize Dukakis, making reference to his lack of "manliness," thereby casting him as unfit to be commander in chief. President George W. Bush was wary of projecting a similar image when he staged a landing on the USS *Abraham Lincoln* in 2003 to announce "mission accomplished" in Iraq. He made sure to remove his helmet as soon as he deplaned. The Kerry campaign was not as responsible when officials allowed their candidate to be filmed at the National Aeronautics and Space Administration wearing a greenish suit that several pundits described as Woody Allen dressed up as the sperm in *Everything You Always Wanted to Know About Sex * but Were Afraid to Ask.* The message here is clear: masculine poses are important, but if improperly staged, they feminize the candidate. Male candidates are held up to masculinist standards and schema and judged by how successfully their attitudes, poses, and dress mesh with their maleness. Women, however, can only put on the "show" of masculinity by displaying character verbally.

The 2004 presidential election pitted the feminine schema against the masculine schema, and the "macho man" prevailed. First, Kerry's erudite and lengthy explanations during debates—a more feminine style of communication—made him look less resolute than President Bush's rough and tough sound bites. President Bush also successfully disparaged Democratic challenger John Kerry by aligning him with the feminine schema trait of flexibility with the "flip-flop" frame. Instead of accepting Kerry's reversal of his position on the Iraq War as a thoughtful policy decision based on emerging information or even a normal part of the complex and ever-changing world of politics, President Bush was able to punch a major hole in the Kerry campaign. In an October 2004 poll, nearly 40 percent of voters reported that the "flip-flop" charge made them less likely to vote for Kerry.[31]

In addition to campaign innuendo linking Senator Kerry to the feminine schema, he was overtly feminized through the ultimate feminizing rhetoric: assertions that he was gay. Conservative reporter James Dale Guckert (who went under the alias Jeff Gannon while working in the White House press corps) wrote that John Kerry "might someday be known as 'the first gay president.'"[32] Fox News was a frequent mouthpiece for this innuendo, alleging that Kerry received a "pre-debate manicure," a topic discussed five times in the three hours leading up to the first debate.[33] The alleged manicure was discussed by former speaker of the House Newt Gingrich on Bill O'Reilly's popular *Factor* program, where Kerry's manicure was compared to Dukakis's helmet debacle, and the senator was further chastised for having gotten a fake tan. O'Reilly used the latter to challenge Kerry's masculinity, stating, "What do you think Osama bin Laden's going to think about this spray-on tan? Is that going to frighten him? I don't know if it will."[34] Only hours after Senator Kerry "won" the presidential debate, Fox posted a fake article on its website in which Senator Kerry refers to himself as a "metrosexual" and fawns over his nails. Fox issued a retraction and apology, but Kerry's possible gayness continued to be the butt of late night talk shows. Senator Kerry responded to his "feminization" by staging sporty photo-ops (windsurfing, snowboarding, tossing a football on the tarmac), but these measures and his battle cry of "bring it on" could not restore his "manliness" in the eyes of the public. On paper, President Bush is not as macho as Kerry, as measured by the latter candidate's combat history, but President Bush was better able to perform hypermasculinity than Kerry.

The presidency is soaked to the bone in masculinist ideology in overt and insidious ways that make it difficult for American women and men to imagine a woman as a legitimate occupant of the office. The gendering of the presidency is displayed and enforced through gendered language, referring to female leaders with informal nicknames, masculinist posturing by presidents, and the gendering of campaigns, even when both candidates are male. Women are also distanced from the presidency by their inability to be full citizen-soldiers.

Citizen-Soldiers and the Presidency

The masculine traits culturally associated with the presidency are heightened by another cultural belief that diminishes the electability of women to that office. The president also holds the unique position of commander in chief, or head of the military. Two-thirds of the forty-two men who have served as president have had prior military experience, which suggests that it is an important prerequisite for the presidency. Cultural beliefs about military experience and the presidency hinder women in that they are less likely to have such experience, but even if they do, cultural ideas about who can be a "real" soldier tend to exclude women. Military experience also indirectly stymies female presidential candidates, in that the ideal citizen is supposed to engage in both civic and martial (military) practices, but women who join the military are undermining the close alliance of men and the military and cannot fully carry the mantle of citizen-soldier.[35] President Bush explicitly linked good citizenship with the citizen-soldier in his stock speech to military families in 2005: "The citizen soldiers of Idaho are making history. You're fighting to ensure that our freedom, like the state of Idaho, may endure forever. Americans are grateful for your devotion to duty and your courage under fire. We live in freedom and peace because of your determination to prevail" (August 24, 2005).

Female candidates to date have not fit the ideal of the citizen-soldier that the office of the president demands, and it is debatable whether it is even possible, given that female soldiers do not stand on equal footing with their male counterparts. Beyond restrictions to the duties they can perform, high-profile cases of female soldiers in recent years highlight the "othering" of women in the military. National attention was paid to the Navy's Tailhook convention in 1991 where female sailors were groped by their male counterparts, and women in the military continue to face an unusually high rate of rape, or what is officially termed "unprofessional gender-related behavior." In 2003–2004, the Department of Defense reported nearly 2,000 incidents of sexual assault among the four military branches, and one-fifth of the Air Force Academy's women had reported experiencing at least an attempted sexual assault in 2003.[36]

The case of the first woman, Shannon Faulkner, admitted to the all-male Citadel in 1994 epitomizes the othering of women in the military. Faulkner had sued to be admitted to the Citadel, and during testimony a top-ranking alumnus relayed that the ultimate insult used to demean cadets was to be compared to a "female": "And if the term 'woman' was used, then that would be a welcome relief, compared to the large majority of the terms you were called, [which] were gutter slang for women. And it goes on all the way down to the genitalia, and that's where the criticism was. And the point was, if you are not doing what you are supposed to do, you are not a man, you are a woman, and that is the way you are disciplined in the barracks every day, every hour."[37] Military institutions that feminize soldiers to demean and discipline them are not equipped to accept women into their ranks as true citizen-soldiers.

Even seemingly positive portrayals of military women in popular culture reflect their othering. The rescue of Jessica Lynch framed her as a hero, but upon closer inspection, her heroism came from being a damsel in distress who was able to survive until she was rescued. Her depiction as a hero illustrates different societal expectations for military men and women, highlighting the fact that women continue to be excluded from the realm of the "real" soldier. The title of Lynch's biographical account of her ordeal, *I Am a Soldier, Too: The Jessica Lynch Story*, illustrates her second-class soldier status.[38]

Military institutions that do not accept women as full members uphold existing societal beliefs about proper femininity that make being a citizen-soldier and a woman incompatible. Despite presidential scandals and other shortcomings, this citizenship ideal is a requirement for the presidency. Women's exclusion from the citizen-soldier ranks is a major barrier to an elected and effective female president, a barrier that has become more ominous in the post-9/11 environment.

Pat Miller argues that modes of masculinity are reimagined depending upon the national need.[39] For example, the heightened masculinity offered in World War II was followed by a period of peace in which the conventional masculinity of the war was maligned.[40] President Bush has taken the presidency to new macho heights through political rhetoric post-9/11 (e.g., "smoke 'em out"; catching Osama bin Laden "dead or alive"); his spectacular performances (e.g., landing on the USS *Abraham Lincoln*; rolling up his sleeves while touring the wreckage of Hurricane Katrina flanked with a crew of bulky firefighters flown in for the event); his rancher/cowboy image; and his masculine posturing, whether he is addressing a major audience, a group of reporters, or a camera. Leonie Huddy and Nayda Terkildsen find that voters are significantly more likely to vote for a presidential candidate whom they deem competent to handle military crises, a strength stereotypically associated with male candidates.[41] In a comprehensive assessment of the issue, Jennifer Lawless finds an unequivocal gender bias favoring male candidates and elected officials post-9/11.[42] When it comes to handling national security and military crises, citizens clearly prefer male leadership and male characteristics and find men to be significantly better able to respond to the circumstances of these terrorist attacks. "As a result of this stereotyping, levels of willingness to support a qualified woman presidential candidate are lower than they have been in decades."[43]

Separate Spheres Ideology

Widespread beliefs about the "proper" roles for women and men present another hurdle for women on their way to the White House. Separate spheres ideology, or gendering of the public and private spheres of life, has persisted despite women making great numerical strides in public sphere activities (e.g., working outside the home, holding political positions). Carole Kennedy notes that a majority of Americans "still subscribe to the notion that women are primary caregivers for children as well as being primarily responsible for family social obligations."[44] The liberal feminist motto of the second wave of feminism in the 1970s, that a woman can do anything a man can do, effectively validated men's activities and the public sphere without a commensurate valuation of women's activities or the private sphere. Thus, although women have moved en masse into the public sphere, few men have moved into the private sphere, and women who work outside the home do twice the amount of housework as their husbands.[45]

Separate spheres ideology is of particular significance to the White House because the president is analogous to the head of the household, the protector. Given prevailing cultural notions of gender role delineation in the household, it is difficult to envision women as the head of the household and, thus, difficult to imagine a woman as the symbolic head of the national household. The caretaker role is simply not presidential. The misfit between being a woman and protector is seen in the paucity of such roles in popular culture. There are rare exceptions when women are cast as the protectors, such as Sigourney Weaver's character Ripley in the *Alien* movies (which portrayed her as a failed protector), but in general, women are systematically excluded from the protector role and instead cast as the object of protection or the damsel in distress in popular culture. The hypermasculine presidential context of the "era of terrorism" heightens the importance of the male role as protector, a role that woman are hard-pressed to play convincingly in the popular consciousness.

The general acceptance of separate spheres ideology also makes it difficult to imagine a female president who is unconstrained by familial obligations. Existing research indicates that women face more questions about their family responsibilities on the campaign trail than men,[46] and voters are concerned that female candidates will neglect their families if they gain public office.[47] Similar concerns are not generally raised for male candidates at any level of office. The association of women with the private sphere and mothering runs counter to conceiving female presidential candidates as sufficient protectors and focused leaders without familial obligations pulling them away from their duties. These cultural narratives are echoed in and reinforced by popular culture depictions of women, a topic revisited later in this chapter.

Female Objectification

The normalization of female objectification in American culture in the past two decades is an emerging topic of study that has implications for the possibility of a female presidency. "Sexual objectification occurs when a woman's body is treated as an object (especially as an object that exists for the pleasure and use of others), and is illustrated interpersonally through gazing or 'checking out,' and in the representation of women in the media."[48] The general acceptance of female objectification is verified by the increasing number of objectified female images in popular culture, lack of a vocal public critique of such images, and the rise of "consensual objectification," or the false consciousness of girls/women who revel in their own object status.[49] Images from television, video games, films, magazines, and many other sources disproportionately use female bodies to hawk products, and the camera frame often focuses on female body parts rather than the whole picture in an objectifying manner.[50] Girls get the message that they should accept the male gaze as little children. They learn early on that the holy grail of female existence is the production of a high-quality product (their body), and boys get the message that it is their job/right/entitlement to consume these products. "Girls are taught to view their bodies as 'projects' that need work before they can attract others, whereas boys are likely to learn to view their bodies as tools to use to master the environment."[51] This fundamental difference in the way little boys and girls view their bodies and identities has profound effects for politics and the possibility of a female presidency as importance is increasingly placed on women's beauty at the expense of other more substantive personal characteristics. The rise of "beauty culture" solidifies the subject/object gender dichotomy, the smart/attractive dichotomy that lends to denial of female expert status, and the female phenomenon of self-objectification that discourages women from imagining themselves in and striving to attain positions of power. These gendered beliefs, discussed further below, present additional barriers to women's political ambitions at every level of office.

The subject/object cultural dichotomy that has become entrenched in recent years with broad acceptance of female objectification presents another barrier to women being perceived as powerful political actors. Simply put, in the male/subject–female/object split, women are inherently in a less powerful position. Objects are possessed, acted upon, and are therefore not considered legitimate purveyors of power. If both men and women evaluate women by the worth of their bodies, as bodies, it poses a fundamental barrier to women gaining equivalent authority to men, especially in domains saturated with (male) subjectivity, such as politics.

The rise of beauty culture has furthered the mind/body dichotomy in the collective consciousness. Female candidates for any office will have to balance expectations that they be sufficiently attractive with the fact that this will increase perceptions of their femininity and hurt their electoral chances. Once they gain positions of power, women are still expected to maintain a physically pleasing (object) status. This was epitomized in the gallery of the US Capitol, where students visiting during a class trip were privy to twenty minutes of then-House Minority Leader Nancy Pelosi applying makeup on the House floor prior to giving an on-camera speech. More recently, Katherine Harris, Florida secretary of state during the embattled 2000 presidential election, alleged that major news organizations had doctored her makeup in pictures to make her look bad. Regardless of the validity of this allegation, the fact that Harris's appearance is important enough to be discussed is a uniquely female phenomenon in politics. Likewise, political coverage of Elizabeth Dole's bid for the 2000 Republican Party nomination mentioned her physical appearance significantly more than her male competitors.[52] Perhaps the most troubling example of the expectation that female leaders will continue to be objects, regardless of the power they hold, is the public fascination with Hillary Clinton's hairstyle. A now-defunct website dedicated to the First Lady's coifs was one of the most popular websites during the 1990s, and numerous media stories have covered the topic, leading the New York senator to comment, "If I want to knock a story off the front page, I just change my hairstyle." How can a female presidential candidate fit the norms of beauty culture expected of women (in general and women in politics) while also projecting an image of heightened masculinity?

In addition to the double bind of beauty culture and masculinity that female presidential candidates face, the pressure to be physically appealing on the campaign trail works against candidate viability and perceptions of competence. In their experimental study, Lee Sigelman, Carol Sigelman, and Christopher Fowler found that increased attractiveness for a female candidate increased voter perceptions of her femininity.[53] That poses a problem for female presidential candidates, given that "women who are considered feminine will be judged incompetent."[54] The present heightened state of women as sex objects adds another layer: The more a woman succeeds at being a valuable body, the less the world views her as knowledgeable and competent.[55] Ideals of womanhood in American culture involve traits that directly conflict with presidential traits.

The Cartesian split between mind and body that pervades American culture would adversely affect any group whose primary valuation is physical, since such dichotomies encompass implicit hierarchy. The male/mind–female/body split is intensely present in American society, despite the mass entrance of women into high education in the past thirty years. Feminist theorist Lorraine Code examines the operation of the mind/body dichotomy in precluding women from being possessors of knowledge. "It is no exaggeration to say that anyone who wanted to *count* as a knower has commonly been male."[56] Women's object status, or the ability of men to instantly reduce them from a subject to an object that exists for the visual consumption of men, feeds the idea that women cannot truly possess knowledge. Objects are acted upon; they are not agents of thought or other action. Professional men automatically garner credibility when they walk into a boardroom, a courtroom, or other positions of power. Professional women, however, have to work to earn credibility. Given that an important masculine/presidential trait is intellectual strength, the denial of female expert status on the part of both male and female audience members ties into foundational beliefs about who can be a possessor of knowledge and is an impediment to the election of a female president.[57]

In addition to altering expectations of female candidates among the electorate, the normalization of female objectification in American society also influences personal ambition. Researchers have discovered a disturbing new trend of self-objectification, in which girls/women increasingly internalize the male gaze, viewing themselves through this lens as a result of pervasive sexual objectification. Self-objectification is causally related to a variety of mental health disorders, including clinical unipolar depression,[58] "habitual body monitoring," body shame, diet restriction, symptoms of anorexia and bulimia, shame about menstrual cycles, and "gaze anticipation" leading to social physique anxiety.[59] Self-objectification has also been linked to lower cognitive functioning,[60] less physical motility,[61] and a lower average grade point average in college.[62] Self-objectification also has consequences for politics beyond lowered self-esteem and cognitive functioning. The more a woman objectifies herself, the lower her external political efficacy.[63] This finding has serious implications, considering that an increasing percentage of each generation of girls self-objectify, and political efficacy is linked to the likelihood of voting as well as actually running for office. Widespread female embrace of the male gaze solidifies the subject/object binary and makes it difficult to reform gender stereotypes about women's cultural identity that militate against the electoral chances of a female presidential candidate.

The President in Popular Culture

Popular culture both reflects cultural values and shapes them through images and content. Visual entertainment media are particularly important when it comes to shaping national consciousness, given the power of images. Movies and television are able to present "reality," or something like it, as well as fantastic stories that bend time, space, gravity, and even tradition at times. Equality, justice, redemption, democracy: these elusive ideals can be explored and realized in fictionalized settings. But despite the potential to topple existing societal hierarchies—gender, race, economics, and so on—popular culture tends to reflect and therefore reinscribe, normalize, strengthen, and perpetuate these hierarchies. Novelty may pull in viewers, but bending accepted cultural norms too far will alienate mainstream audiences and work against the commercial end goal of the entertainment industry.

Depictions of presidents on the big and little screens both reflect and shape cultural perceptions of who is worthy and capable of occupying this office. Cultural critics conclude that masculine hegemonic narratives are generally upheld. "Heterosexuality, masculine authority and feminine nurturance are made normative by the dominant media story-lines and entertainment genres."[64] Male and female presidents in popular culture are portrayed in ways that further stereotypes and societal beliefs that harm women's advancement to the White House. More specifically, film and television present very few women in this position, conflate masculinity and the presidency, normalize male leadership, uphold separate spheres ideology, and promote the objectification of women. These themes are explored further in the following brief analysis of presidents on the big and little screens and in a comparison of two popular television programs portraying a male and female president.

Presidents on the Big Screen

A steady stream of high-budget, popular movies about male presidents have been released in recent years featuring Hollywood "A list" actors: *Dave,* starring Kevin Kline and Sigourney Weaver (1993); *In the Line of Fire,* with Clint Eastwood and John Malkovich (1993); *The American President,* featuring Michael Douglas as the president (1995); *Independence Day,* with Will Smith and Bill Pullman as a heroic, "warrior" president (1996); *Wag the Dog,* starring Dustin Hoffman and Robert De Niro (1997); *Air Force One,* featuring Harrison Ford as another heroic, "warrior" president (1997); and the recent remake of *The Manchurian Candidate* with Denzel Washington (2004). Without exception, these movies show a masculine (sometimes hypermasculine), white, male president. According to the Internet Movie Database, only three movies (that the reader has likely never heard of) have featured a female president. First, *Kisses for My President* (1964), starring Polly Bergen and Fred MacMurray, tells the story of Leslie McCloud, the first woman to be elected president. The movie is more a running joke about the gendered responsibilities of the First Gentleman than his wife's historic position. The 1998 comedy *Jane Austen's Mafia!* also portrays a minor female character winning the presidency, while the third female president on the big screen was featured in the low-budget movie *PI: Post Impact* (2004). To date, no wide release movie has featured a female president.

Women in popular culture have rarely been shown in the vice presidential role, including Joan Allen as Senator Laine Hanson in *The Contender* (2000); Glenn Close as the vice president in *Air Force One*; and the second *Brady Bunch Movie* (2002), in which President Mike Brady appoints his wife vice president. The American public is more comfortable with a woman in the vice presidential rather than presidential role, and popular culture reflects this in allowing a few female characters to serve as the second in command.[65]

The paucity of female presidents on the big screen naturalizes the notion that the presidency is for men only. Furthermore, the typical hypermasculine portrayal of "warrior" presidents frames presidential politics as a masculine pursuit. The most notable examples are Harrison Ford's character in *Air Force One,* who personally foils a terrorist attempt, and Bill Pullman's character in *Independence Day,* who uses his fighter pilot skills to save the world. Manly leadership is often taken to the extreme in movies portraying the president, giving a platform for the performance of hypermasculinity that has become a major staple in contemporary political rhetoric.

In addition to normalizing a male presidency and masculine leadership, Hollywood tends to portray women as interlopers in the world of politics. One poignant example is the 2004 remake of *The Manchurian Candidate*, in which Meryl Streep plays an incestuous, maniacal mother who attempts to gain the White House by brainwashing her son and getting him elected to the presidency. The movie is sprinkled with thoughtful comments about women being barred from the Oval Office, but they are overshadowed by the lengths Streep's character goes to in attempting to gain presidential power. The message is that women have been barred from the presidency, but that is acceptable because they cannot handle the job.

Presidents on the Little Screen

Television executives have made history in recent years with two programs featuring female presidents: *Battlestar Galactica* (the remake, beginning in 2003) and *Commander in Chief* (the 2005–2006 season). President Laura Roslin's character in *Battlestar Galactica* is unusual in that the series is set far enough in the future that there have been other female presidents and the plots do not revolve around her gender or novelty. The now-cancelled series *Commander in Chief,* however, focused on the novelty aspect of a female in the Oval Office. A comparison of *Commander in Chief* to *The West Wing* illustrates the inability of Hollywood to portray a female president without reflecting and reinscribing the gendered societal beliefs previously discussed.

In 2005, for the first time in television history, two prime-time programs—*Commander in Chief* and *The West Wing*—revolved around the life of the US president. It was also the first time a female president was featured, an ideal situation for analyzing her portrayal relative to her male counterpart. The highly acclaimed and popular television series *The West Wing* ended its seven-year run on NBC in 2006. Martin Sheen played Josiah (Jed) Bartlet, a liberal-minded president on a program that pulled in political junkies as well as a more mainstream audience. Bartlet fits well in his role as Hollywood's dream of a liberal president, modeled after Bill Clinton, who often talked about doing the "right thing" but was rarely able to in the rough and tumble world of Washington politics.[66] Viewers tuned in religiously to follow the interesting character arcs and lives of those working closest with the president. Women have a conspicuously high profile in the Bartlet White House: the press secretary is a tough-as-nails female; many competent women have been featured on the show as political consultants, lobbyists, campaign workers, and members of Congress; the first lady is a medical doctor who is active behind the scenes in policy decisions (reminiscent of Hillary Clinton); and even the female administrative assistants are multidimensional characters. Martin Sheen's Bartlet is a convincing presidential figure, and the political and personal narratives of *The West Wing* made it a very popular television program.

In contrast to President Bartlet from *The West Wing,* President Allen from *Commander in Chief* is unconvincing due to problems with gender and the presidency. ABC introduced Geena Davis as President Mackenzie "Mac" Allen (note the masculine nickname) in the series *Commander in Chief* in 2005. Series creator Rod Lurie also wrote and directed *The Contender*, featuring Joan Allen as a plausible female vice-presidential candidate. The short life of this initially popular program highlights the societal beliefs and practices that make being a women and being president fundamentally incompatible at the present time. This television program enjoyed record-breaking opening audiences—the biggest launch in five years[67]—earning Geena Davis a Golden Globe award in 2006—but it was laid to rest after its first season. Given the novelty of a female president and the deep-seated societal ideologies that work against it, as well as Hollywood's overriding goal of making money by appealing to a wide audience, the creators had one of two general options: change the woman or change the office. The first option would have entailed portraying Mac as an imposing, masculine figure, defying gender norms. Putting aside the question of whether a stunning Hollywood star could truly transcend gender norms for the moment, this path was not chosen. The second general option was to tailor her characterization of the presidency to fit with socially acceptable standards for women. This option was selected, and the result was a sappy, laughably unrealistic depiction of the presidency that turned off the political junkies who avidly followed *The West Wing,* feminists who were excited to see the historical debut of a female president in popular culture, and those tuning in to see a good drama. Lurie (who was later replaced by Steven Bochco of *NYPD Blue* fame) presented "Mac" as active in both the public and private spheres, unambitious, above the partisan fray, and sexualized.

Lurie was straightforward about the fact that Mackenzie Allen would not be another Jed Bartlet: "I don't want to get bogged down with the minutiae of lawmaking. *The West Wing* is rather arcane and deals with a lot of issues. We're going to deal a lot with how the president gets her kids to school and goes trick-or-treating. We'll have some East Wing and some West Wing stuff."[68] In other words, President Allen would be a parent first and president second. This was epitomized in the first episode when Mac's youngest daughter spills juice on Mac's shirt in the limousine on the way to her first congressional address. Mac handles the situation by cleverly putting a scarf over the stain, demonstrating her merit as a mother. The series includes many similarly unrealistic scenes where Mac's parental duties compete with presidential responsibilities, forwarding the notion that a female president's time would be divided between two jobs. In contrast, *The West Wing* also involves familial storylines, but President Bartlet's parental responsibilities do not compete with his "other" job, a reflection of different cultural standards of what it means to be a "good mother" and a "good father." When Bochco took the reigns of *Commander in Chief* to restore ratings, he was explicit in his desire to place more emphasis on Mac's private life. This gendered strategy backfired, as it would have if the hypermasculine *NYPD Blue* revolved primarily around the home lives of detectives instead of crime solving. Drama and the private sphere are gendered feminine, and they do not mix well with the hypermasculine office of the presidency.

In addition to President Allen straddling the public/private divide in a highly gendered fashion, the show's creators also depicted President Allen as a champion for women's rights: a situation with a Nigerian woman facing death because of extramarital relations; a woman on death row; revival of the ill-fated Equal Rights Amendment. These narratives may have appealed to feminists, but they also gendered the office by not illustrating the range of policy issues a president typically faces. The plots also reflected male stereotypes: the First Gentleman caught in a seemingly compromising position with an intern; President Allen's son getting into fights at school to defend his father's "manliness." But by far the most damaging aspect of the plots of *Commander in Chief* was a lack of realism as a result of trying to change the office to accommodate the implausibility of a female president at the present time.

The pilot for *Commander in Chief* set up an unrealistic presidency in a number of ways. First, Mackenzie Allen assumed the presidency through the vice presidency. Mac was put in a more palatable second-in-command position, thus allowing the show's creators to avoid the sticky question of under what conditions the country would elect a woman. The plot became exceedingly untenable when the dying president requests that Mackenzie Allen step down because it is understood that her ideology as an Independent is not properly aligned with his. As if presidents overriding the Constitution to handpick their successors and electing an Independent vice president were not enough fantasy, Mac intends to step down until she is needled in a sexist fashion by Nathan Templeton, the Speaker of the House. Templeton, played by Donald Sutherland, was set to assume the presidency when Mac stepped down.

The lack of realism in *Commander in Chief* both mirrors societal beliefs and sends some clear gendered messages about women and the White House. First, Mac's "accidental" presidency upheld stereotypes of women as not being ambitious. The pilot shows flashbacks to the future president recruiting her for the vice presidency, and Allen, a former member of Congress and college chancellor at the time, is openly resistant to reentering politics. Not coincidentally, President Roslin from *Battlestar Galactica* is also an "accidental" president who is forty-second in line for the job until an emergency shortens the list. This prevailing popular culture theme for female presidents mirrors broader societal conceptions that "good" women are not ambitious.[69] Furthermore, the portrayal of President Allen as an Independent both discounts the power of partisan politics in Washington and reinforces the stereotype of women as a moral check in politics. On its face, President Allen rising above the partisan fray may appear to be an affirming portrayal of women in politics, but it ultimately others her in a gendered fashion.

Commander in Chief also reinforces beauty culture ideals that fit poorly with presidential traits and public perceptions of competence. Geena Davis's sexy presentation of President Allen has been noted in numerous news articles about the show. As Ellen Goodman notes: "Like every female candidate with a hemline and a hairdo, more media attention was paid to her appearance than her position papers."[70] The Allen administration has been described as the "Jolie administration," while Davis is described as "robust" with "bee stung lips," "smart, beautiful, and dressed to the nines."[71] In general, press coverage of *Commander in Chief* exhibited highly gendered, demeaning language that focused on Davis's physicality. Tom Shales of the *Washington Post* writes: "Geena Davis can veto my legislation anytime. Starring as the first woman to hold the highest office in the land, Davis reminds us what we have missed in most of our past, real-life presidents: cuteness. She's got a twinkle in her eye, a twinkle in her smile, a twinkle everywhere. She's President Twinkle—just what we need to tame the extreme, charm the militant, inspire the troops."[72]

Press coverage focusing on Davis's physicality was reminiscent of reporters' treatment of Elizabeth Dole during her bid for the 2000 Republican Party nomination. Dole's hair, clothing, and even her sex life were discussed in numerous news articles about her candidacy. For example, one reporter commented on Dole's hair: "Fabric will shine, crinkle, stretch, seem like paper, have a sheer veneer or be tougher than, say, Elizabeth Dole's hairdo."[73] Dole's male competitors did not receive similar coverage about their physical appearance, nor did Martin Sheen's character on *The West Wing*. The undignified gendered language used to describe Davis's fictional presidency and Dole's actual presidential candidacy epitomizes the role of popular culture—both entertainment and news—in maintaining the maleness of the presidency.

Some of the blame for demeaning press coverage of Davis's president in *Commander in Chief* falls on the show's creators, who decided she would be a highly sexualized character with bright red lipstick and suggestive blouses. Davis's sexualized presidency fits well with the proliferation of female objectification in popular culture. It is difficult to imagine a prime-time television program featuring a professional female protagonist who is not sexualized (e.g., the female characters in the original *Law and Order* and its spin-offs, *Grey's Anatomy, Desperate Housewives,* and *Sex and the City,* to name a few). However, the presidency is unique in its association with masculinity, and female presidents cannot be portrayed in the same way as female attorneys or doctors. President Allen's sexual image carried with it the damaging side effect of diminishing her status as a possessor of knowledge, making her character's position as the most powerful political leader in the country implausible. Additionally, as a sexualized, feminine being without military experience, President Allen was not a citizen-soldier. She lacked many of the informal credentials required for the presidency that are difficult, if not impossible, for women to acquire.

Although some of the critical media coverage of *Commander in Chief* was warranted, much coverage was dismissive of the program or Geena Davis without necessary explanation. One reporter wrote, "Any way you slice it, Geena Davis is not a president, period. . . . President of the Junior League, but not the president of the United States."[74] This statement was provided without discussion of why Davis is unconvincing as president, as though the basis was obvious. Yet another reporter shot down the show early in the season: "Geena

Davis makes history tonight, taking an oath as the nation's first female president. OK, it's just pretend. But we can see what it might be like for her, her children, and her husband, who is now the first gentleman. Will he select china and state dinner menus? Will the military respect her? Not with all that lipstick on, Geena."[75]

These few examples are indicative of a general tendency of reporters to not take the show seriously because it featured a female president, some even before *Commander in Chief* debuted. Elizabeth Dole also faced seemingly inexplicable negative coverage early on in her candidacy for the Republican Party nomination that is best explained by gender bias.[76] Similar to the press coverage questioning Dole's viability, President Allen's viability was challenged through constant critiques of the program's prospects for success.

Conclusion

The short-lived television series *Commander in Chief* reflects the impossible job of portraying a realistic female president, given ingrained beliefs about gender that permeate conceptions of the presidency, including its connection with masculinity, public/private role expectations, the citizen-soldier requirement that women cannot embody, and the proliferation of female objectification that runs against the grain of legitimate leadership. The television show revolved around President Allen's gender in the same way that female presidential campaigns revolve around gender, whether the candidate wants them to or not. Elizabeth Hanford Dole insisted that her candidacy was not about her gender, but in the end, she was resigned to the fact that gender played a central role in her failed candidacy. Gender also cost *Commander in Chief* its candidacy for the hearts and minds of American viewers. It is a prime example of popular culture reinforcing existing beliefs that serve as barriers to women gaining the White House, despite good intentions to the contrary. (Geena Davis is personally involved in See Jane, an organization that seeks to increase the number of female characters and decrease gender stereotyping in children's television programming. Lurie, the show's creator, openly advocates for a female presidency.) For all its faults, however, *Commander in Chief* at least attempted to imagine the possibility of a female presidency and opened up new territory in the imagination—however flawed—for the viewing public, although its failure might have closed the door on future programming of this nature.

Popular culture plays a key role in both reflecting and upholding sexist beliefs when portraying presidents. This observation is based on only a handful of examples because only a few are available. Analysis of popular culture phenomena does not effectively function as proof in a scientific sense, but it is a good manifestation of cultural practices and ideologies. This examination of *Commander in Chief* uncovered gender biases in the show's content and media coverage that are indicative of broader cultural ideas about gender and the presidency.

This chapter is premised on the normative assertion that artificial constraints on who can hold public office are undesirable in a democratic republic that prides itself on seeking equality of representation. The presidency is the most visible and most powerful political position in the United States, and as such, fair representation in this office is more symbolically important than other offices. In this sense, equitable presidential elections are a basic requirement for a functioning democratic republic. However, widely held cultural beliefs mitigate democratic representation in American politics by barring a majority of the population from holding the highest position, namely: the marriage of masculinity and the presidency; the exclusion of women from the ranks of citizen-soldiers; the persistence of separate spheres ideology; and the normalization of women's objectification in American culture.

It is important to recognize how deep beliefs about the president run and the strength of their current when considered in totality. Many Americans are supportive of electing a woman as president in a general sense but will likely be hesitant to support an actual female candidate, given incompatibilities in how gender and presidential roles are conceived. These attitudinal barriers, in combination with reiterative structural barriers (e.g., lack of party recruitment of and support for female candidates; lack of and biased media coverage for female candidates; etc.) for women seeking the White House, seem insurmountable at the present time. A woman will be elected to the presidency at some point, but it will happen in spite of major impediments, not as an inevitable consequence of some natural forward trajectory of women's progress in politics.

Notes

1. Yahoo News, "Madonna: 'America Not Ready for a Female President.'"

2. This opening line was inspired by Meredith Conroy's unpublished essay, "Are You Man Enough? The Gendering of Presidential Candidates by Print Media."

3. Center for American Women and Politics, "Women in Elective Office, 2007."

4. This point was made previously in Thomas and Wilcox, "Introduction," *Women and Elective Office*.

5. CBS Poll, "Ready for a Woman President?"; Cannon, "You Go, Girls: Growing Support for Women Presidential Candidates."

6. CBS Poll, "Ready for a Woman President?"

7. Rasmussen Reports, "72% Say They're Willing to Vote for Woman President."

8. Sears et al., "Is It Really Racism?"

9. Kennedy, "Is America Ready for a Woman President?" p. 313.

10. CBS Poll, "Ready for a Woman President?"

11. Ibid.

12. Rasmussen Reports, "72% Say They're Willing to Vote for Woman President."

13. WNBC/Marist Poll, "National Poll: Campaign 2008."

14. Ibid.

15. See Witt, Paget, and Matthews, *Running as a Woman*.

16. See Borrelli, "Gender, Credibility, and Politics."

17. See Duerst-Lahti and Kelly, *Gender Power, Leadership, and Governance*; Borrelli, "Gender, Credibility, and Politics"; King, "Sex Role Identity and Decision Styles"; and Jamieson, *Beyond the Double Bind*.

18. See Darcy, Welch, and Clark, *Women, Elections, and Representation*; Ford, *Women and Politics*; Wilson, "Is America Ready for a Woman President?"; and Gordon, "From the Guest Editor: A Woman President."

19. See Bystrom et al., *Gender and Candidate Communication*; Kahn, *The Political Consequences of Being a Woman*; and Heldman, Carroll, and Olson, "'She Brought Only a Skirt.'"

20. See Burrell, *A Woman's Place Is in the House*; Witt, Paget, and Matthews, *Running as a Woman*; and Carroll, *Women as Candidates in American Politics*.

21. See Duerst-Lahti and Kelly, *Gender Power, Leadership, and Governance*; and Borrelli, "Gender, Credibility, and Politics."

22. See Huddy and Terkildsen, "The Consequences of Gender Stereotypes for Women Candidates"; Cook, "Voter Reaction to Women Candidates"; and Kenski and Falk, "Of What Is the Glass Ceiling Made?"

23. Duerst-Lahti, "Reconceiving Theories of Power," p. 11.

24. See King, "Sex Role Identity and Decision Styles."

25. Norton and Norris, "Feminist Organizational Structure in the White House," p. 478.

26. Ibid., p. 191.

27. Borrelli, "Gender, Credibility, and Politics," p. 182.

28. For an extended discussion of women in positions of power, see

Duerst-Lahti and Kelly, *Gender Power, Leadership, and Governance*; and Winsky Mattei, "Gender and Power in American Legislative Discourse."

29. Use of the male pronoun has been justified on the grounds that only men have held this office. However, the term "president" refers to an office, not a specific person. It is grammatically correct to refer to the president as "he or she."

30. See Conroy, "Are You Man Enough?"

31. Pew Research Center for the People and the Press, "Race Tightens Again, Kerry's Image Improves."

32. See Kurtz, "Jeff Gannon Admits Past 'Mistakes,' Berates Critics."

33. See Media Matters for America, "Cameron's Fake Kerry Story Capped FOX Commentators' Manicure Fixation."

34. Ibid., p. 2.

35. See Snyder, *Citizen-Soldiers and Manly Warriors.*

36. See Smith, "Sexual Assaults in Army on Rise."

37. Faludi, *Stiffed*, p. 144.

38. See Bragg, *I Am a Soldier, Too.*

39. See Miller, "From Paradigm to Parody."

40. Ibid., p. 122.

41. See Huddy and Terkildsen, "The Consequences of Gender Stereotypes."

42. See Lawless, "Women, War, and Winning Elections."

43. Ibid., p. 480.

44. Kennedy, "Is America Ready for a Woman President?" p. 316.

45. See Morin and Rosenfeld, "With More Equity, More Sweat."

46. See Mezey and Gluck, "Does Sex Make a Difference?"

47. See Whicker and Isaacs, "The Maleness of the American Presidency."

48. See Slater and Tiggeman, "A Test of Objectification Theory."

49. See Heldman and Holmes, "Consumer Culture and the Gaze"; and Levy, *Female Chauvinist Pigs.*

50. See Kilbourne, *Still Killing Us Softly*; and Archer, Kimes, and Barrios, "Face-ism: Five Studies of Sex Differences in Facial Prominence."

51. See Stephens, Hill, and Hanson, "The Beauty Myth and Female Consumers."

52. See Heldman, Carroll, and Olson, "'She Brought Only a Skirt.'"

53. See Sigelman, Sigelman, and Fowler, "A Bird of a Different Feather?"

54. Jameison, *Beyond the Double Bind*, p. 16.

55. See Matschiner and Murnen, "Hyperfemininity and Influence."

56. Code, *What Can She Know?* p. 9.

57. See Borrelli, "Gender, Credibility, and Politics."

58. See Fredrickson and Roberts, "Objectification Theory"; and Muehlenkamp and Saris-Baglama, "Self-Objectification and Its Psychological Outcomes for College Women."

59. See Fredrickson and Roberts, "Objectification Theory"; Noll and

Fredrickson, "A Mediated Model"; Muehlenkamp and Saris-Baglama, "Self-Objectification and Its Psychological Outcomes"; and Calogero, "A Test of Objectification Theory."

60. See Fredrickson and Roberts, "Objectification Theory"; and Gapinski, Brownell, and LaFrance, "Body Objectification and 'Fat Talk.'"

61. See Fredrickson and Harrison, "Throwing Like a Girl."

62. See Heldman, "The Political Consequences of Female Objectification."

63. Ibid.

64. See Connell, *Masculinities.*

65. See Kennedy, "Is America Ready for a Woman President?"

66. This observation is based on a conversation with a writer from *The West Wing.*

67. See De Moraes, "Steven Bochco by a Landslide."

68. Givhan, "In the Oval Office, Pumps and Circumstance," p. C1.

69. See Carroll, "Political Elites and Sex Differences in Political Ambition."

70. See Goodman, "TV Series May Hurry History."

71. Poniewoznik, "Hail to the She," p. 90.

72. See Shales, "Geena Davis Sweeps Up the Oval Office," p. C1.

73. See Quintanilla, "Premiere Vision."

74. See Goodman, "Fall TV Preview: Addicted to Fall TV."

75. See Ryan, "All Hail the Chief."

76. See Heldman et al., "'She Brought Only a Skirt.'"

3

The Significance of Social and Institutional Expectations

Sue Thomas and Jean Reith Schroedel

The recent elections of "female firsts" such as Chancellor Angela Merkel in Germany, President Michelle Bachelet in Chile and President Ellen Johnson-Sirleaf in Liberia render the question of when the United States will join the more than eighty countries worldwide that have had women heads of state more timely than ever. With a modern history of two female secretaries of state and increasing numbers of women in statehouses and in Congress, the near-term possibility of a woman president of the United States does not seem far-fetched. Indeed, the topic was often broached with respect to the imagined 2008 Hillary Rodham Clinton–Condoleezza Rice match-up.

The media questions about the first woman president are all but endless—will she be a Republican or a Democrat? A conservative or liberal? A senator or governor? From the West or the South? Someone with a military record or a record of alternative service? Will she have made her political reputation on foreign or domestic policy? Bowing to Geena Davis's character in *Commander in Chief*, will the first woman president be a vice president who is elevated either through the resignation or death of a sitting president, or someone who runs in and wins a presidential election? Moving from political factors to personal ones, will she be a scion of a political family or a self-made woman? In light of the increasing importance of religion in shaping political preferences and the influence of "morality" issues in electoral victories, to what extent will her religious perspective enter political debate and assessments of candidate credibility?

And finally, what role will "women's" issues play in the rise of the first woman president of the United States? How will she deal with those topics that resonate with traditional women and how will she deal with topics perceived as feminist issues? How will a woman president's credibility be affected by her stance on both those types of women's issues, and how will that differ from men's approach to them? Issues of reproductive choice are especially relevant to such debate—particularly since so many, like abortion, are high profile and heavily contested.

In this chapter, we address these questions by situating them in a very particular context—one related to societal and institutional gendering—or, put another way, how our sociocultural expectations about the proper, traditional, or natural roles of men and women in public and private life affect societal and institutional dynamics, structures, and ideologies. We argue that, to the extent that American society perceives significant divisions of public (especially political roles) and private labor along gender lines (which are reflected in our dichotomization of some issues as "women's" issues and some as "everyone's" issues), and to the extent that our collective image of "president" envisions a male figure, only an occasional "exceptional" woman will have a chance to be president of the United States. The exceptional woman will be someone who is poised to run when the electoral context is most favorable and who can successfully, albeit gingerly, negotiate around women's issues and perceptions of women's abilities—or who ascends to the position in the event that a sitting president is no longer able to serve. Conversely, only when gendered social roles are largely eradicated will women in executive positions, including presidential positions, become routine. It is also at that point that those issues presently referred to as women's issues will no longer be seen as single-interest or marginal, and female candidates will no longer have to prove that they are as capable and qualified as male candidates. Women, along with men, will be seen as being tough enough to handle such issues as foreign policy, war, and terrorism. And men, along with women, will consider issues such as education, health care, and child care as centrally important to the national agenda.

Societal Gendering and Its Impact on Women's Political Opportunities

If women are routinely to contend for the highest political office in the land, it will first require a comprehensive shift in our views of the roles of both sexes in the public and private realms. As illustrated by results of survey research on public perceptions about women's proper roles within society, that shift is still incomplete. Since 1972, the percentage espousing support for gender equality has increased from 47 percent to 78 percent.[1] Although that represents a remarkable increase in a relatively short space of time, a substantial portion of the populace does not support equal roles for men and women. There still are deeply embedded perceptions of the tasks for which women and men are better suited and the personality traits, worldviews, and levels of vigor thought to flow from those tasks. These disparate perceptions, which can exist on an unconscious level even for those who endorse egalitarianism, privilege men while simultaneously inhibiting women.[2]

In the work world, the jobs of physician or secretary, human resources director or chief executive officer, teacher or superintendent, firefighter or librarian, bookkeeper or certified public accountant, minister or choir member, soldier or seamstress, nursing home attendant or truck driver conjure up images of either men or women. In the twenty-first century, by no means are any of these roles filled exclusively by men or women. Nevertheless, as Table 3.1 illustrates, each of the roles tends to be peopled more by one sex than the other—and, perhaps, most importantly, the skills and perspectives required in these roles are generally ascribed to one sex or the other.[3] So, even when women work in what is usually a male arena, they start from the assumption that stellar or even adequate performance will take abnormally elevated levels of effort or skill. Men are the "norm," whereas women are the "other."

A deeply embedded unconscious gendering is operational with respect to the presidency. All forty-two presidents have been male. When 79 percent of respondents to a recent Roper poll indicated they were comfortable with the idea of a woman serving as president, the results were touted as a breakthrough. What has been less discussed are the implications of the fact that 21 percent of respondents were not comfortable with the idea.[4] Moreover, a 2006 CBS/*New York Times* poll revealed that only 55 percent of respondents believed that the country was ready for a female president.[5]

The personality traits and worldviews ascribed to men and women also relate to their roles in the private sphere. Because men are, most often, the primary breadwinners for families, they are perceived as ambitious, hard-charging, tough, strong leaders, able to get a job done, and good in crises. Because women are, most often, the caretakers of the home, the children, and elderly or disabled relatives,

Table 3.1 Employed Person by Occupation and Sex

Category	Percent Women
Management occupations	36.7
Architecture and engineering occupations	13.8
Community and social services occupations	61.1
Lawyers	29.4
Education, training, and library occupations	73.4
Physicians and surgeons	29.4
Registered nurses	92.2
Dental hygienists	98.8
Protective service occupations	21.7
Personal care and service occupations	77.6
Sales and related occupations	49.3
Office and administrative support occupations	75.9
Construction and extraction occupations	2.5
Installation, maintenance, and repair occupations	4.6

Source: US Department of Labor, Bureau of Labor Statistics. "Labor Force Statistics from the Current Population Survey." www.bls.gov/cps/wlf-databook2005.htm. Accessed February 24, 2006.

they are perceived as nurturing, compassionate, soft-hearted, warm, honest, and expressive.[6] When women move from private sphere roles to public roles, they often find themselves faced with those stereotypes. Thus, they feel it necessary to establish credibility by overcoming gender stereotypes that suggest a lack of toughness or decisiveness and a reluctance to take bold actions. One telling example of this double bind comes from the realm of women officeholders. Public perceptions of women legislators, for example, are that they are more compassionate, more honest, more task-oriented, more interested in issues related to education, poverty, health care, the environment, and the welfare of children and families than men. Men, however, are seen as dominant, tougher, decisive, in possession of technical expertise, and stronger on issues of crime suppression and punishment, economic performance, military and foreign policy matters, trade, taxes, agriculture, security, and terrorism.[7] Because the latter set of issues is foundational in the public sphere, not to mention the territory of the presidency, men are generally seen as "naturals" in the role of president. When a particular woman compares well with men, she is seen as "exceptional." Margaret Thatcher's appellation as the "Iron Lady" attests to this point of view.

Social psychology studies have found that the desire for a prototypical leader is particularly strong in times of uncertainty and stress, such as is the case today on both the domestic and international fronts.[8] Since the essence of the office of the presidency involves dealing with high levels of uncertainty and stress, women may find it difficult to overcome the public's unconscious need for leaders whose ascriptive characteristics conform to those of the prototypical leader. For example, Jennifer L. Lawless found evidence of these attitudes in a poll conducted a year after the 9/11 attacks. A total of 61 percent of respondents indicated that male leaders were better than female leaders at handling military crises. On specific questions related to fighting terrorism and the Middle East conflict, the proportion indicating men were more competent ranged from 30 percent to 40 percent.[9]

It is not only in the public sphere that women are at a disadvantage compared to men. Their private sphere roles and responsibilities make public sphere experiences very different for each sex. That is, even when women deviate from traditional private sphere roles to participate actively in the public sphere, they are more often than not expected to perform double duty in the home and "at work." For women, entering public life does not mean leaving the bulk of private responsibilities to others.[10] In the political realm, studies of legislators and potential legislators indicate that, despite holding public office, women bear the brunt of work inside the home.[11] One consequence, revealed by recent political science scholarship, is that private responsibilities may dissuade women who have considered running for office and are well situated to do so from running.[12] In short, simply extending public life to women who were once excluded does not result in equally situating women and men with respect to political opportunity or success. Until both sexes have full opportunity to embrace public and private roles, women who seek political office, especially high political office such as the presidency of the United States, will be at a disadvantage. And the impact of these gendered social roles on perpetuating American views of what is "natural" for men and women is that men continue to be seen as "presidential." Under such circumstances, women who seek that office will continue to be seen as a novelty or even an aberration.

From Societal Gendering to Institutional Gendering: The Political World

Another way to analyze the impact of gendered sociocultural roles on the ascent of women to the presidency is to explore the ways in which they are replicated in institutional life. In what ways can institutions be said to be "gendered"? Scholars of institutional gendering point out that gender adheres not just to individuals but also to the organizations and institutions to which they belong. Sociologist Joan Acker, who introduced the concept, notes that the totality of institutional life, including stereotypical expectations for women and men's attributes, behavior and perceptions, personal relationships, dominant ideologies, distributions of power, and organizational processes, is gendered.[13] Institutional gendering results in disadvantage to one sex or the other, depending on which is dominant. The issue is not just that, for example, rules and practices—formal and informal, tacit and explicit—privilege some over others; it is that they do so in a disparate fashion. Hence, those structures, behaviors, and perspectives that conform to the gendered expectations of the institution—in the case of political bodies such as legislatures, courts, and the executive, the expectations are male—are rewarded. Further, to the extent that women's preferences are distinctive, they are likely to be devalued and attenuated.[14]

One vehicle for institutionally disadvantaging women may be reactions to the issues they bring to the table and those on which they place priority. Research on congressional and state legislatures indicates that women officeholders have worked to shift governmental agendas by bringing issues previously relegated to the private sphere squarely onto public agendas (such as domestic violence), transforming issues long hidden from public view from whispered conversations to public crimes (such as sexual harassment), and expanding the education of men and influencing their policy choices on topics with which they are unfamiliar (such as funding for research for breast cancer).[15] These efforts have resulted in successful passage of legislation often referred to as "women's issues."[16] The effects of institutional gendering may mean that women achieve lower status and earn fewer rewards for concentrating on issues perceived to be of secondary importance.

Apart from the mix of issues that women bring to the agenda and prioritize, their approach to issues may also accord them less success and status than men. In a study of the Colorado legislature, Lyn Kathlene found that legislative women were more likely than men to be contextual in their political outlook (to perceive that people's lives are interdependent, based on a continuous web of relationships). Men were more likely to be instrumental (to see people as autonomous individuals in a hierarchical, competitive world). Consequently, when formulating policy solutions, legislative women relied on different and more sources of information and created prescriptions that reflected not just an individual aberrant action, but also the impact of societal opportunities and lifelong experiences on those actions. The complexity of women's legislative proposals and their contextual nature also meant lower success rates for bill passage. As Kathlene notes, women's approach was "at odds with the instrumental institutionalized discourse" that devalued or marginalized contextualism in legislative institutions.[17]

Moving from legislatures and the ways in which gender conditions institutional environments to the presidential level, political scientist Georgia Duerst-Lahti notes:

> An institution becomes gendered because it takes on characteristics or preferences of the founders, incumbents, and important external actors who influence it over time. In doing so, these founders and influential incumbents create the institutions' formal and informal structures, rules, and practices, reflecting their preferred mode of organizing. If men have played an overwhelming role in an institution's creation and evolution, it is only "natural" that masculine preferences have become embedded in its ideal nature. It takes on a masculine gender ethos. This is what has happened to the US presidency.[18]

Presidential historian Forrest McDonald's comments further explain the pervasiveness of the masculine ethos of the US presidency:

> For in addition to the powers and responsibilities vested in the presidential office by the Constitution and those acquired over the years, the office inherently had the ceremonial, ritualistic, and symbolic duties of a king-surrogate. Whether as warrior-leader, father of his people, or protector, the president is during his tenure the living embodiment of the nation.[19]

Indeed, political scientists Caroline Heldman, Susan J. Carroll, and Stephanie Olson sum up the male ethos of the presidency this way: There is "perhaps no political position where gender stereotypes work more to women's disadvantage than the highly masculinized office of the US presidency."[20]

Institutional Gendering and Religious Institutions

Illustrating institutional gendering in private institutions, such as marriage and the family, and public ones, such as the political arena, tells only part of the story of how the American sociocultural ethos affects the possibility of a woman president—either in 2008 or beyond. All social institutions—educational, economic, legal, military, and religious—are gendered. It is the latter that may be particularly relevant to analysis of the possibility of a woman president in the near future. Although, in the early 1940s, Paul Lazarsfeld identified religion as an important determinant of political preferences, his findings did not fit with the era's dominant voting model and were discounted.[21] However, recent research indicates that religious belief is a strong predictor of political views, and that, in some cases, it trumps class as a determinant of voting.[22] Not only are religious institutions as deeply gendered (if not more so) than political institutions, a subset of them, those of evangelical Christians, are grounded in explicit, direct subjugation of women in public roles.[23] Further, over the past half century, Protestant sects that endorse women's work in the home have gained members, while those advocating social equality between men and women have lost members.[24] An example of a growing sect is the Southern Baptists, who, at their 1998 annual convention, revised their Baptist Faith and Message to read: "'A wife is to submit graciously to the servant leadership of her husband even as the church willingly submits to the headship of Christ' and then went on to state that a wife 'has the God-given responsibility to respect her husband and to serve as his helper in managing her household and nurturing the next generation.'"[25] Two years later, the Southern Baptist Annual Convention voted to limit church leadership positions to men.[26] Most importantly, socially conservative Protestants believe that female submission to male leadership is appropriate in the political sphere, as well as within the church and family. Marvin Olasky, an early advisor to President George W. Bush, explains it thus:

> God does not forbid women to be leaders in society, generally speaking, but when that occurs it's usually because of the abdication of men. As in the situation with Deborah and Barak, there's a certain shame attached to it. I would vote for a woman for the presidency, in some situations, but again, there's a certain shame attached. Why don't you have a man who's able to step forward?[27]

What bears most directly on when the first women ascends to the presidency and when women's presence as contenders is considered routine is the extension of private religious beliefs to the public, political stage.[28] The role of religion in politics has both grown and been transformed in the recent political era. In particular, the role of evangelical Christians in direct political action has had a deep effect on American politics in terms of candidate selection, issue positions of candidates and parties, and electoral victories.[29] From the 1950s onward, there have been repeated attempts by Republicans to mobilize evangelical Protestants into a mass-based social movement in the United States, but only in the mid-1970s did they succeed in reaching beyond church leaders to politically mobilize the rank-and-file members.[30] The Supreme Court's 1973 legalization of abortion in *Roe v. Wade* was the catalyst. Large numbers of conservative Christians came to believe the nation was heading in the wrong direction. Appalled at what they considered to be assaults on traditional morality and family values, conservative Protestants formed advocacy groups and became politically active for the first time in half a century.[31] In "politicized" churches, pastors used the pulpit to argue that contemporary society had turned away from biblical teachings and risked divine retribution unless actions to reverse course were taken.[32] Ronald Reagan's victory in the 1980 presidential election was a direct outgrowth of this mobilization, as was George W. Bush's presidency.[33] In 2000, he received 68 percent of the white evangelical vote and 78 percent in 2004.[34] Overall, evangelical Christians comprised more than one-third of all Bush voters in 2004.[35] According to Anna Greenberg, socially conservative Christians have gained control of many state party apparatuses and are particularly influential in Republican primaries.[36]

Perhaps the best illustration on the effects of the rise of socially conservative Protestants as a political force that bears on the questions of when or whether a woman wins the presidency is recent research showing an inverse relationship between socially conservative mobilization and the propensity of a state to elect women to political office. To test whether socially conservative Christians exert a dampening effect on women's ability to achieve elective office, researchers compared state-level data on the percentage of women in elected office in 2002 and 2004 to the percentage of Baptists across the states, and the percentage of each state's population that belong to churches associated with the National Association of Evangelicals (NAE).[37] The NAE, which is composed of forty-nine socially conservative churches, is an activist organization that lobbies government on a wide range of social and political issues.[38] Even though the research models in these studies included a host of control variables that might account for differences across states in numbers of women in office,[39] the authors found a strong inverse relationship between membership in socially conservative churches and women's representation in electoral office. In particular, as the NAE percentage increased in a state, the measure of women in elected office decreased. Whether that impact is manifested by women's desire for or willingness to stand for office or by voters' unwillingness to vote for women who do run or both, religion does appear to have a strong impact on women's political empowerment in the United States.

Although the rise in political influence of socially conservative Protestants has been marked, its impact is certainly neither solely determinative of political outcomes nor evenly distributed across the nation. Still, the effects on presidential elections could be significant in at least two ways. First, the public debate about the suitability of a woman president is likely to be affected by the beliefs of socially conservative Protestant voices. According to Judith Stacey, political discourse has become increasingly dominated by "family values" rhetoric, which would likely be exacerbated if a woman were to run for the Oval Office.[40] As Rebecca Klatch notes, "The social conservative world, then, is rooted in a firm conception of the proper and separate roles of men and women, which divinely ordained, are essential to the survival of the family and to the maintenance of a moral, ordered, and stable society."[41] Any serious female candidate running for the presidency will have to confront these essentialist views about women's nature and divinely mandated roles.[42]

Second, it is precisely because the presence of socially conservative Christians is not randomly distributed across the states that winning the presidency may be especially difficult for a woman. Because federal elections are determined not by national popular votes, but by votes of the members of the Electoral College (which, in turn, are based on the candidate who wins the majority of votes in each state—with each state voting in the College based on its state population), candidates must win in the College.[43] Careful analysis of 2004 state voting patterns in relationship to party, Electoral College strength, and NAE membership suggests that a woman of either party faces serious obstacles to winning the presidency in the near term.

First, if the Republican Party selects a woman nominee and wants to replicate the 2004 victory strategy of securing the solid South and a large chunk of the heartland, its members will have to convince voters whose religious orientation is opposed to female leadership to vote for a woman for president. That is because the states with the highest proportion of NAE members (twelve states) were those that Bush carried easily in 2004.[44] The population of each of them belonging to NAE-affiliated churches ranges from 33 to 47 percent (except Mississippi, with 61 percent of its population in NAE-affiliated churches).[45] Although only 51 percent of the nationwide electorate favored Bush in 2004, the percentage supporting Bush in the high NAE states was 57.3 percent. As Table 3.2 suggests, the twelve states with the highest levels of NAE populations add up to 112 Electoral College votes (or 42 percent of the total) out of the necessary 270. To the extent that votes are influenced by religious beliefs, and to the extent that NAE-affiliated churches question the capacity of a woman to be president, a Republican woman (in contrast to a Republican man) will face real challenges putting together an electoral majority using this geographical strategy. Moreover, a Republican, either man or woman, will have a hard time winning the presidency without the region of the country that has given the party its strongest recent support.

Alternatively, if the first woman nominee for president were a Democrat, the Republican-dominated southern states with large shares of socially conservative Protestants would be unlikely to deliver votes to her. The interaction of party and gender might tempt a Democratic woman to write off the southern states. Instead, she might pursue a majority in the Electoral College by holding the Democratic base in the Northeast and West while attracting additional votes from the Midwest and, possibly, the Southwest. Naturally, this

Table 3.2 Top Quartile of National Association of Evangelicals States and Electoral College Votes

State	Electoral Votes
Alabama	9
Arkansas	6
Georgia	15
Kentucky	8
Louisiana	9
Mississippi	6
North Carolina	15
Oklahoma	7
South Carolina	8
Tennessee	11
Virginia	13
West Virginia	5

strategy contains it own set of risks. First, the future candidate must hold all the states won by John Kerry in 2004. The most likely states to stick with a Democratic candidate, female or male, are those places where Kerry received more than 55 percent in 2004. Only five states (almost all in the Northeast), with a total of sixty Electoral College votes fall into this category.[46] Additionally, if the Democratic nominee held the Pacific Coast states that Kerry carried (California with 54.6 percent of the vote, Hawaii with 54 percent, Washington with 53 percent, and Oregon with 51.5 percent), seventy-six Electoral College votes could be added to the total needed to win.[47] Although the 2004 margin in these four states was less than 5 percent, it is plausible that a strong Democratic woman could carry them, especially because each of these states have small NAE populations, and, in accord with the research on correlates of the presence of women officeholders introduced above, nearly all these states have a strong tradition of electing women to high political office.[48] Should such a strategy succeed, however, the total Electoral College vote of all the high-probability states is 136—or just over half of what is needed to win.

Extending the strategy outlined above to raise the Electoral College total increases the challenge. Moving from 136 Electoral College votes to the required 270 means that the future candidate will need to win all the remaining ten states that favored Kerry in 2004. One-third of them (Connecticut, with 54.3 percent, Delaware, 53.3 percent, and Maine, 53.1 percent) have moderate NAE membership levels and a strong enough history of supporting female candidates to suggest that antifemale bias will not be likely to overwhelm the small Democratic margins in each of them (however, Maine splits its Electoral College votes, indicating that neither major party candidate will automatically earn all of Maine's votes).[49] Next, although each of the remaining seven states that voted Democratic in 2004 have low levels of NAE membership, each also supported Kerry by either a razor-thin margin of victory or has a poor history of electing women or both. Among the thin-margin states, Minnesota and New Hampshire have 10 percent or less NAE membership and strong records of supporting women candidates; Wisconsin and Michigan have midlevel records with respect to electing women and are mixed on levels of NAE membership (Wisconsin's NAE membership is less than 10 percent, but Michigan's is slightly above 20 percent). Although Pennsylvania has a very small NAE membership total, it has earned one of the worst records in the nation in electing women.[50] The remaining two states (Illinois and New Jersey) had 2004 vote margins in the 2 percent range, although both have been slightly favorable to women candidates in the past and both have low levels of NAE membership.[51]

Alternatively, if a Democratic woman presidential candidate chooses to put together a coalition of states in the West and Midwest that voted Republican in 2004, her best prospects are in states with the smallest voting margins for Bush, those in which women candidates have done relatively well in the past, and those with lower levels of NAE membership. In 2004, Bush barely prevailed in several Western states (New Mexico, with 50 percent; Nevada, 50.5 percent; and Colorado, 52.5 percent),[52] all of which have strong records of electing women to political office and relatively low levels of NAE church membership.[53] However, they provide only twenty-nine Electoral College votes. In the Midwest, the best chances for a Democratic woman to prevail are in Iowa, Ohio, and Missouri, which voted for Bush by 50.1 percent, 51 percent, and 53.4 percent, respectively.[54] Although none of these states has been particularly supportive of women candidates, a Democratic woman might succeed in Iowa, which has a low proportion (8 percent) of its population belonging to NAE churches.[55]

In sum, the influence of socially conservative Protestants in US politics suggests that, absent a remarkable set of electoral circumstances, it will be challenging for a woman candidate to win the presidency in 2008 or immediately thereafter. Even a Republican woman who is conservative and experienced in the military or foreign policy will likely face cognitive dissonance among conservative religious citizens who may prefer to elect men for this important leadership position.[56] And a Democratic woman may not attract the majority of voters in as many states as previous male contenders of her party—especially those states closer to party balance, those with moderate or higher levels of NAE membership, and those without a strong history of electing women to other political offices. To be clear, this analysis is not meant to suggest that socially conservative Protestants are monolithic political thinkers, that they single-handedly control the political arena, or even that their views are held by the majority. However, the elements of US elections related to the two-party system and the existence and form of our Electoral College amplify their influence. Because conservative Protestants are particularly strongly positioned in the Republican Party and in the southern states, the effects on both the party nominations and votes in the general election are likely to be significant.

Societal and Institutional Gendering and the Pipeline for the Presidency

The foregoing analysis suggests that the effects of societal and institutional gendering in many spheres place political women and those issues associated with them in a disadvantageous political position compared to men. The result diminishes women's chances to be nominated to a major party ticket and to be elected to the US presidency. That fact may discourage some women from running at all. Indeed, evidence gathered from lower-level elective political offices suggests that the phenomenon is operative in political roles far less demanding than the presidency. After more than twenty-five years of incremental progress elevating the proportion of women in state and federal legislatures, it appears that a plateau may have been reached. As Table 3.3 demonstrates, for the first time since the late 1960s and early 1970s, the election cycles of the new millennium have resulted in either a slight decrease in the number of women in office (in Congress, statewide elected executives, and state legislatures) or only small gains. Following the 2006 midterm elections, the percentage of women in Congress increased only slightly from 2001, from 13.6 to 16 percent; the percentage of women in state legislatures had increased only 1.1 percent; and the percentage of women in statewide elected executive office had decreased in every electoral cycle from 2001 to 2007.[57] In addition, in 2007, there were still only nine women governors (in Alaska, Arizona, Connecticut, Delaware, Hawaii, Kansas, Louisiana, Michigan, and Washington), one more than in 2006.[58] This latter set of statistics is vitally important because modern history shows that gubernatorial offices are springboards to the presidency. Of the five most recent presidents, four were governors (Carter, Reagan, Clinton, and George W. Bush).[59]

Naturally, many factors may explain these patterns. However, research at the state legislative level suggests that gendered environments may contribute to them. Surveys of state legislators reveal that the costs for success in this arena are higher for women than men. Studies consistently reveal that women legislators continue to perceive discriminatory environments based on sex. The result is that women face and must work to counteract collegial perceptions that they are not as effective as men. To do so, they need to prove themselves by working harder and more precisely to achieve the same levels of respect and success. This atmospheric double standard may be overt or subtle, but women across the nation appear to agree on its

Table 3.3 Women in Elective Offices, as a Percentage

Year	Congress	Statewide Elected Executives	State Legislators
2001	13.6	27.6	22.4
2003	13.6	26.0	22.4
2004	13.8	26.0	22.5
2005	15.0	25.7	22.7
2006	15.0	25.1	22.8
2007	16.0	24.1	23.5

Source: Center for American Women and Politics. *Women in Elective Office 2007 Fact Sheet.* http://www.cawp.rutgers.edu/Facts/Officeholders/elective.pdf.

existence. For example, Sue Thomas's survey of state legislators revealed that, when asked about the biggest obstacles to their careers, fully one-quarter of women noted that the double standard was the culprit.[60] The problem was stated in terms of their status as wives and mothers, being a woman in a male environment, being treated as second-class legislators, being perceived as solid only on certain issues associated with women, being isolated, and being unrepresented in leadership. Combined with the persistent double duty at work and in the home referenced earlier in this chapter, this atmospheric discrimination may well depress the numbers of women who are interested in political office but unwilling to pay the higher price demanded of them. If so, it will, in turn, result in a smaller group of women with the experience and credentials to run for the presidency.

Gendering and the Framing of Women's Issues: The Delicate Balance

As discussed earlier in this chapter, one indicator of the prevalence and depth of societal and institutional gendering is the ways in which key political issues are dichotomized into "women's issues" and "men's issues," with men's issues often perceived as "everyone's" issues. Topics accorded lesser status in the hierarchy of politically important concerns in the United States include (1) family life, such as child care, elder care, child support, parental leave, and flexible work schedules; (2) women's health issues, such as reproductive rights and funding for and research into a host of diseases that predominantly affect women; (3) education; (4) health care availability and affordability; and (5) employment, including equal access to the full range of occupations and pay equity. Even with the emergence of the gender gap in 1980 and the competition to win women's votes, these issues are still considered to be single-interest and at the margins of political importance.[61] Rarely are they accorded the respect and attention other issues receive, issues usually considered to belong more centrally to the "masculine" arena of politics. That may be especially true after September 11, 2001, when issues of war, terrorism, security, and the economy are seen as of primary importance. Indeed, in 2004, the Republican Party was said to be targeting women's votes by appealing to "security moms" and largely ignoring other issues of concern to women.[62]

An important consequence of bifurcating issues by gender and privileging "men's" issues over "women's" issues is that, at present, women who run for any political office have to calibrate their presentations of self to recognize, maximize, and counteract widely held gender stereotypes across issue domains. As many of the chapters in this volume illuminate, women candidates can sometimes be advantaged by the prevailing stereotypes about issue competence and can often be disadvantaged. In times and places in which "women's issues" are highly salient to electorates, women candidates can be advantaged by highlighting them. But when other issues come to the fore, issues on which women are assumed to be less capable, candidates risk loss by emphasizing women's concerns.[63] And when issues related to war, foreign policy, terrorism, and economic decline are uppermost in the minds of the electorate, as has been the case in the post–9/11 world, whether or not women candidates emphasize women's issues, their assumed lack of competence on "men's" issues will be difficult to overcome.

This effect of stereotypes about women and men's issue competence and the need for a women presidential candidate to be carefully positioned on women's issues is likely to be exacerbated by the interaction of party and gender. As Republicans are seen by the wider electorate as better at handling those issues also associated with male competence, a Democratic woman running in the present electoral environment will have a great many obstacles to overcome. And a Republican woman will need to surmount the difficulties that may arise if she has been a champion of women's issues or is seen as weakening or abandoning the party's position on the status of women.

Perhaps the most highly charged women's issue presently on the political agenda relates to reproductive rights—particularly abortion. Although a majority of Americans are pro-choice, people often take that position while approving of various restrictions on the practice. Whether the restrictions pertain to parental consent or notification, waiting periods, informed consent, or spousal consent, the right to reproductive choice regarding abortion is neither legally protected as absolute nor deemed to be appropriate to be otherwise. Indeed, public opinion on abortion has been stable for the more than thirty years it has occupied center stage in policy debates. Says the Pew Research Center for the People and the Press:

> A consistent majority of Americans (65 percent) are opposed to overturning the 1973 *Roe v. Wade* decision establishing a woman's right to abortion. But most Americans also favor restrictions on abortion. Nearly three-quarters (73 percent) favor requiring women under age 18 to get parental consent before being allowed to get an abortion. Members of both political parties are divided in views of the availability of abortion. Nearly two-thirds of liberal Democrats (64 percent) believe abortion should be generally available to those who want it. That compares with only about a third of moderate and conservative Democrats (34 percent). About one-in-five conservative Republicans (22 percent) believe abortion should not be permitted at all; just 1 percent of moderate and liberal Republicans agree. And roughly twice as many conservative Republicans as GOP liberals and moderates say abortion should be banned, or allowed only in cases of incest, rape or to protect the life of the woman (71 percent vs. 36 percent). There also are wide differences among religious groups over this question. Most seculars (60 percent) believe abortion should be generally available, and a plurality of white mainline Protestants agree. About two-thirds of white evangelicals (68 percent) believe abortion should not be permitted or allowed only in cases of rape, incest or to save the woman's life. White Catholics are deeply divided over abortion, with about three-in-ten (31 percent) saying it should be generally available, and 43 percent saying it should be banned or only legal in cases of rape, incest or to save the life of the mother.[64]

A woman candidate for the presidency will face a series of delicate choices surrounding her position on reproductive rights and the extent to which she is willing to take on or fit into her party's position on them—especially abortion. To date, Democrats who run for president have been expected to support the party position in favor of choice. A pro-choice Democratic woman who runs for president may be more disadvantaged than a pro-choice Democratic man. Because women are assumed to be more concerned with and committed to issues of reproduction than men, a woman candidate may be seen as dangerously subjective about the subject. And what of a Republican woman candidate? Running as a pro-choice candidate, even in the mildest way, would likely create furor among the Republican Party's base, including those who are socially conservative Protestants. Being antichoice, however, might anger enough Independent and swing voters that a Republican woman candidate would lose their votes.[65] Certainly, that could be the case for a Republican male candidate as well, but the consequences for a female candidate are greater. Any woman candidate, including Republicans, is likely to be perceived by the electorate as more sympathetic to women's issues than a male candidate. Countering that stereotype on reproductive issues may create more dissatisfaction among voters with a female antichoice candidate. Either way, as reflected in the analysis of Electoral College votes, a woman candidate for president must navigate a much more difficult and delicate path than her male counterparts.

The preceding discussion of the possibility of an antichoice Republican woman losing the votes of independent and swing woman voters raises the question of whether a woman running for president would garner a greater share of women's votes than a male candidate. The answer, as extensively explicated elsewhere in this volume, is, possibly, but not necessarily. Although the historic nature of the race would attract women's interest and open the wallets of women campaign contributors, just as Geraldine Ferraro's race for the vice presidency did in 1984, it may or may not translate into a greater share of votes than a similarly situated male candidate.[66] Much depends on the electoral context, including whether the race is an open one, salient campaign issues, the party and issue positions of the woman candidate, and the competition. Who the opposing male candidate is and his party and issues positions will matter tremendously. Only in the unlikely scenario of both parties nominating a woman (as was widely speculated on in the "Hillary versus Condi" media discussion during 2005 and 2006) does the issue of gender and women's issues take on a different dimension entirely. Then, it would be reasonable to suppose that the Democratic and Republican women who run in the general election will present themselves similarly to the Democratic man and Republican man who would otherwise have stood in their places. In that circumstance, the influence (although not the import) of women's issues will, to some extent, be neutralized. That is not to say that women running for the presidency from both parties will silence or dampen public attention and media attention to their status as women; it will only render stereotypical views about women candidates' positions on women's issues less volatile than they might be otherwise.[67]

In sum, the influence of women's issues, especially reproductive rights issues, on the successful candidacy of the first woman running for president on a major party ticket are likely to be considerable. Whether Democrat or Republican, the woman in question will need to forge a path beyond stereotypes and false options. She will have to redefine the role of presidential candidate so that it ceases to be seen as an entirely masculinized role and redefine critical issues so that they are not seen as the primary province of one sex or the other. The successful woman will have to the largest extent possible reframed the debate.[68]

Conclusion: Madam President—How Soon and How Often?

In this chapter, we have sought to frame analysis of the effect of issues stances by female candidates for the US presidency, particularly on women's issues, in a broader discussion of societal and institutional gendering. The very appellation "women's issues" is indicative of the bifurcation of roles with which both sexes contend—in and out of the political arena. The following questions remain: Will a woman be elected in 2008, or will she take office a great deal later, and what will be the circumstances that propel her into the Oval Office? When will issues that are important to men, women, and children cease being seen as political liabilities and move instead to become routine elements of presidential agendas, and at what point in history will the question of the candidate's sex cease being a novelty that will dominate all else in an election? We conclude that only when women and men are given full opportunities and responsibilities in both public and private spheres will women contenders for the presidency on major party tickets be more than historical anomalies.

Yet, surely, before then, circumstances will align to propel at least one woman into the presidency.[69] Beyond Hillary Clinton's declared candidacy, there are several women who are regularly mentioned by the White House Project (a national, nonpartisan organization that works to advance a critical mass of women into the political leadership pipeline) as possible contenders in the near future, such as

Senator Susan Collins (R-ME) and Governor Janet Napolitano (D-AZ).[70] Among this group is one woman who has been quoted repeatedly as being interested in running for the presidency. Senator Kay Bailey Hutchison (R-TX and Republican Conference Secretary) has said that, in 2008, "quality and qualifications" will be more important than the sex of the candidate. "It's just the right woman, who wants the job, who will run for the job, with the right credentials. I really think we're there."[71] It will be exciting to see if she is right.

Notes

1. Dolan, "How the Public Views Women Candidates," p. 42.
2. Rashotte and Webster, "Gender Status Beliefs," p. 630.
3. Anderson, *Thinking About Women*, pp. 19–23.
4. Feminist Daily News Wire, "Nearly 100 Percent of Americans Would Vote for a Woman President."
5. Ibid.
6. See Gordon and Miller, "Does the Oval Office Have a Glass Ceiling?"; and Dolan, *Voting for Women*, pp. 7–12.
7. Dolan, *Voting for Women*, pp. 7–12, 78–84.
8. See Hogg, "Organizational Orthodoxy and Corporate Autocrats"; and "Uncertainty, Social Identity, and Ideology."
9. See Lawless, "Women, War, and Winning Elections."
10. See Cooper and Lewis, *Managing the New Work Force*; Hochschild, *The Second Shift*; and Holtzman and Williams, "Women in the Political World."
11. In addition to the job of legislator, women remain primarily responsible for all matters of home and hearth in ways male legislators do not. These responsibilities include child care, cooking, cleaning, shopping, washing dishes, and doing laundry. See Thomas, "The Personal Is Political."
12. In their study of the "eligibility pool" in New York state—individuals whose background makes them plausible candidates to run for high-level political office—Fox and Lawless (2003) found sharp gender differences among the male and female respondents with respect to sex-role socialization. The typical male respondent interested in running for political office held traditional views about gender roles (e.g., opposed abortion, opposed the Equal Rights Amendment, held negative views of feminism, and considered men to be better suited than women for politics). In contrast, the typical female respondent held views that would be considered feminist.
13. See Acker, "Gendered Institutions."
14. See Duerst-Lahti and Kelly, *Gender Power, Leadership, and Governance*; Duerst-Lahti, "Governing Institutions, Ideologies, and Gender"; Duerst-Lahti, "Knowing Congress as a Gendered Institution"; Kathlene, "In a Different Voice"; Kathlene, "Power and Influence in State

Legislative Policymaking"; and Kenney, "Field Essay: New Research on Gendered Political Institutions."

15. See Levy, "Do Differences Matter?"; Kedrowski and Sarow, "The Gendering of Cancer Policy"; Walsh, "Enlarging Representation"; Norton, "Transforming Policy from the Inside"; Thomas, *How Women Legislate*; Dolan, "Support for Women's Interests in the 103rd Congress"; and Dodson, "Representing Women's Interests."

16. See Saint-Germain, "Does Their Difference Make a Difference?"; Thomas, *How Women Legislate*; Dodson and Carroll, *Reshaping the Agenda*; Vega and Firestone, "The Effects of Gender on Congressional Behavior"; Tamerius, "Sex, Gender, and Leadership"; Dodson, "Representing Women's Interests"; Dodson, "Acting for Women"; Dolan and Ford, "Change and Continuity Among Women State Legislators"; Dolan and Ford, "Are All Women State Legislators Alike?"; Swers, *The Difference Women Make*; Bratton and Haynie, "Agenda Setting and Legislative Success in State Legislatures."

17. See Kathlene, "In a Different Voice"; and Kathlene, "Power and Influence in State Legislative Policymaking."

18. Duerst-Lahti, "Presidential Elections: Gendered Space and the Case of 2004," p. 23.

19. McDonald, *The American Presidency*, p. 425.

20. Heldman, Carroll, and Olson, "'She Brought Only a Skirt,'" p. 316.

21. Swatos, "The Politics of Gender and the 'Two-Party' Thesis," p. 24.

22. See Greenberg, "Race, Religiosity, and the Women's Vote"; and Whistler and Wekkin, "Religion and Politics Among Southern High School Seniors."

23. See Sherkat, "'That They Be Keepers of the Home.'"

24. Swatos, "The Politics of Gender and the 'Two-party' Thesis," p. 30.

25. Stammer, "A Wife's Role Is 'to Submit,' Baptists Declare," pp. A1, A26.

26. Mead and Hill, *Handbook of Denominations in the United States*, p. 66.

27. Wegner, "The Impact of Feminists," p. 5.

28. Several studies have found that support for traditional gender roles is higher among Protestants than among other religious identifiers and those holding secular worldviews. See, for example, Lottes and Kuriloff, "The Effects of Gender, Race, Religion, and Political Orientation"; and Greenberg, "Race, Religiosity, and the Women's Vote."

29. The terms "evangelical" and "fundamentalist" are often used to describe socially conservative Protestants. Beck explains, "Evangelicals and Fundamentalists both believe three essential doctrines: (1) the supreme authority of the Bible for matters of faith, (2) salvation only through personal faith, and (3) the Christian imperative to tell others about Jesus." For much of the twentieth century, fundamentalists withdrew from worldly concerns, viewing modern society as hopelessly corrupt. In contrast, evangelicals were more likely to remain engaged. Since the 1970s, as fundamentalists became

reengaged in political and social life, the distinction between the two groups has diminished sharply. See Beck, "Fundamentalists," pp. 111–112.

This increased participation by evangelicals may be explained by the dramatic shift in religious adherence away from more liberal Protestant sects toward socially conservative denominations since the 1970s. See Masci, *CQ Researcher: Religion and Politics*, p. 7. For example, the Southern Baptists, with 16 million members, is one of the fastest-growing denominations, as well as being one of the most socially conservative sects in the country. See Mead and Hill, *Handbook of Denominations in the United States*, p. 64.

30. Wilcox, "The Christian Right in Twentieth-Century America," p. 665.

31. Ibid, p. 668.

32. Kaufmann, "The Partisan Paradox," p. 492.

33. Masci, *CQ Researcher: Religion and Politics,* p. 14.

34. See Pew Research Center, "Religion and the Presidential Vote."

35. Ibid.

36. Greenberg, "Race, Religiosity, and the Women's Vote," p. 64.

37. See Schroedel, Merolla, and Foerstel, "Women's Relative Lack of Electoral Success"; and Merolla, Schroedel, and Holman, "The Paradox of Protestantism."

38. Schultz, West, and Maclean, *Encyclopedia of Religion in American Politics*, p. 322.

39. These independent variables include the following: proportion of the population that is Catholic, proportion that is nonevangelical, two measures of women's status in the states, two measures of the state economies, the presence or absence of term limits, and two measures of state ideology.

40. See Stacey, "The Rhetoric and Politics of 'Family Values.'"

41. Klatch, "Women of the New Right in the United States," p. 371.

42. See Peek and Brown, "Sex Prejudice Among White Protestants."

43. Electoral College votes are allocated on a winner-take-all basis (except in Maine and Nebraska, which allocate their votes on a proportional basis).

44. See Schroedel, Merolla, and Foerstel, "Women's Relative Lack of Electoral Success"; and Merolla, Schroedel, and Holman, "The Paradox of Protestantism."

45. The following are the percentages of each state's population belonging to NAE-affiliated churches and their ranking with respect to women in elected office: Alabama, 41 percent and forty-fourth: Arkansas, 47 percent and twentieth; Georgia, 41 percent and fortieth; Kentucky, 39 percent and forty-ninth; Louisiana, 38 percent and twenty-second; Mississippi, 61 percent and forty-eighth; North Carolina, 42 percent and fortieth (tied with Georgia); Oklahoma, 37 percent and forty-second; South Carolina, 47 percent and fiftieth; Tennessee, 44 percent and forty-third; Virginia, 33 percent and forty-fifth; and West Virginia, 35 percent and forty-sixth. See Merolla, Schroedel, and Holman, "The Paradox of Protestantism"; and Institute for Women's Policy Research, *The Status of Women in the States,* p. 78.

Nearly all of the high NAE states also fall into the lowest quartile of states with respect to women's economic status, as measured by the percentage of women with health insurance, percentage with four years or more of college, percentage of women-owned business, and percentage of women living above the poverty line. The following are the rankings of high NAE states with respect to women's economic autonomy: Alabama, forty-fifth; Arkansas, forty-ninth; Georgia, thirtieth; Kentucky, forty-seventh; Louisiana, forty-sixth; Mississippi, forty-eighth; North Carolina, thirty-fifth; Oklahoma, forty-second; South Carolina, forty-third; Tennessee, forty-fourth; Virginia, eighth; and West Virginia, fiftieth. See Institute for Women's Policy Research, *The Status of Women in the States,* p. 80.

46. These states were Massachusetts, at 62.1 percent of the vote; Rhode Island, with 59.5 percent; Vermont, with 59.1 percent; New York, with 57.8 percent; and Maryland, with 55.7 percent of the vote. See CNN, "Election 2004–US President."

47. Ibid.

48. See Center for American Women and Politics, "Women in State Legislatures, 1985–2005 Fact Sheet."

49. See Federal Election Commission, "Distribution of Electoral Votes."

50. In Pennsylvania, which ranks forty-seventh in the country with respect to electing women to political office, only 11 percent of the population belongs to NAE churches. However, the percent Catholic, which also is negatively associated with women's electoral representation, is relatively high. See Merolla, Schroedel, and Holman, "The Paradox of Protestantism."

51. See CNN, "Election 2004–U.S. President."

52. Ibid.

53. The chances for a Democratic woman in most of the remaining Western states are bleak. Their percentages going to Bush in 2004 are as follows: Utah, 71.1 percent; Wyoming, 69 percent; Idaho, 68.5 percent; Montana, 59.2 percent; and Arizona, 54.9 percent. See ibid. Arizona, which in the past was strongly Republican, may provide the best opportunity for a Democratic woman. It currently has a Democratic woman serving as governor.

54. Ibid.

55. Ohio has a moderate level of NAE membership, but Missouri has 25 percent of its population belonging to NAE-affiliated churches.

56. In their analysis of data from the 1998 General Social Survey, Lieberman and Mooney ("Southern Attitudes Toward Working Women") found that southerners were more likely than respondents in other parts of the country to agree with the statement, "It is much better for everyone involved if the man is the achiever outside the home and the woman takes care of the home and family."

57. These offices include governor, lieutenant governor, secretary of state, attorney general, state treasurer, state auditor, state controller/comptroller, chief agricultural officer, chief education officer, commissioner

of insurance, commissioner of labor, corporate commissioner, public service commissioner, and railroad commissioner.

58. See Center for American Women and Politics, "Women in Statewide Elective Executive Office 2007."

59. Perhaps more telling, as of 2006 only twenty-eight women have ever held gubernatorial positions in the United States (across twenty-one mostly small states). Of these twenty-eight, eighteen were elected outright, three replaced spouses, and seven gained office through constitutional succession. See ibid.

60. See Thomas, "The Personal Is Political."

61. Since 1989, women have made up a larger share of the voting-age population, have voted in greater proportions than men, have generally been more ideologically liberal, and have been more inclined than men to vote for Democratic presidential candidates. In 2004, women made up 54 percent of the voters. See CNN, "Election 2004–U.S. President," and Center for American Women and Politics, "Fact Sheet: Sex Differences in Voter Turnout."

62. See Burrell, "Gender, Presidential Elections, and Public Policy."

63. Ibid.

64. See Pew Research Center, "Abortion and Rights of Terror Suspects Top Court Issues."

65. There is some evidence that the salience of reproductive issues, particularly abortion, is increasing as threats to reproductive choice become greater. In 2006, in South Dakota, the legislature passed a bill signed by the governor that institutes a near-complete abortion ban. Yet a referendum campaign was launched to repeal the law and passed in November 2006. A recent statewide poll found that 57 percent of South Dakotans want the ban repealed, many indicated regret for previously voting for Republican legislators who put the ban in place, and many respondents said they had not anticipated that the legislature would go so far as to ban abortion. See Simon, "Abortion Ban Foes Petition for a Choice."

66. See Clift and Brazaitis, *Madam President: Women Blazing the Leadership Trail.*

67. It is difficult to imagine a presidential race either in 2008 or subsequently in which women headed the major parties' tickets without a male third-party candidate entering the race. The difficulty some voters, both male and female, would have voting for a woman suggests that a male alternative would present himself. This situation would probably aid the Democratic nominee because Republican voters are more likely than Democratic voters to defect to the male third-party candidate.

68. The question of self-identification as a feminist or not will almost surely be one of the ways the debate on women candidates and women's issues is framed. It is likely that the first woman running for the presidency on a major party ticket will need to gracefully elude the topic—perhaps by redefining the term "feminist" in a fairly benign and neutral fashion.

69. For discussion of the historical and current political environment

for black women candidates for president, see McClain, Carter, and Brady, "Gender and Black Presidential Politics."

70. Given the Republican Party's position on reproductive issues, Collins, who is pro-choice, faces more obstacles than does equally pro-choice Democrat Napolitano.

71. See CBS News, "The Quest to Become Ms. President."

4

Shaping Women's Chances: Stereotypes and the Media

Gina Serignese Woodall and Kim L. Fridkin

Louisiana governor Kathleen Babineaux Blanco faced intense scrutiny after Hurricane Katrina destroyed much of her state in the summer of 2005. According to a *New York Times* article published in the wake of Hurricane Katrina, Governor Blanco "was being mocked as weepy and indecisive by radio talk show hosts who derided her as 'momma governor.'"[1] Troy M. Hebert, a state representative from Louisiana, said, "People can't stop comparing her to Rudy Giuliani. . . . When 9/11 came, [Giuliani] looked like he was doing something. I'm not sure he was. But he looked like it." Governor Blanco acknowledged the comparison with Giuliani and dismissed some of the criticism against her as sexist, saying, "I'm not a guy. I can't be Rudy, whatever that is."[2]

Governor Blanco's staff was concerned with improving Blanco's image in the aftermath of Katrina. For example, Governor Blanco's spokeswoman, Denise Bottcher, worried that the governor was "doing too many 'first lady' things and not enough John Wayne." Bottcher continued by explaining that "women are easily portrayed as weak, which [the governor] has had a hard time over coming. I will say again: men cry—compassion: women cry—weak."[3]

While she was being derided for her "weakness" and "emotionality" over the crisis, Governor Blanco and her staff tried to combat such criticisms by bolstering her image as "tough." For example, the governor asserted that "she was far tougher than her critics allowed, noting that when she used phrases like 'locked and loaded,' it was because she knew how to handle a gun."[4]

The unique situation faced by Governor Blanco illustrates a common dilemma for female politicians: Do women political candidates need to hide their compassion and showcase their toughness to be seen as competent public leaders? Or will voters punish women politicians for being too tough? And will women candidates receive any electoral dividends by highlighting their empathy and sensitivity? According to Kathleen Hall Jamieson, common gender stereotypes create a double bind for women politicians in American society. In particular, women leaders are often punished if they act in a way that reinforces sex role expectations (e.g., showing emotion signifies weakness), *and* they may be punished if they act in a way that conflicts with commonly held stereotypes (e.g., acting tough signifies insensitivity).[5]

The double bind, as articulated by Jamieson, is a product of two interacting factors. First, people hold stereotypes about what constitutes proper feminine and masculine behavior. Second, people have ideas about desirable traits in a leader. The double bind is created because people's stereotypes about strong leadership traits do not overlap with people's views regarding women's stereotypical strengths.[6] As Ruth Mandel observed in 1981, "If you're assertive and aggressive enough to do the job, you're unfeminine and therefore unacceptable. If you're not aggressive enough, you can't do the job—and, in either case, good bye."[7]

Gender Stereotypes and Women Candidates

Since common stereotypes drive the double bind, it is important to understand the content and persistence of gender stereotypes. Scholars have examined the prevalence of gender stereotypes since the 1950s. Their research suggests that men, generally, are perceived as possessing agentic traits, such as being bold, rational, and unemotional, whereas women, generally, are perceived as possessing communal traits, such as sensitivity, empathy, and passivity.[8]

Political science research has shown that people apply these gender stereotypes to the political arena. Furthermore, these stereotypes lead people to view men and women candidates as having distinct areas of policy expertise. In particular, women candidates are viewed as being more competent at handling "compassion" issues, such as poverty, education, the environment, child care, and health care policy, whereas men are seen as more competent at dealing with male issues, such as the economy, foreign policy, and other defense issues.[9]

These issue and trait stereotypes are robust and have been identified by researchers using a variety of different methods, including surveys[10] and experiments.[11] Stereotypes persist when one is examining students as subjects[12] or a more representative population.[13]

In a classic study of gender stereotyping in politics, Virginia Sapiro examined people's evaluations of male and female candidates by giving experimental subjects a speech by Senator Howard Baker that had no clear ideological or party leanings. She told some subjects that John Leeds, a candidate for the House, had given the speech, but other subjects thought that House candidate Joan Leeds made the speech. Sapiro found that people differed in their evaluations of John and Joan Leeds, even though people were given identical information about these candidates. In particular, subjects viewed John Leeds as more competent at dealing with military issues and farm issues, whereas Joan Leeds was seen as better able to deal with health and educational issues.[14]

Over twenty years have passed since Sapiro conducted her study. The political landscape for women has changed a great deal in the interim. When Sapiro's study was published, the US Senate had only two women senators, and only twenty-one women served in the US House of Representatives. As of 2007, there were seventy-one women in the US House and sixteen women serving as US senators. However, gender stereotypes about male and female candidates persist. For example, Ann Gordon and Jerry Miller asked students at a midwestern university to read a newspaper article about an "up-and-coming" member of Congress, Representative Wilson. Representative Wilson was portrayed as a likely candidate for the White House in 2008. In one article, Wilson was a man (John) and in the other article, Wilson was a woman (Jessica). As in Sapiro's study, the information provided about the potential presidential candidate was identical; only the gender of the candidate varied. Like Sapiro, Gordon found people distinguished between John and Jessica Wilson on issue and trait dimensions. For example, subjects viewed John Wilson as more competent at dealing with economic and military issues, whereas Jessica Wilson was advantaged on civil rights.[15]

In addition, recent survey research shows that gender stereotypes about men and women candidates persist. In the fall of 2002, Jennifer L. Lawless asked respondents whether male or female politicians were more or less likely to possess a specific trait or competency level for dealing with a specific issue. Lawless, like previous researchers, found respondents were more likely to view male politicians as self-confident, assertive, tough, and aggressive and more likely to view women politicians as compassionate, compromising, sensitive, and emotional. For example, 58 percent of the respondents said women politicians were more compassionate than men, 2 percent said male politicians were more compassionate, and 40 percent said men and women politicians were equally likely to be compassionate.[16] Similarly, 46 percent of the respondents said men were more likely to be tough, 6 percent said women were more likely to be tough, and 48 percent said men and women politicians were equally likely to be tough.

Furthermore, Lawless's results showed that people continue to view men and women as having distinct areas of expertise. For example, 61 percent of the respondents thought a male politician could handle a military crisis better than a woman, whereas 62 percent of the sample believed a woman candidate or officeholder would be more likely to improve children's welfare, compared to a man.[17]

Finally, research has suggested that gender stereotypes lead people to view men as more likely to possess leadership or executive traits[18] and that people believe these "male" traits are more important in top leadership positions, compared to "female" traits.[19] Again, contemporary research shows that people continue to view certain male traits as more important for successful leaders. For example, Lawless presented respondents with a list of four stereotypically masculine traits (assertive, tough, aggressive, self-confident) and four stereotypically feminine traits (compassionate, sensitive, emotional, compromising) and asked respondents to choose the four traits most important for political candidates and officeholders. Of the top four traits chosen by respondents, three were masculine traits (tough, self-confident, assertive), and only one was a feminine trait (compassionate).[20]

Respondents also believed that women candidates were less viable than male candidates.[21] For example, Sapiro found subjects viewed John Leeds as significantly more likely to win election to the US House of Representatives, compared to Joan Leeds.[22] Similarly, Gordon and Miller found that John Wilson was viewed as a more viable candidate for president in 2008 than Jessica Wilson. In Gordon and Miller's experiment, 44 percent of the subjects viewed Jessica Wilson as viable or somewhat viable, compared to 71 percent for John Wilson. Subjects viewed Jessica Wilson as more viable as a vice presidential candidate, with 63 percent of the sample evaluating her as viable or somewhat viable. John Wilson, however, still had an advantage, with 88 percent of the subjects calling him viable or somewhat viable.[23]

Gordon and Miller explored the reasons subjects gave for their views regarding the candidates' viability. In general, many of the subjects did not think Americans were ready for a female president. For example, one subject said, "I feel that a woman President would not be respected." Another subject speculated, "I'm not sure a woman would deal with situations as effectively as men." And, a third subject thought that other nations "may try to take advantage of the fact that [the President] is a woman."[24]

Differences in the viability ratings given to men and women candidates can be consequential, harming women in the electoral arena. In particular, viability, or electability, is a cue that voters sometimes use when developing overall impressions of candidates. People's views about a candidate's viability can influence their eventual vote.[25]

To explore Americans' readiness to elect a woman president, the White House Project commissioned Roper to conduct an Internet poll of more than 1,000 respondents to measure their comfort level with women holding various positions of power in the United States.[26] The results of the poll illustrated that Americans were more comfortable with women in certain positions. For example, 97 percent of respondents were very or somewhat comfortable with a woman as head of a large retail company. Similarly, almost all respondents (97 percent) were very or somewhat comfortable with a woman being the head of a charity organization.

However, respondents were less at ease with the idea of a woman general in the military, with only 73 percent of the respondents indicating that they would be very or somewhat comfortable with a woman general. Similarly, only 80 percent of the respondents said they would be very or somewhat comfortable with a woman as a head coach for a professional sports team.

With regard to political office, 95 percent of the sample felt very to somewhat comfortable with a woman as a member of Congress, and 84 percent were comfortable with a woman as vice president. Only 79 percent of the sample, however, said that they were very or somewhat comfortable with the idea of a woman as president.

A CBS/*New York Times* poll published in January 2006 showed greater support for a woman president.[27] When respondents were asked if they would vote for a woman for president "from their own political party if she were qualified," 92 percent of adults said "yes." Support for a qualified woman president has almost doubled since Gallup began asking this question in the 1950s. For example, in 1955, 52 percent of respondents said they would vote for a woman for president. Support for a woman president rose to 73 percent in 1975, 82 percent in 1987, and 91 percent in 1999.

Although most people said they would vote for a qualified woman candidate for president, not as many thought the United States was ready for a woman president. In the 2006 CBS/*New York Times* poll, 55 percent of respondents said the United States was ready for a woman president, in contrast to 1996, when only 40 percent of respondents in a Gallup poll thought the country was ready for a woman president.

Another recent study by the White House Project, which examined the electorate's readiness for a woman president, involved an experiment conducted during the 2002 gubernatorial elections.[28] Voters viewed a sample of over 400 advertisements and recorded their reactions by moving a dial. Subjects turned up the dials when they saw or heard character traits they deemed effective and turned down the dials when they saw or heard character traits they deemed ineffective. Marie C. Wilson found that, before the ads even started, voters reacted to the mere presence of the candidates' appearance onscreen. Specifically, "Women stayed even or were dialed down, but men were dialed up from the first second."[29] These findings suggest that the mere image of a male or female candidate is a powerful and distinguishing component of political campaigns.

Interestingly, the gender of the citizen may or may not influence one's willingness to vote for a woman president. The CBS/*New York Times* study found that men and women were equally likely to say they would vote for a qualified woman for president. However, the Internet survey commissioned by the White House Project found that women were more "comfortable" with the idea of a female president. For example, 83 percent of the female respondents said they were very or somewhat comfortable with a woman as president of the United States, whereas only 75 percent of the men indicated they were somewhat or very comfortable with the idea of a woman president. Some research on gender stereotyping of politicians showed that women respondents are more likely to hold stereotypes that favor women. For example, Kim Fridkin Kahn found that female subjects were more likely than male subjects to view women candidates as more compassionate and as better able to deal with education and health care issues, compared to identical male candidates.[30]

Common stereotypes may constrain women's campaigns for political office. Therefore, a woman candidate for president needs to be cognizant of people's conceptions of women's perceived strengths and weaknesses when designing a campaign strategy for capturing the White House. In addition, a woman candidate for president needs to consider how the news media is likely to portray her candidacy. The news media play a critical role in electoral campaigns because political candidates rely on the media to reach voters, and citizens use information disseminated by the media when evaluating candidates.[31] In other words, the media serve as a crucial information *link* between candidates and the public. Is the media likely to be an obstacle for female candidates, or can the media be a crucial ally for female candidates as they run for political office? We turn now to a review of the pertinent literature.

Media Coverage of Women Candidates

Political scientists have found that the media do not cover all political candidates equally. Senate candidates generally garner more media coverage than House candidates,[32] competitive candidates receive more media attention than their noncompetitive counterparts,[33] candidates who spend more money on their campaigns receive more coverage,[34] and incumbents garner more attention than challengers.[35] Furthermore, the news media's coverage of candidates does not always accurately reflect the messages disseminated by the candidates.[36]

Additionally, we know that the news media differ in how they cover male and female political candidates.[37] For instance, Kahn finds that in statewide office races, women candidates receive less attention than their male counterparts, even when controlling for incumbency and the competitiveness of the race. Moreover, the coverage that women candidates do receive is more negative than that for their equivalent male counterparts, often focusing on their lack of viability.[38]

James Devitt examined news coverage in six statewide races (five gubernatorial campaigns and one campaign for attorney general) and found that male and female gubernatorial candidates received about equal amounts of news attention. However, the news media were more likely to focus on the women candidates' personal life, appearance, and personality, whereas male candidates received more news attention for the policy positions and policy priorities.[39]

Furthermore, female candidates often expressed frustration with media coverage of their own campaigns. For example, newspaper coverage of Christine Gregoire's 2004 gubernatorial campaign in Washington emphasized her toughness, ambition, and self-confidence—in a negative fashion—but her own campaign advertisements stressed her humble beginnings and experience as attorney general.[40] More commonly, when female candidates run for public office, reporters often focus on frivolous matters, such as physical appearance and personality, making it difficult for women candidates to secure the media attention for their views on substantive issues. For example, after Hillary Rodham Clinton claimed victory in the 2000 New York Senate race, the *New York Times* ran the following headline: "First Lady's Race for the Ages: 62 Counties and 6 Pantsuits."[41] In a similar vein, the *Milwaukee Journal Sentinel* wrote how Clinton "whittled her figure down to a fighting size 8" and mentioned that she had eaten "little more than a lettuce leaf" during her fundraisers.[42] With the media focusing on such matters, it may signal to voters that women are not as serious or as competent as their male counterparts, since the press does not cover men in the same fashion. For example, it is difficult to imagine the press focusing on a male candidate's apparel or eating habits or chiding a male candidate for having a successful career.

Dianne G. Bystrom, Marcy C. Banwart, Lynda Lee Kaid, and Terry A. Robertson examined the universe of mixed-gender Senate and gubernatorial newspaper coverage in 1998, 2000, and 2002. They found the media tended to stereotype women in terms of their sex and marital status more so than men. Moreover, the news media continued to associate male candidates with male issues (defense) as well as male traits (competence and aggression) but associated women candidates with female issues (education) and female traits (honesty and warmth).[43]

Additionally, when examining the 2002 congressional campaigns, Bystrom and her colleagues found that the news media paid significantly more attention to the personal backgrounds of women candidates and the competence of male candidates.[44] They also found that the media were more likely to link issues that resonate with voters (the economy) with male candidates than female candidates.[45] Although Bystrom and her colleagues did not find significant differences in the quantity of coverage given to men and women candidates, the persistence of coverage that reinforced traditional issue and trait stereotypes might place women candidates in an unfavorable position when running for political leadership positions.[46]

Overall, the research examining news treatment of male and female candidates illustrated significant and persistent gender differences in coverage. Furthermore, experimental research examining the electoral consequences of these gender differences in coverage showed that people develop less favorable impressions of candidates covered so as to emphasize gender. For example, candidates who are covered like women candidates are viewed by citizens as less viable and less competent than candidates who are covered like male candidates.[47]

Scholars have also investigated what men and women candidates choose to talk about in their controlled media messages. For example, researchers have examined a variety of campaign messages, such as televised political advertisements, speeches, web pages and direct mail to see whether men and women articulate different campaign themes.[48] The vast majority of these studies suggest that men and women candidates focus on different issues, with women focusing on female issues like education and health care and men stressing male issues like the economy and foreign policy.[49] This research suggests that men and women campaign on issues that highlight their stereotypical strengths.

However, candidates embrace a different strategy when it comes to personality characteristics. In particular, women candidates try to eradicate trait stereotypes by emphasizing their embodiment of stereotypically male traits. In particular, women are more likely than men to emphasize male traits like experience and leadership. Male candidates adopt a similar strategy by highlighting their possession of typically female traits, focusing on their empathy and integrity.[50]

Although men and women candidates emphasize alternative issue and trait messages in their campaigns, research on US Senate and gubernatorial campaigns indicates that the news media do not cover the messages of men and women candidates in equivalent ways. In particular, the news media much more faithfully represent the messages of male candidates, virtually mirroring the content of their political communications. In contrast, the news media are less accurate in their representation of the messages of women candidates, often distorting the messages of these candidates.[51] In general, the news media's coverage of men and women candidates differs in regard to the sheer amount of coverage, the emphasis, and the tone.

The research on media coverage of men and women candidates has focused almost exclusively on statewide or local campaigns. Will gender differences in media coverage persist in a national contest for president? Will gender differences in media coverage be exacerbated or mitigated when women run for the White House?

"Ma" President? Elizabeth Dole

Elizabeth Dole was a standout candidate in the 2000 pre-primary campaign for the Republican nomination for president; she began to test the waters for a possible presidential run on March 10, 1999, and decided to drop out of the race on October 20, 1999, citing lack of funds. During this period, public opinion polls showed Elizabeth Dole running a strong second to George W. Bush and well ahead of the rest of the field, including John McCain and Steve Forbes. Furthermore, Elizabeth Dole was widely popular among the public, with 75 percent of the general population having a favorable impression of Dole, compared to 69 percent reporting a favorable impression of Bush. Finally, trial heat questions during this period showed Dole beating Democrat Al Gore in a hypothetical general election contest.[52]

Elizabeth Dole's candidacy for president of the United States, even though short-lived, represents the most recent and most viable presidential bid by a woman candidate. A number of scholars have examined how Dole's candidacy was treated by the news media.[53] To begin, Caroline Heldman, Susan J. Carroll, and Stephanie Olson collected two datasets of news coverage. One dataset, consisting of 421 news stories from forty different major papers in the United States, compared news coverage of Dole with her Republican rivals (Gary Bauer, George W. Bush, Steve Forbes, Alan Keyes, and John McCain). The second dataset, consisting of 155 news stories from thirty-one different US papers, allowed Heldman and her colleagues to examine in-depth coverage of Dole.[54]

According to Heldman and her colleagues, the office of president presents women with unique challenges because of the highly masculinized nature of the office. The president's role as commander in chief of the military and as manager of the country's economy highlights men's stereotypical strengths while corresponding to women's stereotypical weaknesses. If reporters hold common gender stereotypes, coverage of women candidates for president may suffer.[55]

In Heldman and her colleagues' analysis, Elizabeth Dole did receive less favorable and more stereotyped coverage. For example, Dole received less coverage and less serious and less sustained coverage than Bush and McCain, even though Dole was leading McCain in public opinion polls at the time.[56] In addition, the press reported horserace coverage more often for Dole, and the coverage of Dole's viability was negative, focusing on her lack of fundraising abilities.

Reporters covered Elizabeth Dole's personality and appearance more than the traits and appearance of her opponents.[57] Diane J. Heith, for example, pointed out reporters' descriptions of Dole as "robotic," a "control freak," and "over-rehearsed."[58] Similarly, another columnist described Dole's public speaking style as sounding and looking like "Tammy Faye Baker meets the Home Shopping Network."[59]

The in-depth coverage of Elizabeth Dole emphasized her gender more than other aspects of her candidacy and framed her coverage as the "first woman" to be a serious contender for the presidency. By using the "first woman" frame, the news media may have been encouraging citizens to view Dole as a novelty and as a candidate not to be taken seriously.[60]

Karrin Vasby Anderson also examined the news coverage of Elizabeth Dole's campaign from July 1998 until she withdrew from the race in newspapers, newsmagazines, and on the television news. Anderson's findings were similar to those of Heldman and her colleagues. First, Anderson's analysis showed that Dole was covered—first and foremost—as the woman candidate for president. Second, both studies indicated that the office of the president is masculinized and that "it is *just as* gendered as it *has always been.*"[61] The focus on Dole's gender was emphasized in the media portrayal of her candidacy, "making it harder for a voter to imagine her as president."[62] Anderson concludes by saying that the "US presidency remains a bastion of masculinity," making it more difficult for women to mount a competitive campaign for president.[63]

Finally, Sean Aday and James Devitt conducted a content analysis of 462 stories taken from the *Des Moines Register,* the *Los Angeles Times*, the *New York Times*, *USA Today*, and the *Washington Post* from August 1, 1999, to October 20, 1999, comparing the coverage of Dole's presidential campaign to that of Bush, McCain, and Forbes. Once again, differences were found both in quantity and quality of coverage. In terms of quantity, Dole received significantly less coverage than Bush but more than McCain or Forbes. Additionally, Dole received less issue coverage than any of her male colleagues but more personal coverage (personality and physical descriptions) than any of her male opponents. For example, the *New York Times* reported that "Dole prepares so thoroughly for appearances that she even requires aides to count the steps she must take to the podium. Though roughly as fragile as Margaret Thatcher, she is also famously thin-skinned, and has been known to burst into tears over unflattering press."[64] Yet descriptions of her male colleagues' personality and image were not as negative and not as prevalent. These differences in news coverage likely reinforced gender stereotypes among voters.

Aday and Devitt also found that male and female reporters differed in their coverage of Elizabeth Dole. Female reporters were more likely than their male counterparts to describe Dole's position on issues (25 percent of the articles by women reporters discussed Dole's issue views, compared to 14 percent for male reporters). Male reporters, however, were more likely than female reporters to focus on Dole's personality traits (39 percent of the articles written by men mentioned Dole's personality, but only 27 percent of the female reporters' news stories discussed Dole's personal traits).[65]

Some of Dole's harshest criticism came from women journalists. The Pulitzer Prize–winning *New York Times* columnist Maureen Dowd noted in a March 31, 1999, column: "It's hard to imagine the woman who likes to coordinate the color of her shoes with the color of the rug on the stage where she gives a speech, dealing with any crisis that involved a lot of variables."[66]

Similarly, in a column in the *Washington Post* in October 1999, Mary McGrory said, "Some men call her a 'Stepford wife,' an over-programmed perfectionist. And women from outside the South found her deep-fried effusiveness off-putting. . . . Despite her considerable credentials she brought only a skirt to the proceedings and in the end offered only the novelty of the first serious presidential run by a woman."[67]

Dole's communications director, Ari Fleischer, often expressed his frustration at the way Dole was covered. Why were male politicians "on message" and women "scripted"? George W. Bush's inaccessibility rivaled Dole's, but he was praised for being "disciplined" and having "a controlled message," while Gary Trudeau portrayed Dole as a "Stepford-like personality who spouts sound bites on command, never varying so much as a semicolon."[68]

Although Elizabeth Dole's campaign was plagued by a number of political shortcomings in the pre-primary season of the 2000 presidential election, one was not of her own making: the inequitable and stereotyped media coverage she received. With the news media focusing on her physical characteristics, being a "first woman" candidate, as well as judging her "type-A" personality traits pejoratively (while praising the same characteristics in George W. Bush), the media unfairly disadvantaged Dole. The media treatment may have signaled to voters that Dole was not a viable contender, or was unimaginable as commander in chief, when coverage focused on her "well-coifed" appearance and perfectionist personality traits. According to the major public opinion polls published in 1999, voters initially liked Elizabeth Dole. Yet the public may have turned away from her candidacy because of the superficial and negative media treatment she received.

Wartime Versus School Time: A Gendered Political Climate

Stereotypes that people hold about men and women may be more likely to hurt women candidates at certain times and may help them at other times. In particular, when the salient issues of the day stress male candidates' stereotypical strengths and women candidates' stereotypical weaknesses, women politicians will be at a disadvantage. As an illustration, when the country is at war or when the US economy is in recession, economic issues, foreign policy, and defense issues will top the national agenda. These are precisely the issues that people believe men can handle better than women. If the economy is strong and the nation is at peace, however, the public's attention may turn to other issues, such as education, health care reform, and the environment. During these times, the issues on top of the public agenda correspond to women's stereotypical strengths, which may assist women politicians at the ballot box.

The linkage between political context and the prospect for women candidates corresponds with fluctuations in women's electoral gains since the late 1970s. During the 1980s, when the United States was still in a Cold War with the Soviet Union and the national economy was sluggish, only 8 percent of women running as nonincumbents for the US Senate won their election bids. During the 1990s, when the Cold War had come to an end and the US economy was rebounding, women made impressive gains in the US Senate. In particular, 31 percent of the women running as challengers and for open seats won their Senate contests. However, after 9/11, when the "War on Terror" and the Iraq War became prominent, women's electoral success diminished. In fact, only 8 percent of women nonincumbents running for the US Senate were successful in 2002 and 2004.

Lawless systematically examined the power of gender stereotypes and the connection between the political climate and the fortunes of women candidates in 2002. She found that one year after 9/11 and shortly following the US invasion of Afghanistan, two-thirds of all respondents did not believe men and women were equally competent at dealing with military issues. Of these respondents, 95 percent thought men were better able to handle these issues than women. Moreover, 30 percent of respondents thought a male presidential candidate would be more effective than a female presidential candidate in bringing peace to the Middle East.[69]

In addition, Lawless found that support for a woman for president was lower among respondents who thought foreign policy was an important issue. And, more generally, public support for a woman president dipped during this post-9/11 period: only 80 percent of Lawless's respondents were willing to vote for a woman for president, even if she were qualified and the nominee of the respondent's party.[70] In contrast, in the most recent CBS/*New York Times* poll, cited earlier and published in January 2006, 92 percent of respondents said they would vote for a woman for president "from their own political party if she were qualified." And, a Gallup poll published prior to 9/11, in 1999, found that more than nine out of ten people would vote for a qualified woman for president. These results suggest that persistent gender stereotypes about men and women's areas of political expertise tie women's political fortunes to the prevailing political climate.

Fiction on American TV Equals Reality in Other Countries

In the United States, the prospect of a woman president, especially during periods of international unrest and economic uncertainty, seems improbable. However, a cursory look around the world suggests a more optimistic view may be warranted. Fourteen women are currently serving as president or prime minister in countries as diverse as Bangladesh, Chile, Finland, Latvia, Jamaica, and New Zealand.

For instance, Ellen Johnson-Sirleaf, a Harvard-trained banker and survivor of Liberia's violent politics, recently became Africa's first woman to be elected head of state in 2005. Additionally, Michelle Bachelet was elected in January 2006 as president of Chile, a conservative, male-dominated, deeply Roman Catholic country. And in late 2005, conservative Angela Merkel became the first female chancellor of Germany.

France may be almost ready to elect its first woman president.

Media buzz surrounding Ségolène Royal, a member of parliament, regional president, and former minister, was intense. According to the *New York Times*, in the aftermath of the immigrant youth riots, followed by violent protests, "Ms. Royal...is the only politician who looks good."[71] However, critics faulted her for a lack of experience in economic and national security matters. Nonetheless, Royal received a great deal of positive press attention in France, appearing on four French magazine covers, with one proclaiming, "The Irresistible Ascension."

In the United States, a woman has never been nominated by a major party to run for president. However, a woman president has made it to prime-time television. Mackenzie Allen, played by Geena Davis, was president of the United States on ABC's now-cancelled *Commander in Chief.* Although Allen was not elected to the presidency—she was elected vice president and succeeded the president when he died from a massive stroke—she acted presidential on the show, which debuted on September 27, 2005. Organizations such as the White House Project promoted the show as a way of turning "the fiction of a woman president into reality by shaping ideas about women as leaders."[72] Perhaps by seeing a woman acting presidential, dealing effectively with terrorism, foreign policy mishaps, and economic turmoil, people will begin to alter their stereotypes about women politicians. In addition, and probably more importantly, the increase in the number of women in high-level elective office as well as an increase in women in leadership positions, such as Nancy Pelosi as Speaker of the US House of Representatives and Condoleezza Rice as secretary of state, may help reduce people's stereotypes about men and women's unique strengths and weaknesses. When these stereotypes are eliminated or at least reduced, the road to the White House will be easier to navigate for the next woman candidate for president.

Notes

1. Dao, "After Storm, She Tries to Mend State, and Career."
2. Ibid.
3. Ibid.
4. Ibid.
5. See Jamieson, *Beyond the Double Bind.*
6. Ibid.
7. Mandel, *In the Running*, p. 43.
8. See McKee and Sheriffs, "The Differential Evaluation of Males and Females"; Sheriffs and McKee, "Qualitative Aspects of Beliefs About Men

and Women"; and Parson and Bales, "Family Socialization and Interaction Process."

9. See Leeper, "The Impact of Prejudice"; Mueller, "Nurturance and Mastery"; Rosenwasser and Seale, "Attitudes Toward a Hypothetical Male or Female Candidate"; and Sapiro, "If US Senator Baker Were a Woman."

10. See Alexander and Andersen, "Gender as a Factor"; Cook and Wilcox, "Women Voters"; Dolan, *Voting for Women*; Fox, *Gender Dynamics in Congressional Elections*; Koch, "Candidate Gender and Assessments"; Koch, "Do Citizens Apply Gender Stereotypes?"; Koch, "Gender Stereotypes and Citizens' Impressions"; McDermott, "Voting Cues in Low-Information Elections"; Niven, "Party Elites and Women Candidates"; and Sanbonmatsu, "Political Knowledge and Gender Stereotypes."

11. See Dolan, "Gender Differences in Support for Women Candidates"; Huddy and Terkildsen, "Gender Stereotypes"; Huddy and Terkildsen, "The Consequences of Gender Stereotypes"; Kahn, *The Political Consequences of Being a Woman*; King and Matland, "Sex and the Grand Old Party"; Leeper, "The Impact of Prejudice"; Riggle, Shields, and Johnson, "Gender Stereotypes and Decision Context"; Rosenwasser and Dean, "Gender Role and Political Office"; Rosenwasser and Seale, "Attitudes Toward a Hypothetical Male or Female Candidate"; and Sapiro, "If US Senator Baker Were a Woman."

12. See Sapiro, "If US Senator Baker Were a Woman"; Rosenwasser and Dean, "Gender Role and Political Office"; Huddy and Terkildsen, "Gender Stereotypes"; Huddy and Terkildsen, "The Consequences of Gender Stereotypes"; Leeper, "The Impact of Prejudice."

13. See Kahn, *The Political Consequences of Being a Woman*; and King and Matland, "Sex and the Grand Old Party."

14. See Sapiro, "If US Senator Baker Were a Woman."

15. See Gordon and Miller, "Does the Oval Office Have a Glass Ceiling?"

16. See Lawless, "Women, War, and Winning Elections."

17. Ibid.

18. See Huddy, "The Political Significance of Voters' Gender Stereotypes"; and Witt, Paget, and Matthews, *Running as a Woman*.

19. See Huddy and Terkildsen, "Gender Stereotypes"; and Rosenwasser and Dean, "Gender Role and Political Office."

20. See Lawless, "Women, War, and Winning Elections."

21. See Huddy and Terkildsen, "Gender Stereotypes"; Huddy and Terkildsen, "The Consequences of Gender Stereotypes"; Kahn, *The Political Consequences of Being a Woman*; Leeper, "The Impact of Prejudice"; Sapiro, "If US Senator Baker Were a Woman"; and Gordon and Miller, "Does the Oval Office Have a Glass Ceiling?"

22. See Sapiro, "If US Senator Baker Were a Woman."

23. See Gordon and Miller, "Does the Oval Office Have a Glass Ceiling?"

24. Ibid.

25. See Bartels, "Candidate Choice and the Dynamics of the

Presidential Nomination Process"; and Brady and Johnston, "What's the Primary Message?"

26. The White House Project is a national, nonpartisan, nonprofit organization that aims to increase women's presence in leadership roles, up to the US presidency. The poll results can be found at http://www.thewhitehouseproject.org/v2/researchandreports/roperreport/White%20House%20Project%20poll%209-05.pdf.

27. This CBS/*New York Times* poll was published on February 5, 2006. See http://www.cbsnews.com/htdocs/pdf/020306woman.pdf.

28. See Wilson, *Closing the Leadership Gap.*

29. Ibid., p. 19.

30. See Kahn, *The Political Consequences of Being a Woman.*

31. See Aldrich, "A Dynamic Model of Presidential Nomination Campaigns"; Paletz, *The Media in American Politics*; Patterson, *The Mass Media Election*; and Iyengar and Kinder, *News That Matters.*

32. See Krasno, *Challengers, Competition, and Reelection*; Westlye, *Senate Elections and Campaign Intensity*; and Jacobson, *The Politics of Congressional Elections.*

33. See Herrnson, *Playing Hardball*; and Kahn and Kenney, "Do Negative Campaigns Mobilize or Suppress Turnout?"

34. See Westlye, *Senate Elections and Campaign Intensity.*

35. See Herrnson, *Playing Hardball.*

36. See Paletz, *The Media in American Politics*; and Kahn, *The Political Consequences of Being a Woman.*

37. See Fox, *Gender Dynamics in Congressional Elections*; Kahn, *The Political Consequences of Being a Woman*; Williams, "Gender, Political Advertising, and the 'Air Wars'"; and Kropf and Boiney, "The Electoral Glass Ceiling?"

38. See Kahn, *The Political Consequences of Being a Woman.*

39. See Devitt, "Framing Gender on the Campaign Trail."

40. See Bystrom, "Advertising, Web Sites, and Media Coverage."

41. Ibid., p. 172.

42. Ibid.

43. See Bystrom et al., *Gender and Candidate Communication.*

44. Ibid.

45. Ibid.

46. "Stereotypical" coverage also includes discussion of women candidates' relationships with their husbands and children, as well as making their gender an issue. Focusing on such issues may conjure up images of women as wives and mothers, encouraging voters to perceive women candidates as one-dimensional, potentially hampering views of their viability. See Bystrom et al., *Gender and Candidate Communication*; and Bystrom, "Advertising, Web Sites, and Media Coverage."

47. See Kahn, *The Political Consequences of Being a Woman.*

48. See Dabelko and Herrnson, "Women's and Men's Campaigns"; Iyengar et al., "Running as a Woman"; Kahn, *The Political Consequences of Being a Woman*, and Larson, "'Running as Women'?"

49. See Dabelko and Herrnson, "Women's and Men's Campaigns"; Iyengar et al., "Running as a Woman"; Kahn, "Does Being Male Help?"; Kahn, "Gender Differences in Campaign Messages"; Kahn and Goldenberg, "Women Candidates in the News"; Kahn and Gordon, "How Women Campaign for the US Senate"; and Witt, Paget, and Matthews, *Running as a Woman*.

50. See Iyengar et al., "Running as a Woman"; Kahn and Goldenberg, "Women Candidates in the News"; Kahn, "Does Being Male Help?"; and Kahn, "Gender Differences in Campaign Messages."

51. See Kahn, *The Political Consequences of Being a Woman*.

52. See Heldman, Carroll, and Olson, "'She Brought Only a Skirt.'"

53. See Aday and Devitt, "Style over Substance"; Anderson, "From Spouses to Candidates"; Bystrom, McKinnon, and Chaney, "The First Lady and the First Estate"; Heith, "Footwear, Lipstick, and an Orthodox Sabbath"; and Heldman, Carroll, and Olson, "'She Brought Only a Skirt.'"

54. See Heldman, Carroll, and Olson, "'She Brought Only a Skirt.'"

55. Ibid.

56. Bystrom, McKinnon, and Chaney, in "The First Lady and the First Estate," their examination of media coverage in Iowa, also found that Elizabeth Dole received less news coverage than George W. Bush and Steve Forbes.

57. See Bystrom, McKinnon, and Chaney, "The First Lady and the First Estate"; and Heldman, Carroll, and Olson, "'She Brought Only a Skirt.'"

58. See Heith, "Footwear, Lipstick, and an Orthodox Sabbath."

59. See Heldman, Carroll, and Olson, "'She Brought Only a Skirt,'" p. 324.

60. See Heldman, Carroll, and Olson, "'She Brought Only a Skirt.'" Heith (2001) also finds evidence for the "first woman" frame in her analysis of news coverage of Elizabeth Dole's bid for the US presidency.

61. Anderson, "From Spouses to Candidates," p. 125 (emphasis in original).

62. Ibid., p. 107.

63. Ibid.

64. Aday and Devitt, "Style over Substance," p. 12.

65. Ibid.

66. Clift and Brazaitis, *Madam President*, p. 149.

67. See Heldman, Carroll, and Olson, "'She Brought Only a Skirt.'"

68. Clift and Brazaitis, *Madam President*, pp. 148–149.

69. See Lawless, "Women, War, and Winning Elections."

70. This statistic is valid only when the "Don't know" option was included as an attribute. When the "Don't know" attribute is excluded, only 65 percent of respondents indicated they were willing to vote for a woman. See Lawless, "Women, War, and Winning Elections."

71. Sciolino, "Is France Ready to Elect a Woman?"

72. http://www.thewhitehouseproject.org/v2/programs/perception/CIC/index.html, accessed 4/2006.

5

Masculinity on the Campaign Trail

Georgia Duerst-Lahti

With cameras running and news reports filed on the campaign trail, John Kerry played hockey, went windsurfing, shot geese, and touted his heroic actions during the Vietnam War; and George W. Bush flew a fighter jet, drove a racing boat, cleared brush, and continually talked tough about killing terrorists. Manly men, doing manly things, in manly ways. Or at least that is what each wanted to project to the voting public, arguably because that is what the public expects in the presidency, especially in time of war.[1] The 2004 election dripped with projections of masculinity.

More often than not, however, even when masculinity was at the center of campaigning, it also hid right in front of us, not the direct subject of analysis or comment. Just ordinary. Occasionally though, the press took up the subject explicitly. One op-ed piece focused on "political virility" and declared "real men vote Republican."[2] Another analyzed "how Kerry became a girlie-man."[3] A long analysis article led with the claim that "when it comes to the presidency, macho is good, and it probably always has been."[4] These articles reflect an empirical truth about presidential elections: From war hero and ultimate founding father George Washington onward, presidential elections have been very much about picking the right or best man for the job. Yet Americans appear to pick "the man" without really thinking about men as having gender. They may be aware of the choice among types of men but seem to cast this choice in individual terms rather than explicitly distinguishing among types of masculinity. All the time, however types of masculinity operate as a subtext. In 2000, for example, Al Gore was cast as the intellectual policy wonk who resorted to the "big kiss" to project his virility. George W. Bush, in contrast, became the guy you could like at a backyard barbeque, solid and dependable, an "everyman" whom voters could feel comfortable around, even if—or maybe because—he did not seem "real smart." Types of masculinity have always been in play in presidential campaigns, whether or not Americans notice.

Another gendered aspect of presidential campaigns that seems more implicit than explicit is found in the link between the masculinity of the presidency and the behaviors and symbolic meanings inherent in campaigns. For example, heroes have always had an edge in elections, and 2004 was no exception as Democrats opted for John Kerry in large part because he was a war hero. But the concept of hero itself is masculine. Men are heroes. Women are assigned its feminine counterpart, heroine, whose connotations are not wholly synonymous. An example of a campaign practice, the common act of taking off the coat and tie and rolling up the sleeves, signals a casual candidate, even a workingman capable of laying bricks or otherwise taking care of ordinary men's duties.[5] However, such a gesture only works for a woman if she is attired in men's clothing, and then, arguably, such a move does not convey quite the same meaning. One suspects many would see her as a woman trying to act like a man. In a third illustration, the notion of "attacks" in presidential campaigns suggests gendering, a point that will be explored later. Whether attacking other candidates or having campaigns go on the attack, the concept of attack operates differently for women than men. This difference was demonstrated by the now infamous attack by Rick Lazio on Hillary Rodham Clinton during the debate in their 2000 New York Senate race. Lazio merely approached her too closely and vigorously, triggering a reaction because it seemed an inappropriate physical attack by a man on a woman. Certainly, any kind of attack has never been consistent with femininity.

Because most Americans only have contact with presidential campaigns through news coverage, that news coverage shapes understandings of the presidency and presidential campaigns. In such coverage, the expectations of presidential candidates, rituals and processes of campaigns, and the very language of coverage largely function to exclude women; yet in only a few areas does coverage consistently recognize this fact. The most notable area is poll questions about whether Americans are ready for a female president. This question makes clear that we expect the president to be a man. One other—perhaps insulting—area of coverage concerns whether female voters find a candidate to be (sexually) attractive, a question that goes back to John F. Kennedy's campaign in 1960, when much commentary suggested women would vote for a candidate because he is handsome. Nonetheless, throughout most news coverage, instead of explicit cognizance of candidates' masculinity, several assumptions function to naturalize men as president and render their gendering invisible.

This chapter attempts to make visible that which has always operated at the center of presidential campaigns but only sometimes has been explicitly acknowledged: masculinity. Using the lens of gendered institutions and the process of gendering, I consider the 2004 presidential election for the ways in which masculinity was evident on the campaign trail. I then extend the analysis into the early stages of the 2008 presidential election to explore the dynamic of individuals emerging as "presidential possibilities." To do so, I draw upon press coverage in eight national and regional newspapers and explore the gendered use of words associated with presidential campaigns and candidates. I also look at the campaign context by undertaking a gender analysis of issues and events during the 2004 election cycle, and again through 2005, in order to consider implications for the 2008 cycle.

Presidential Campaigns and Masculinity in Relationship to Femininity

Are women capable of participating in manly activities such as playing hockey, shooting geese, flying fighter jets, or clearing brush? The answer is, of course, of course. With very few exceptions, at least some women have always done things men do. On almost any behavioral or attitudinal measure we find far more differences among men and among women than between them.[6] Most men do not play hockey, and very few have ever flown a jet fighter; some women do each, although fewer than the number of men. Further, and closely related, women are no more of like mind than are men.[7] Again, far more differences exist among women and among men than between them. Studies that find sex differences generally use "on average" comparisons between a group of male and female subjects. This measure obscures in-group differences. It is possible, often, to tease out some distinctions between women and men in their ideas about politics and other matters, and certainly women and men behave somewhat differently in any number of ways, but overlap always remains. For example, innumerable studies of legislative voting find that political party affiliation matters more than gender, although instances of gender differences can be identified as well. Both men and women can deliver a political speech, although they likely will choose to emphasize somewhat different topics, utter somewhat different words, and display somewhat different co-verbal behaviors.

This sharing of and divergence in ideas might best be thought of as rooted in compound ideology, in which the conventional liberal-conservative ideology overlays gender ideology of masculinism and feminalism (an ideology that encompasses women across the ideological spectrum).[8] This compounded view of gender and political ideas and ideology helps to interpret how women and men both share and diverge in their views about proper gender roles and the ways government policy should be structured to support or sanction some kinds of gender arrangements and not others. It also helps to make sense of why a groundswell of women will not arise to support a female candidate. This lack of support makes sense when potential supporters diverge on the liberal-conservative continuum. Alternatively, but not necessarily discretely, their gender ideology may either not allow them to admit that gender matters at all (equality as the same), or their gender ideology may not allow for women in such public positions. Still, some female voters may swing toward a woman candidate precisely because she is a woman. Similarly, men may opt to support a female candidate because of partisan ideological agreement. Alternatively they may agree as partisans but still be sufficiently masculinist to cling to the notion that a man is the better choice for president. In all instances in which gender ideology militates against supporting a woman candidate, such thinking leaves the power of the presidency in the masculine realm.

But gender is more complicated than two ideational overlays allow. Gender is, in its simplest definition, the cultural construction of biological sex. In general—which is a point challenged by the growing transgendered movement—both biological sex and gender has been constructed as dualisms with the sexes and genders being opposites. For this reason, the boundaries of masculinity hinge upon the construction of femininity, with masculinity being set as not-feminine. Such a construction, of course, eliminates the tremendous overlap between women and men and creates difference when none really exists. Both women and men have legs, for example, but women's legs are sexualized, and culturally women are urged to distinguish their legs from men's by the gendered practice of shaving them. In campaigns, women's appearance—including their legs—receives a level of scrutiny well beyond that of male candidates. Artificial differences are culturally imposed, and maintaining these differences is particularly important for the gender identity of those whose ideology favors gender complementarity, or difference.

In presidential campaigns this need for gender dualisms has at least two major consequences. First, male candidates often have their credibility challenged through attacks upon their masculinity, which are cast in terms of their being too feminine. This dynamic is one area in which press coverage of presidential candidates does seem to explicitly recognize masculinity, or the lack thereof. Coverage often focuses on whether a candidate is manly enough. George H.W. Bush, for example, suffered from the "wimp factor," Bill Clinton was chastised for his quivering lip when he felt another's pain, and John Kerry was cast by his opponents as "French," a code for effeminate. In such instances, the feminine is deployed to denigrate the man and his masculinity. Interestingly, this construction can be quite fluid: Ronald Reagan was praised for his sensitivity when a tear came to his eye during emotionally moving moments, such as at the Normandy cemetery in a speech commemorating the fortieth anniversary of the Normandy invasion in 1944. If masculinity is questioned through charges of being too feminine, and we expect masculine candidates, then female candidates face the double bind. They do not match the expected gender performance for their sexed bodies, or they act in feminine ways and hence perform in a manner used to denigrate presidential candidates. This dynamic reflects the second major consequence of gender dualism: Women are expected to be feminine, but presidential candidates are judged by the quality of their masculinity.[9] Therefore, women candidates must continually negotiate how to be womanly while projecting the manliness expected of presidents. Gender is anything but simple.

Gender operates both as a set of categories common to dualisms—male and female, men and women, masculine and feminine, masculinism and feminalism—and as a process that imbues practices, behaviors, ideas, words, institutions, and other social, cultural, and political phenomena with gender and masculine or feminine association. That is, we understand such behaviors as throwing a ball like a girl or fighting like a man to be gendered. We associate the military or engineering with men and masculinity and nursing or elementary school teaching with women and femininity. We commonly refer to issues such as health, education, reproductive rights, and welfare as "women's issues," even though far more men than women work on them in legislatures and the executive branch. These associations relate to the longstanding "separate spheres doctrine" that held women were to attend to the private sphere of home, hearth, and family care while men were to handle the public sphere of politics, business, and providing for the family. Under these gender arrangements, politics has been gendered as a "man's game," which women have only begun to enter in substantial numbers since the 1970s. As women enter, a process of gender transformation occurs as political institutions move from homogeneous conditions of all men and masculinity to one of varying degrees of heterogeneity that incorporates women and femininity.

The process of gendering interacts with extant gender expectations. As a result, women's issue areas have been relatively open for women to enter, even though administrative departments devoted to these issues were largely populated by men when they were created and for decades hence. The first female cabinet secretary, Frances Perkins, headed the Department of Labor from 1933 to 1945. It is probably no coincidence that the Women's Bureau was located in this department and therefore the process of regendering the department to allow a female to head it was less difficult than with other departments. Similarly, women—on average—are understood to be good with language and to be gracious and tactful, all skills associated with diplomacy. Men—on average—are thought to be aggressive and are culturally expected to protect. Given these associations, it is not surprising that two women have become secretary of state, but none have yet headed the Department of Defense.

In gendering processes, once homogeneity has been breached, it is easier for women to enter and not be entirely novel, although the process is unlikely to be consistent or smooth. As more women enter, the process of transforming to a condition in which it is open to either women or men eases, and the area can become transgendered—appropriate for either males or females to cross over, even though the meaning is not entirely synonymous when they do so. Clearly a regendering of the executive branch is already underway. Women have served as cabinet secretaries for the Department of Labor six times and Health and Human Services four times, although men continue to serve, too.[10] Women have also entered state legislatures and Congress. In many states and in Congress their numbers are large enough and they have been present long enough that the institution now accepts and expects that women will be members. In Maine, California, and Washington, both US senators are currently women, which suggests a substantial gender transformation of this post. Since 1972, a number of women have emerged as potential presidential candidates, although none has yet made it to the first primary or caucus. For 2008, two names were regularly mentioned in the press, Hillary Rodham Clinton and Condoleezza Rice. The regendering process keeps moving in the direction of accepting a woman as president, although we have not yet accomplished this feat. Whether 2008 becomes the election cycle when women break into elections from campaigns remains to be seen. One thing is certain and is already evident, especially about Hillary Clinton; throughout regendering processes, resistance and backlash are not uncommon. Arguably, this is so in large part because gender also carries power.

Gender power, or the power that accompanies masculinity or femininity, is not evenly distributed between the two (or more) genders. As currently constituted, masculinity carries much more power than femininity. Gender difference becomes gender dominance. Women, for example, generally have more gender power in terms of the custody and care of children, particularly in situations of divorce. However, in policy or politics, other examples of women's gender power advantage are difficult to find. Men and masculinity dominate in politics, as even a casual empirical assessment instantly confirms. With dominance comes the capacity to set norms and ideas about what is right, just, proper, good, and plain old ordinary. Because in most of politics, men dominate, masculinity sets the terms of normal, and these terms—whether for institutions or practices and processes related to them—have been masculinized. What is important for rethinking the possibility of a Madam President is the power of masculinity to mask its dominance because of its ordinariness. Only when we gain the capacity to "see" gender and gender power in the presidency will we be able to address their consequences.

It is always easier to see the ordinary when something out of the ordinary appears. In the case of the presidency, female candidates help us to notice how overwhelmingly male the candidates have been. Such observations, however, tend to bog down in individuals. Further, even fewer recognize that campaigns themselves are highly gendered phenomena. In contrast, common polling questions tap more directly into the masculine assumption for the presidency. The Center for American Women and Politics has collected a series of poll results, from January 2003 through March 2006, querying about the possibility of a female candidate for president. A sample of these results is shown in Box 5.1.

Box 5.1 Polls About a Woman President, 2005–2006

- Gallup found that 87 percent in 2000 agreed they would vote for a woman if their party nominated a qualified one for president.
- In a Rasmussen poll in April 2005, 72 percent of Americans said they would be willing to vote for a woman for president, but only 49 percent thought their family, friends, and coworkers would vote for a woman candidate.
- CNN/*USA Today* found that nearly half of Americans (46 percent) thought the United States would have a female president within the next ten years, and an additional 41 percent said within the next ten to twenty-five years.
- Roper Public Affairs for the White House Project found that a large majority of Americans (79 percent) were comfortable with the idea of a woman president.
- A WNBC/Marist poll conducted in February 2006 showed that 23 percent of voters would be likely to support a woman candidate for president from either major party, but 27 percent would not be likely to support a woman presidential candidate from either party. For 28 percent, the only woman candidate likely to gain their support would be a Democrat, whereas a Republican woman would draw the votes of 22 percent.
- A Hearst Newspapers/Siena College poll in February 2006 showed that 64 percent said the United States was ready for a woman president.
- In a February 2006 CBS/*New York Times* poll, 92 percent of Americans say they would vote for a qualified woman presidential candidate from their own political party, and 55 percent of those polled think that the United States is ready to elect a woman president, up from 40 percent in 1996.
- Among registered voters in California, 69 percent think the country is ready for a woman president and 24 percent disagree, according to a March 2006 field poll.

Source: Center for American Women and Politics. Samples selected by author.

The simultaneous support for and resistance to a woman president might be the most obvious facts that jump off the page. At most, 92 percent agree that they would vote for a woman from their party, but some recent polls show as few as 23 percent would support a woman candidate. As many as 27 percent say they would not likely support a female candidate, although extrapolation suggests that respondents believe up to 51 percent of other voters would not support a female candidate. Not yet half believe we will have a woman president within ten years. Although the disparate and contradictory assessments of a female candidate's chances of support may be interesting, the phrasing of the questions is more illustrative of the masculine assumptions for the presidency.

Poll questions probe in various ways: Would the respondent vote for a *qualified* woman? Is the United States (or the country) *ready* for a woman president? Is the respondent *willing* to vote for a woman? Are they *comfortable with the idea* of a woman president? And then there is the implication, "although I might support a woman, others will not." The very wording of these poll questions provides clues to the oddity of a woman being president and hence the assumption that a man—and not a woman—should be president. It is this normative *should* that belies masculinism operating as the hegemonic ideology shaping the normal and masking itself in the ordinary.

- Phrasing for a woman candidate must be linguistically qualified with the practical notion that she is actually *qualified.* Such language suggests that respondents might have a difficult time believing any woman could be qualified or, alternatively, need reassurance that she in fact is qualified before agreeing to support her. Notice, to ask whether the respondent is willing to support a man—as a member of a gender category—is absurd because all presidents and most presidential candidates have been men. Polls may question the qualifications of individual men, but never men as a category of candidate.
- To ask if the country is *ready* for a woman president is to suggest that it is something that requires preparation. It also shows the extent to which female candidates are judged as a member of a category and not as individuals.
- Most telling of all, arguably, is phrasing that explicitly says the *idea* of a woman president is the root problem. In this phrasing, no individual, or even the category of women, is

cued; rather, it is the idea. Ideas are the purview of ideology, and masculinism is the ideology that would so deeply entrench the idea that a man should be president.

- Finally, to suggest that you are willing, but that others are not reveals the conservative (small c) expectation that although you have nothing against breaking the normative prescriptions that deem only a man could be president, you do not believe others are so enlightened. (Alternatively, it could be an artifact of the survey process and lack of candor with the interviewer.) It suggests how deeply Americans hold the normative belief that a man should be president.

Several important dimensions of gender and presidential candidates emerge in these questions and their phrasing. First, masculinism has made the very idea of a woman as president something that needs preparation to accept and something that should be questioned. Second, the presidency itself is associated with masculinity in exceptionally strong ways. Third, unlike any man, a female candidate is treated as a member of a category that is suspect and, hence, must first overcome the categorical suspicion before being judged on individual qualifications. This fact makes the challenge of running for the presidency even greater and likely discourages many qualified female candidates from stepping forward. Finally, and on a positive note, the fact that more people are more comfortable with the idea, and are apparently more willing and more ready for this idea, suggests that gender transformations are underway in which the possibility of a female candidacy for president no longer breaks strictly implicit and invisible but deeply held prescriptions. The idea of a woman president has moved inside the bounds of the thinkable for most Americans, even if not everyone likes it.

Masculine Institution, Masculine Campaigns

During the 1980s, scholars of gender came to understand that institutions themselves were gendered. In essence, institutions are reifications that have been created by people, both at their founding and through mundane and major changes by incumbents over time. The social characteristics of those who work in and around the institution, both presently and throughout its history, contribute to its gendering. Particularly important are the characteristics, preferences, and assumptions of the founders. These institutional incumbents embed their preferences and assumptions in the institution's formal and informal structures and processes. Precisely because institutions are invented and sustained by the mind, by the way people think about them, institutions can in theory be anything the founders, and to a lesser extent subsequent incumbents, want them to be. That is why such struggle occurs around the founding of major institutions, for example, the new government in Iraq. It should not then be difficult to recognize that the presidency, sitting atop the executive branch, is a masculine institution.[11]

Mark Kann has written cogently about masculinity in the founding of the US government. He has detailed the explicit culture and grammar of manhood central to the founding fathers and the governmental system they created. They sought to discourage "bachelors and other disorderly men," foster the "family man" as the key to citizenship, vest public leadership in men of the "better sort," and—importantly for the presidency—make the "heroic man" seem more qualified to be president in lieu of a patriotic king.[12] All (especially Federalist) founders generally recognized the need for a heroic man in the presidency, but they cautiously sought those who were "the most wise and good."[13] Thomas Jefferson particularly saw the need for a great leader to support the rule of law but also to contend with "exigencies and opportunities [that] might demand extralegal initiatives, particularly in times of crises."[14] The benefits of having great and heroic men as president were multiple. In addition to procreating a new nation in the midst of crisis, great and heroic men could accrue "sufficient influence to oppose public opinion without provoking mass disobedience."[15] When exigencies demanded unpopular actions, a great leader could model

> independent manhood. His public exhibition of manly prowess heightened the other men's awareness of their own masculine shortcomings and encouraged them to strive for male maturity. His manly language and masterful deeds provided criteria by which most men could measure, judge, and rate one another. His public persona as a self-disciplined man who transcended personal prejudices, parochial loyalties, and factional politics fostered a sense of fraternal solidarity and national pride that bound men together.[16]

In other words, the great and heroic man had particular importance to the founding of the presidency because of its effects on improving and unifying the rest of men. This reasoning might explain the extensive evocation of masculinity during the 2004 campaign. It certainly helps make sense of the longstanding need to pick the right man for the presidency. It also highlights the reaction when a woman—whether another political elite or a voter—raises questions about a man's masculine shortcomings.

Not incidentally for rethinking Madam President, the great-man model of the presidency also had the advantage of reinforcing traditional patriarchy if the great man "separated himself from women and conquered antagonistic female forces," consistent with a line of thought running from Plato through Machiavelli and clearly to the founding fathers. "He kept women at a distance to avoid distraction, temptation, and seduction from public duty. . . . The Heroic Man was a patriarch who exercised authority in opposition to women and womanhood."[17] This rendering smacks of the same forced and artificial demarcation used to hold sex and gender dualisms in place. Not only was the presidency established as a masculine institution, but its masculinity also demanded the exclusion of women. Perhaps gender conditions have changed sufficiently since the founding so that the masculinity of the presidency no longer requires the opposition of women and femininity. However, as is true with all institutions, the preferences embedded at its founding leave an enduring mark. Institutions continue to operate either in continuity with these preferences or in a dialectic relationship. Given the assumed masculinity and the preferences for a particular type of great man, any Madam President must contend with these initial great man assumptions.

One way to explore the extent to which the presidency continues to be cast in masculine terms is to look at the words used in coverage of presidential campaigns. If words commonly associated with masculinity appear more than words commonly associated with femininity, then we have some indication of the persistence of masculinity in presidential campaigns. If the usage is similar, then the institution and its campaigns has been substantially transformed and regendered from its highly and deliberatively masculine origins. To identify terms as either masculine or feminine, however, requires relying upon gender stereotypes, which causes several problems. First, stereotypes do not reflect empirical reality and tend to exaggerate differences found on average at the expense of the tremendous and otherwise recognized differences among women and among men. Stereotypes also obscure the overlap between men and women. Second, to use stereotypes is in some ways to reinforce them rather than to transform them. I greatly prefer the latter and recognize the great limitations to stereotypes and the danger involved in this approach. Third, reliance upon stereotypes does not adequately capture the many gender transformations that have occurred since second-wave feminism began to influence the commonwealth. With these important caveats in mind, I nonetheless employ stereotypic words whose gendering is quite obvious. In order to compare, I have matched terms in their gender equivalents to the extent possible. In some instances, no directly "opposite" words exist. Other times, I found no use of a feminine term in this dataset that would approximate a masculine one simply because feminine terms are not as common to coverage of presidential elections. In fact, this list is brief in part because my research team and I were challenged to find sufficient feminine terms for analysis.[18] We discovered far less use of words associated with women and femininity than men and masculinity in coverage of presidential campaigns. Further, as was discussed earlier, often the feminine words were used to denigrate a male candidate. We ran a preliminary search of nearly 100 words before settling upon the ones used in this research.

The words are drawn from a database of over 15,000 news articles and op-ed pieces in the *Washington Post*, *New York Times*, *Los Angeles Times*, *Boston Globe*, *Atlanta Journal-Constitution*, *Houston Chronicle*, and *St. Louis Post Dispatch*. For 2005 onward, the *Seattle Times* was added to the search. The articles from 2003 and 2004 were selected from Nexus and/or ProQuest by searching for the terms "presiden!" and "candida!"; these "wildcard" searches gather articles that include all terms based upon that root word, such as president, presidency, candidate, candidates, and so on. The database contains all articles with these words, with the exception of Associated Press articles, duplicates reprinted in a second paper, music and movie reviews, news briefs, and articles about President Bush that had nothing to do with the campaign. For 2005 and 2006, I searched for the terms "presiden!" and "2008." Table 5.1 shows the relative frequency of masculine and feminine word pairs.

As is quickly evident, masculine words vastly outweigh feminine words in frequency of use with two exceptions. The term "wildcard=femini!," which picks up "femininity," "feminist," and "feminism," is used more often than the term "masculine." Although one might suspect that the masculine is assumed and hence feminine is used more often because it is "marked" as different from the norm, a qualitative look at usage suggests that the words "feminism/ists" cause this anomaly. The other exception is the close frequency of use between "hormone" and "testosterone," although neither appears

Table 5.1 Gendered Words Compared (total N in articles, 2003–2006)

Feminine Words	Number	Masculine Words	Number
Femini!	107	Masculin!	15
Cooperate	523	Compete	2,523
Soft	1,260	Hard	4,636
Intuitive	33	Aggressive	1,070
Sensitive	395	Tough	1,928
Sacrifice	375	Control	2,347
Hormone	17	Testosterone	15

often. It is interesting that women and hormones emerge about as often as testosterone because words associated with women are so scant. In all other word pairs, the masculine term is used far more often than the feminine term: "Hard" is used roughly four times as often as "soft." The pairs "compete-cooperate" and "tough-sensitive" show roughly five times more use of the masculine than the feminine and "control-sacrifice" six times more masculine use. "Intuition" simply figures very little in contrast to "aggressive," although that may not be a particularly good pairing. "Gut" or "instinct" might pair better as a masculine equivalence of intuition. Yet as tools or means for accomplishing ends, intuition and aggression do pair satisfactorily. In these comparisons, stereotypical masculine words far outweigh feminine ones in frequency of use. Apparently, news coverage of presidential campaigns continues to frame the presidency in heavily masculine language. Female candidates must contend with this constructed reality.

But gender institutions and the processes associated with them are always in flux. They have enduring aspects based upon history but are also influenced by ongoing events that cue gender. For example, the 1992 election became known as the "year of the woman" in large part because the focus was upon domestic issues such as health care and the need to reform a corrupt Congress. That issue, coupled with a major focus on sexual harassment in the Thomas-Hill hearings, highlighted the paucity of women in Congress. These elements of the historical moment shifted the focus toward women and cued their gender as able to handle these areas. In contrast, the 9/11 attack cued a need for masculine protectors and, along with the war in Iraq, put a strong focus on commander-in-chief responsibilities. This focus turned attention away from the early 2001 emphasis on campaign finance reform, tax cuts, patients' rights, and education reform, turning it to the military, terrorism, and the Afghanistan war. The gender climate changed, and the gender cues changed with it.

To assess the gendering of politics caused by current events, I turned to an online chronology of US political events, "Month-by-Month," and used all events listed in domestic politics, as well as selected court cases.[19] From the years 2001 through 2005, a total of 384 events were coded. The coding was based on my judgment about which gender voters would think could best handle a specific event or issue. I used a five-point scale from 2 to –2, with 2 being very masculine and –2 being very feminine. Initial intercoder reliability was above 0.80, and great pains were taken to come to agreement on any differences so that the final coding represents consensus among coders. Twenty-four issue areas emerged from the chronologies. Those considered to be very masculine include defense, war, military, and security. Masculine areas included tax cuts, business, trade, intelligence (e.g., the Central Intelligence Agency), corruption, justice issues (such as prison sentencing), and farm subsidies. Areas that were scored as 0 had elements that could cue both genders and hence canceled a gender cue; they included cloning, family farms, and the 9/11 Commission. One might argue that no feminine issues exist because politics has been and continues to be ensconced in masculinity. That is not my position. Many issues have been deemed to be "women's issues," and gender ideology has always been associated in some areas with women, even if not in the political realm. Further, gender transformations clearly have taken place, and voters do think of some issues as associated with women and hence as women "naturally" handling these areas at least as well as men, and maybe better. The areas deemed feminine for coding were deficits, healthcare, marriage, gay marriage, poverty, civil rights, and anticorruption. Those coded as very feminine are education, the environment, welfare, and abortion. Overall, the percentages of gender areas were very masculine, 24.7 percent; masculine, 29.1 percent; cross-gendered, 14.0 percent; feminine, 23.9 percent; and very feminine, 8.3 percent. To assess the gendered climate, I arrived at a general gender score for each month by calculating the average code for all events. Figure 5.1 presents an average general gender score for each month from 2001 to 2005.

To the extent that such analysis captures the gendered context accurately, several points merit discussion. First, the closer to the general election, the stronger was the cuing of masculinity. Given the widespread awareness of the Republican gender gap that favored

Figure 5.1 Monthly Gender Score of Events, 2001–2005

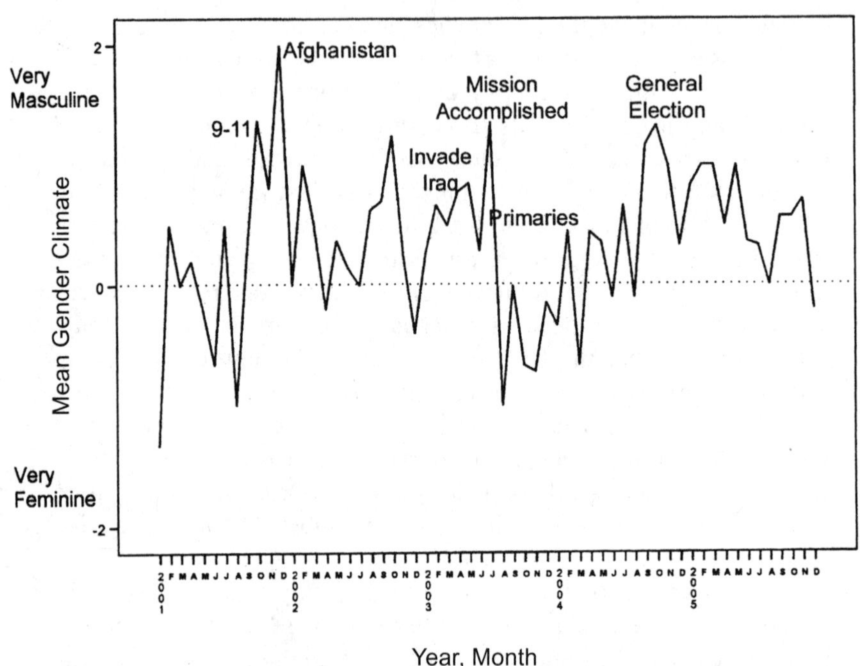

men, emphasizing masculinity made sense for campaign strategist Karl Rove. It suggests both that gender can explicitly be in play in campaigns and that the gender context of 2004 pushed increasingly toward masculine issue areas. Second, during 2003 while Democratic candidates were emerging, abortion, drug plans, deficits, and much concern over the 9/11 report tipped the context away from masculinity. Finally, if issues identified in my coding do indeed cue women as the better gender to handle such issues, then the presidential campaign environment has transformed in positive ways for potential female presidential possibilities. Gender transformation has indeed begun to operate.

Madam President Faces Mr. President

Presidential campaigns are framed in the media such that actions are interpreted through that lens. John Kerry as a "flip-flopper" is an example of a frame that became widespread and seemingly was potent as a lens for interpretation. Words used in news coverage also "prime" an audience by suggesting standards of judgment, both by the nature of the word and by volume. That is, the use of some words and not others sets the stage for deciding whether an item covered is positive or not, worthy or not, and so on. By using terms often, the judgments about some things are primed more than others. Table 5.2 takes a closer look at masculine words covered in a time frame that represents the last two years of the 2004 cycle and the first two years of the 2008 cycle. What standards of judgment are cued by these masculine words?

Of the dozens of words associated with masculinity that I explored, the words used in Table 5.2 proved most common. Of all of them (and their derivatives), "attack" constitutes more than a quarter (26.9 percent) of all words in this sample. "Strong" follows closely behind with more than one-fifth (22.8 percent) of all words, and "hard" occupies 14.5 percent of this sample. "Command," "compete," and "control" have roughly equal totals, although command is much more important in 2004 than other years. This finding reinforces other findings on presidential functions that suggest the commander-in-chief role continues to figure particularly prominently in presidential races, and perhaps especially so for a woman candidate.[20]

Focusing on 2004 shows some of what the first candidate for Madam President likely will face in the general election year. Coverage of the presidential campaign is, of course, greatly elevated in an election year, and the citizenry will be bombarded with words about the campaign. Of the use of these words over four years, 72.6 percent occur in 2004. The 2008 election will likely be framed in terms similar to 2004, unless the United States has ended the war on terror and extricated itself from both Afghanistan and Iraq. Therefore we can particularly anticipate continued heavy use of words derived from wildcards for attack, strength, and hardness. There also is no reason to assume other words will fade. Standards of judging therefore also cue that the potential Madam President must "command," a word relatively more important in 2004 than in the other three years. She will need to compete—presumably aggressively—control, and demonstrate toughness, so that she is recognized as dominating. If 2004 is indicative of other future presidential campaigns, women candidates need to negotiate news priming that leaves them in the position of a victim in a bad horror movie. For female candidates, the challenge will be to seem strong enough to be president without

Table 5.2 Masculine Words by Yearly Totals, in Rank Order of 2004 Use

	Attack	Strong	Hard	Command	Compete	Control	Tough	Aggressive	Dominate	Total
2003	2,290	2,182	1,303	669	865	745	511	338	250	9,153
2004	9,338	7,398	4,636	2,580	2,523	2,347	1,928	1,070	934	32,754
2005	196	295	352	58	113	153	112	49	49	1,377
2006[a]	298	430	250	118	214	228	172	58	58	1,826
Word Totals	12,122	10,305	6,541	3,425	3,715	3,473	2,723	1,515	1,291	45,110

Note: a. Numbers through June 30, 2006, were projected by doubling. Use of these words likely would increase closer to congressional elections in November 2006.

evoking the negative judgment of being an aggressively dominating woman.

Along the Trail

All general election years follow similar patterns, although the particulars change each cycle. Vigorous activity takes place during the primary season, which generally concentrates in January and February and is decided by early March. (In 2004, primaries and coverage had ended entirely by June 3.) Campaigns go into a quieter period from March until the party conventions, although issue groups and the campaigns themselves have since 1992 been more active in running advertisements during this stage of the campaign than had been done previously. The party conventions enliven the campaigns again, with coverage generally running about two weeks prior and a week after each. (In 2004, an unusually long five weeks existed between the conventions: the Democratic convention ran July 26–29, and the Republican convention ran August 30 to September 2.) The debates follow in early autumn. (There were four in 2004: three presidential debates on September 30 and October 8 and 13, and a vice-presidential debate on October 5.) The homestretch frenzy precedes the general election (held November 2, 2004). In other words, we anticipate considerable coverage during the primary season of January and February, a decrease until convention time, with high levels of coverage peaking in October. Table 5.3 looks at the main masculine words according to monthly use levels.

Two results were hypothesized: that levels of coverage, and hence the volume of masculine word use, would be larger during January and October and that evocations of masculinity would increase as the general election neared. As would be expected, overall word usage is heaviest during the early primary months and in September and October, when the campaign heads into the general election. Contrary to expectations, not all masculine words are used more as the general election approached. Further, and somewhat surprisingly, some words are evoked more during the primary than the general election and still others at various times on the campaign trail. These anomalies warrant the closest scrutiny.

"Attack," the most frequently used word, both fits the pattern and offers an anomaly. Not surprisingly, it is used heavily in January and October. It also is evoked often in September, a time when campaigns

Table 5.3 Masculine Word Use by Month, 2004

2004	Attack	Strong	Hard	Command	Compete	Control	Tough	Aggressive	Dominate	Monthly Totals
Jan.	927	1,007	634	204	424	204	262	113	151	3,926
Feb.	742	832	483	209	390	204	257	111	93	3,321
Mar.	944	461	323	71	204	137	156	80	62	2,438
Apr.	758	398	260	174	140	174	146	60	43	2,153
May	496	559	408	292	224	261	150	74	82	2,546
June	673	506	307	197	158	259	117	95	50	2,362
July	813	971	531	253	243	216	181	102	95	3,405
Aug.	1,036	503	325	359	132	149	121	83	71	2,779
Sept.	1,361	743	444	392	191	222	213	113	77	3,756
Oct.	1,356	1,007	675	386	315	382	250	171	141	4,683
Nov.	210	396	222	40	95	133	73	65	68	1,302
Dec.	13	15	24	3	7	6	2	3	1	74
Total	9,338	7,398	4,636	2,580	2,523	2,347	1,928	1,070	934	32,754

swing into high gear and debates, whose coverage is filled with sports and war metaphors, take place. Interesting is the high use of attack in March. Neither the war nor other events on the chronology account for this use of attack; rather, it comes from the launch of the Bush campaign and its attacks on Kerry. Two things are clear for a potential Madam President: She needs to be prepared for direct attacks on her and to respond in a way that does not prime negative judgments. She also must anticipate that the opponents' campaign(s) will devise their attacks with her in mind, including her gender.

"Command" is the second particularly cautionary example for female presidential candidates. Although command did appear frequently during the primary months, many of those uses came from Wesley Clark, who had been a commander, a fact that was often mentioned. Important for female candidates is the very heavy reference to command caused by Swift Boat Veterans for Truth, whose stated purpose was to cast doubt on Kerry's ability to serve as commander in chief. They launched their attack ads in May, and Kerry responded to them with a lawsuit in August. Also, the Republican National Convention touted Bush's experience as commander in chief as evidence that he could serve ably in that role, despite a weak personal record in the military. Command also figures prominently in coverage of the debates, especially the debate focused on foreign policy. Although news coverage seldom directly mentioned that a woman will have a difficult time being accepted as commander in chief, clearly it operates as a critical, and heavily masculinized, subtext on the presidential campaign trail.

Three words (and their derivatives) appeared more often during the primary season than during the general election time: "compete," "tough," and "dominate." I have not yet analyzed these data sufficiently to determine whether they refer more often to the nature of the primary campaigns, the candidates themselves, or some other elements. Suffice it to note that these terms may pose a challenge to a female candidate earlier rather than later on the presidential campaign trail, and that these words are prime judgments during the primary season.

Masculinity in the Campaign During Candidate Emergence

I have concentrated on the 2004 election cycle in order to understand what might occur for 2008. I argued above that the sheer volume of words used in campaign coverage evoked masculinity and caused female presidential candidates real challenges. As we turn to the 2008 election and ask questions about how women often mentioned as potential candidates might actually emerge, scholars should begin to concentrate on an understudied time frame—the first two years of the cycle. In the 2004 campaign, of all who emerged as candidates, only two were first mentioned in the newspapers of this study after 2002, Carol Moseley Braun and Dennis Kucinich. All others were mentioned during 2000 and 2001. Of the twenty-three presidential possibilities mentioned first for the 2004 election, seventeen had been mentioned already in 2000 and another two in 2001 and 2002 each.[21] In other words, scholars of presidential elections tend to begin paying attention well after the press has already designated who possible candidates are. The first two years of the four-year election cycle are crucial.

If the same pattern of early mentions equating to the pool of probable candidates holds for 2008, then most of the presidential possibilities should have already been mentioned. Hillary Rodham Clinton and Condoleezza Rice are the women most mentioned, although only Clinton has launched her campaign and Rice has steadfastly denied any interest in the post. Who else has the press given at least a preliminary stamp of legitimacy by including them in lists of presidential possibilities? Table 5.4 provides a list of names mentioned through the end of 2006 in the *New York Times* and *Washington Post*. As a scan quickly makes evident, among the twenty-seven possibilities mentioned only one other woman appears, Janet Napolitano (D), the governor of Arizona. In other words, less than two years into the 2008 cycle, major newspapers have already identified twenty-seven possible candidates, and twenty-four are men. Masculinity is already underway on the 2008 campaign trail.

One other finding gives pause for the way masculinity might operate early on the campaign trail. Although the volume of exposure to masculine words related to presidential campaigns certainly inundates the attentive public with masculine cues, that measure depends upon the quantity of coverage. To assess the intensity of masculinity evocation in press coverage, I simply calculated the mean number of masculine words used per articles on presidential campaigns. I expected that the peak intensity would correspond with the presidential election year. Table 5.5 reveals a surprising result that has great bearing on the 2008 election.

The highest average use of masculine terms in newspaper stories relating to presidential elections occurred in 2005, not 2004. That is,

Table 5.4 Candidates Mentioned Early for the 2008 Presidential Election

Candidate	Party	Previous Position(s)	Date of First Mention
Hillary Rodham Clinton	D	First Lady, senator (NY)	November 4, 2004
John Edwards	D	Senator (SC)	November 4, 2004
Condoleezza Rice	R	National security advisor, secretary of state	November 5, 2004
Howard Dean	D	Governor (VT)	November 7, 2004
Mark Warner	D	Governor (VA)	November 7, 2004
Bill Richardson	D	Congressman (NM), UN ambassador, secretary of energy, governor (NM)	November 7, 2004
Janet Napolitano	D	Governor (AZ)	November 7, 2004
Phil Bresden	D	Governor (TN)	November 7, 2004
Michael Easley	D	Governor (NC)	November 7, 2004
Rod Blagojevich	D	Governor (IL)	November 7, 2004
John Kerry	D	Senator (MA)	November 9, 2004
Mitt Romney	R	Governor (MA)	November 14, 2004
Chuck Hagel	R	Senator (NE)	November 15, 2004
Bill Frist	R	Senator (TN)	December 21, 2004
Newt Gingrich	R	Congressman (GA)	January 19, 2005
Rudolph Giuliani	R	Mayor (NYC)	January 20, 2005
George Pataki	R	Governor (NY)	January 20, 2005
Sam Brownback	R	Senator (KS)	April 21, 2005
George Allen	R	Senator (VA)	April 29, 2005
John McCain	R	Senator (AZ)	April 29, 2005
Evan Bayh	D	Senator (IN)	April 29, 2005
Joe Biden	D	Senator (DE)	June 22, 2005
Haley Barbour	R	Governor (MS)	July 21, 2005
Tim Pawlenty	R	Governor (MN)	July 21, 2005
Tom Vilsack	D	Governor (IA)	July 21, 2005
Mike Huckabee	R	Governor (AR)	July 21, 2005
Tom Daschle	D	Senator (ND)	October 21, 2005
Russ Feingold	D	Senator (WI)	October 24, 2005

Source: Names mentioned come from the *New York Times* and *Washington Post*.

during the very period when candidates begin their campaigns, testing the waters and lining up supporters, even though coverage was quite scant in comparison to the last two years of the 2004 cycle, the evocation of masculinity was much more intense. Such a result suggests intensified and hidden masculinity early in campaign cycles.

A closer look at the word use shows a different pattern in 2005 than closer to the campaign, however. Of the masculine words analyzed, the rank order of most frequently used words is "hard" (N = 352), "strong" (N = 295), "attack" (N = 196), "control" (N = 153). Different words were cued in 2005 than in 2004. Although strong maintains its place in the second-most-common usage, hard and attack switch order of frequency, and control moves ahead of both command and compete in rank order. What this means for the 2008 election or a possible Madam President is not yet clear.

Some evidence suggests that the gender cuing is changing to be more favorable for a woman, despite the intensity of masculine words. The year 2005 saw Abu Ghraib excesses and system failures with Katrina; scandals reached into the vice president's office; and Congress began to resist President Bush, especially with regard to Iraq and domestic eavesdropping. During 2006, the claim of "mission accomplished" in either Iraq or Afghanistan became tragically farcical as the death toll escalated and the Taliban began to close down girls' schools and otherwise reassert themselves. The gendering of the presidency may in fact shift with the context to the advantage of a potential Madam President.

Although the president's actions do not always accord with his words, he made a remarkable admission during a May 26, 2006, press conference with Tony Blair that lends credence to the possibility of a change in gender climates.

QUESTION: Mr. President, you spoke about missteps and mistakes in Iraq. Could I ask both of you which missteps and mistakes of your own you most regret?

BUSH: Sounds like kind of a familiar refrain here. Saying, "Bring it on"; kind of tough talk, you know, that sent the wrong signal to people. I learned some lessons about expressing myself maybe in

Table 5.5 Rate of Masculine Word Use by Year, 2003–2006

Year	Number of Articles	Number of Words	Mean Words Per Article
2003	5,296	17,933	0.295
2004	10,288	40,216	0.256
2005	532	1,377	3.86
2006 Projected	323	1,826	0.177

a little more sophisticated manner, you know. "Wanted, dead or alive"; that kind of talk. I think in certain parts of the world it was misinterpreted. And so I learned from that.[22]

Tough talk, which so dominated the presidency since 9/11, may finally be recognized as having its downside and framed by the press as such. If so, then perhaps, just perhaps, the campaign trail will evoke less masculinity in 2008. As gender transformation continues and the historically gendered institution responds to the historical moment, 2008 may present a greater opening for a women candidate. Already the discussion about Hillary Clinton is being cast in terms of her potential as an individual candidate and not merely as a "woman candidate." Indisputably, this constitutes progress toward a presidential campaign that women can enter. Incremental progress toward Madam President continues if a female candidate makes her way into the primaries and caucuses. With that, even if she does not ultimately emerge in the 2008 general election, we will be one step closer toward a presidency that reaches the democratic potential of political equality for women and men. No greater symbol could exist of democratic equality than a woman in the White House.

Notes

1. See Lawless, "Women, War, and Winning Elections."
2. See Norlinger, "Political Virility."
3. See Rich, "How Kerry Became a Girlie-Man."
4. See Rainey, "Who's the Man?"
5. See Givhan, "Something Up Their Sleeves."
6. See Rhode, *Speaking of Sex.*
7. See Sapiro, *The Political Integration of Women*; and Burns, Schlozman, and Verba, *The Private Roots of Public Action.*
8. See Johnson, Duerst-Lahti, and Norton, *Creating Gender.*
9. Elsewhere I have offered the concept of feminale, which extends into feminality and feminalism. It allows for associations rooted in that which females prefer with their own agency, and offers a theoretical option for equality that breaks free from masculinism and public patriarchy. Here I stay with the term "feminine" but wish to imbue it with more female agency. See ibid., especially chap. 3, and Duerst-Lahti, "Governing Intuitions, Ideologies, and Gender," and "Knowing Congress as a Gendered Institution."
10. See Center for American Women and Politics, "Women in Presidential Cabinets."

11. The bureaucracy and executive administration, based upon Weberian precepts, were among the first institutions to be analyzed in political science. See Ferguson, *The Feminist Case Against Bureaucracy.*

12. See Kann, *A Republic of Men.*

13. Ibid, p. 133, citing John Adams chap. 6, n. 10.

14. Ibid.

15. Ibid, p. 136.

16. Ibid, p. 134.

17. Ibid, pp. 134–135.

18. Sincere thanks go to Nicholas Stuber and Stuart Kirkpatrick, who once again prove that undergraduates can perform outstanding research. Thanks also go to Jim and Marge Sanger, who support the Sanger Summer Scholars Program at Beloit College and to Beloit College for its ongoing support of faculty research.

19. "See Month-by-Month." Infoplease, Pearson Education, accessed July 29, 2006.

20. See Duerst-Lahti, "Gendering Presidential Functions."

21. See Duerst-Lahti, "Presidential Elections: Gendered Space and the Case of 2004."

22. See "Bush, Blair Hold Joint News Conference."

6

Money and the Art and Science of Candidate Viability

Victoria Farrar-Myers

The 2008 presidential election will be historic in that, for the first time since 1952, neither a sitting president nor vice president will be a candidate for the presidency. But will this election be historic for another reason that many are speculating—that is, will it see the first female candidate running for president since 1972, when Shirley Chisholm ran for the Democratic nomination?[1] This speculation is quickly followed by a discussion of the modern political "arms race," that is, what war chest will be necessary to make any candidate—gender aside—viable to compete in a system where opting out of public financing is becoming the norm among the top candidates, frontloading makes name recognition to compete necessary years in advance, and the invisible primary for the 2008 nomination began the day after the 2004 election ended.[2]

Money is a threshold factor for establishing a viable campaign. With it, candidates can promote their message, operate their campaigns simultaneously in multiple states, and be seen as having a groundswell of support behind their candidacies—in fact, being able to raise campaign funds is sometimes seen as viability itself. Although *financial* viability is a core and necessary factor, it alone is not sufficient to establish a truly viable presidential campaign. Many ingredients go into establishing viability. Successful candidates must not only master the science of viability by amassing money, but also the art of viability whereby they employ the financial war chest they have built to manipulate these ingredients into a winning formula.

When it comes to the money factor and the art and science of viability, a woman presidential candidate will face a number of questions. Can a woman candidate achieve financial viability? Even if she meets this threshold criterion, what else must she do to become a viable candidate for president? What does "viable" mean if not financial viability alone, and does a woman candidate face added issues in establishing viability?

The Money Factor and Viability

The pre-primary period—also referred to as the "invisible primary"—can also be seen as a "money primary" stage in which fundraising is often equated with a candidate's viability.[3] Political contributors can "vote" with the money they donate to a potential candidate. As a result, candidates can go a long way to establishing their viability early by showing they are able to attract funding. Conversely, a candidate can be knocked out of the race before the first vote is even cast by not raising sufficient funds during the pre-primary period—such was the fate suffered by Elizabeth Dole when she explored running for the Republican nomination prior to the 2000 election.[4]

The centrality of money to a presidential candidate's viability raises the question of whether women candidates are able to raise sufficient money to enable them to be seen as viable. One myth of presidential campaign finance is that a woman would not be able to do so.[5] As will be shown below, however, successful women candidates for the House and Senate have been just as effective, if not better, than their male counterparts in raising money.[6] Congress often provides a pipeline for potential presidential candidates, allowing them to gain national recognition and a record of service on which they can base their presidential campaigns. Thus, one could reasonably anticipate that since women have learned to be successful at the campaign finance game at the congressional level, women could succeed in the game at the presidential level as well.[7]

During the 2003–2004 election cycle, the average winning candidate for the House of Representatives, regardless of gender, spent approximately $1.03 million (see Figure 6.1).[8] But when winning candidates are separated by gender, we see that the average female winning House candidate paid out over $1.09 million, while the winning men expended just under $1.02 million on average. Thus, successful women candidates outspent their male counterparts in the House by 7 percent. The twenty-three Republican women elected to the House in 2004 maintained the traditional money advantage that

Figure 6.1 Average Expenditures for Winning House Candidates, 2004

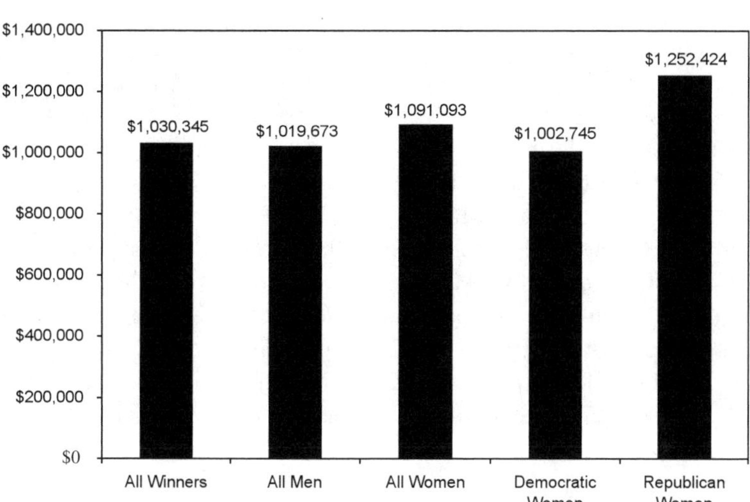

Source: Compiled from Federal Election Commission (FEC) data available at http://www.fec.gov (including data collected and compiled from FEC data by http://www.opensecrets.org).

Note: Democratic women: N = 42. Republican women: N = 23.

the GOP in general normally enjoys over Democrats, spending in excess of $1.25 million, or 21.6 percent above the average, for all winning House candidates that year. The forty-two Democratic women, for their part, actually fell 2.7 percent below the overall mean, averaging just over $1 million.

As for the Senate, similar relationships between successful female and male candidates are found (see Figure 6.2). The three election cycles from 2000 through 2004 saw all 100 seats in the Senate up for grabs, along with two special elections to fill unexpired terms. In these 102 elections, the winning candidate spent on average over $6.4 million. Separating these candidates by gender, though, shows a wide difference between male and female candidates. The average woman spent $10.1 million, or 73.3 percent more, than the average winning male senatorial candidate during this period (under $5.9 million). Given that only fourteen women are included in this analysis,[9] the average is somewhat skewed by the $29 million that Hillary Clinton spent in her 2000 campaign for senator from New

York in 2000.[10] But even if Senator Clinton is omitted from this analysis, the average winning female candidate in the Senate spent $8.6 million, which is 47.4 percent above the average winning male Senate candidate during this period.

The traditional partisan fundraising advantage favoring Republicans is reversed when examining women in the Senate. Democrats (including Hillary Clinton) averaged more than $12.4 million in spending during this period. Without Clinton, the average falls to $8.6 million but still includes four other candidates who spent in excess of $10 million: Maria Cantwell ($11.6 million in 2000), Dianne Feinstein ($11.8 million in 2000), Barbara Boxer ($16.0 million in 2004), and Patty Murray ($12.5 million in 2004). The five successful Republican woman candidates during this period, by contrast, spent on average just shy of $6.0 million, with only one exceeding the $10 million threshold (Elizabeth Dole in 2002, who spent $13.7 million). The Republican numbers, however, also include three

Figure 6.2 Average Expenditures for Winning Senate Candidates, 2000–2004

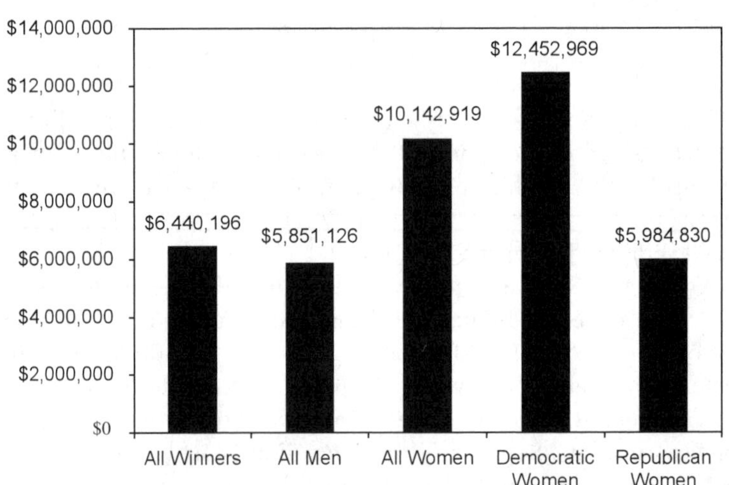

Source: Compiled from data available at http://www.fec.gov (including data collected and compiled from FEC data by http://www.opensecrets.org).

Note: Democratic women: N = 9. 2000: Cantwell (WA), Clinton (NY), Feinstein (CA), Stabenow (MI); 2002: Landrieu (LA); 2004: Boxer (CA), Lincoln (AR), Mikulski (MD), Murray (WA). Republican women: N = 5. 2000: Hutchison (TX), Snowe (ME); 2002: Collins (ME), Dole (NC); 2004: Murkowski (AK).

senators from less populous, small market states—Olympia Snowe of Maine ($2.3 million in 2000), Susan Collins of Maine ($4.1 million in 2002), and Lisa Murkowski of Alaska ($5.5 million in 2004)—as well as Kay Bailey Hutchison (TX) who spent $4.3 million in her 2000 reelection bid against minimal competition. The average expenditures for Republican women, however, still exceeded the average amount spent by successful male candidates during this period.

The fundraising relationships between successful male and female congressional candidates shown above are similar to ones found in a comparable analysis of the 2000 elections.[11] They show that successful women congressional candidates have outspent their male colleagues and have, indeed, learned to play the campaign finance game quite well. But what about the source of their campaign funds—where have these women obtained their financing, and how do their sources compare to those of successful male candidates?

Figures 6.3a–6.3c and 6.4a–6.4c explore these questions, showing the sources of campaign funding for female and male winning House candidates, respectively.[12] Regardless of how the numbers are broken down—by gender and/or by party—the result is largely the same: both men and women received approximately 52–56 percent of their funds in 2004 from individuals, 41–45 percent from political action committees (PACs), and the remaining 3 percent or so from other sources (including themselves). Perhaps the most interesting finding in these charts is the relationship of Democratic women to men when compared to their Republican counterparts. Democratic women received a greater percentage of their funding from individuals (55.7 percent) than Democratic men (53.4 percent). This relationship is reversed for Republicans, where the men received a greater portion from individuals (55.5 percent) than women (52.6 percent).

In breaking down PAC contributions further (see Figures 6.5a–6.5c and 6.6a–6.6c), we see a few other differences between the fundraising profiles of women and men, although these differences are relatively minor.[13] For example, men received a greater portion of their PAC money from business interests (64.8 percent) than did women (55.5 percent). This difference, however, derives primarily from the difference between Democratic men (50.6 percent) and women (43.9 percent), because Republican men and women receive nearly equal percentages from business PACs (77.7 percent and 76.1 percent, respectively). Another interesting, albeit small, difference is the higher percentage of PAC money that women receive from labor PACs as compared to men, regardless of party. The percentage that

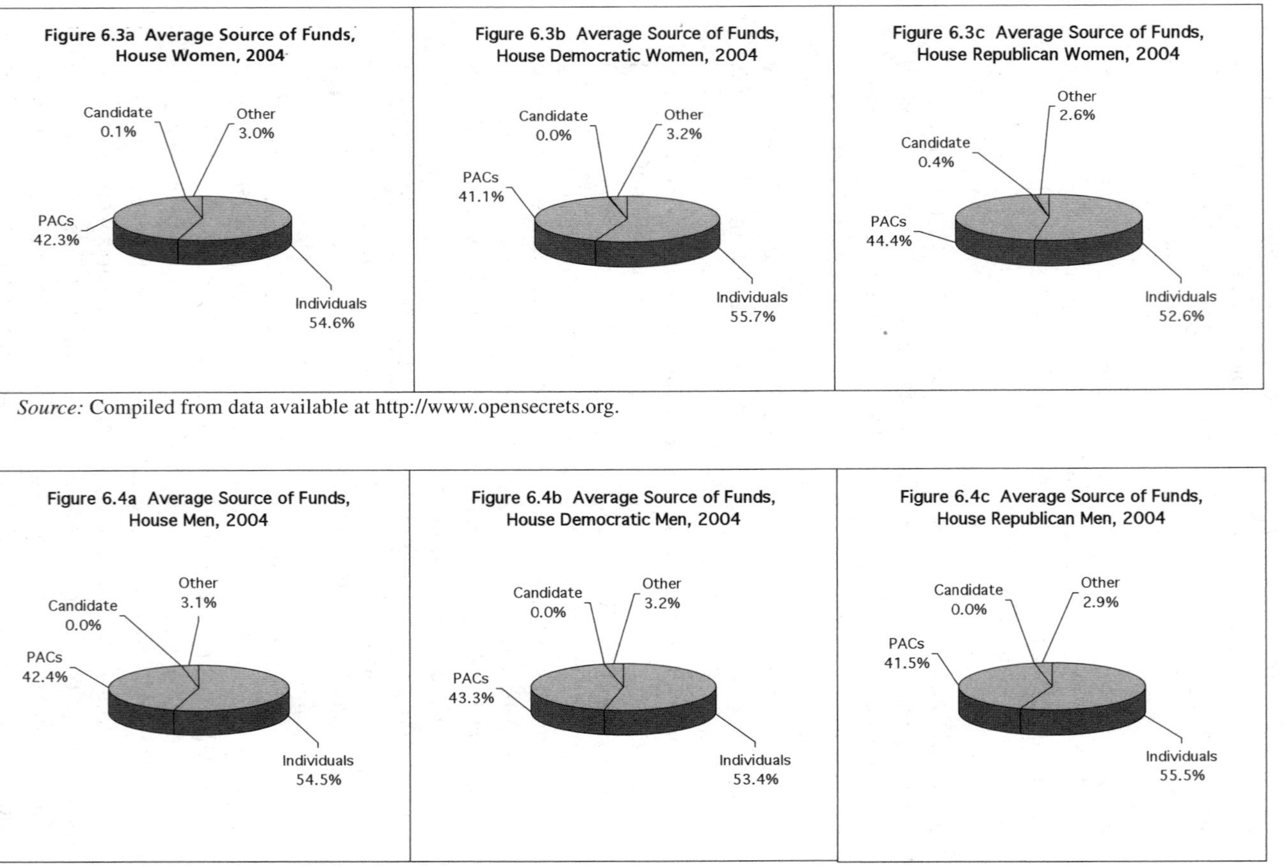

Source: Compiled from data available at http://www.opensecrets.org.

Source: Compiled from data available at http://www.opensecrets.org.

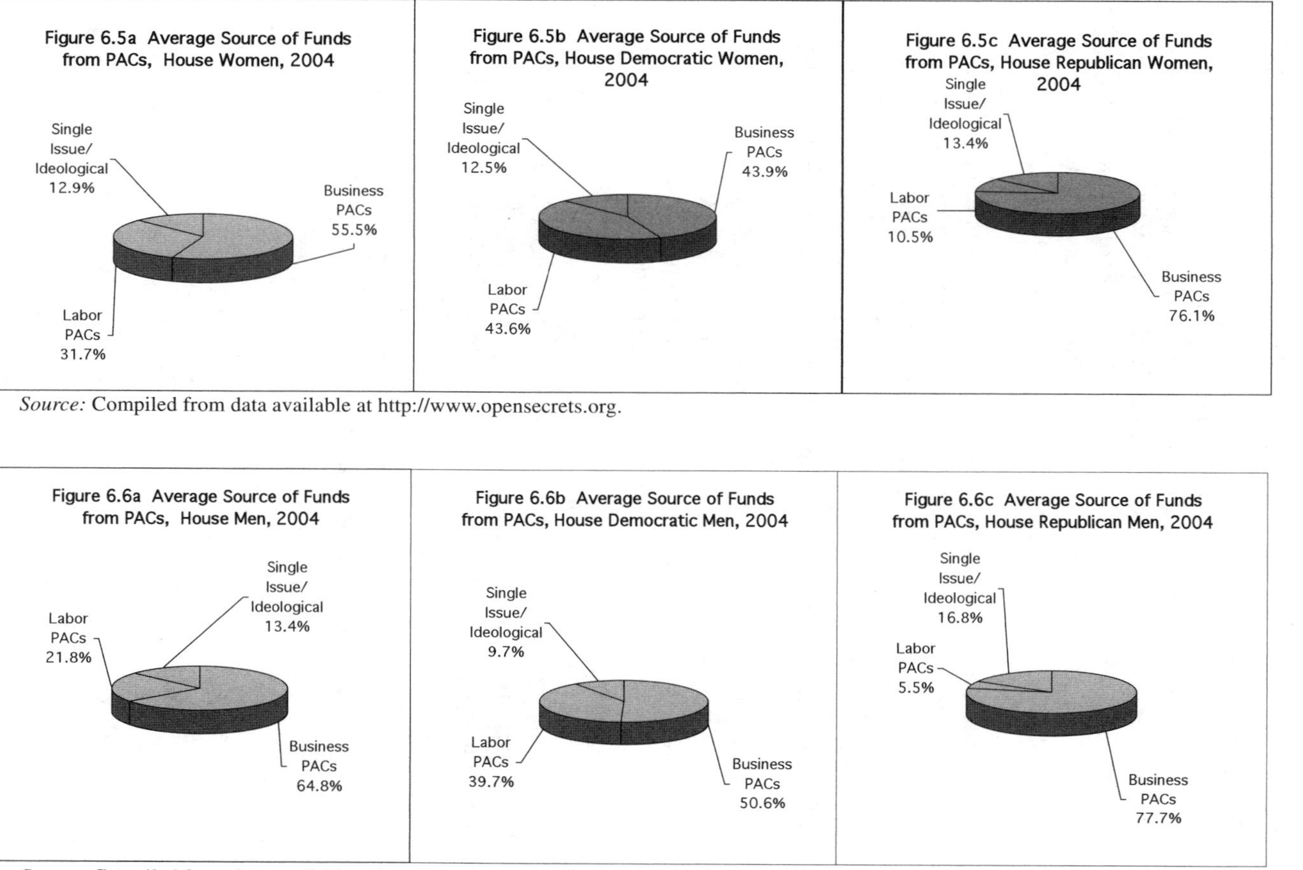

Figure 6.5a Average Source of Funds from PACs, House Women, 2004

Figure 6.5b Average Source of Funds from PACs, House Democratic Women, 2004

Figure 6.5c Average Source of Funds from PACs, House Republican Women, 2004

Source: Compiled from data available at http://www.opensecrets.org.

Figure 6.6a Average Source of Funds from PACs, House Men, 2004

Figure 6.6b Average Source of Funds from PACs, House Democratic Men, 2004

Figure 6.6c Average Source of Funds from PACs, House Republican Men, 2004

Source: Compiled from data available at http://www.opensecrets.org.

Democratic women received from labor PACs was 3.9 percent more than what Democratic men received; for Republicans, this number is 5.0 percent.

The third difference of note relates to single-issue/ideological PACs. Democratic women received a greater percentage of their PAC funds from single-issue/ideological PACS (12.5 percent) than Democratic men (9.7 percent). Much like the finding noted above regarding funding from individuals, though, the relationship is reversed for Republican women (13.4 percent) and men (16.8 percent).

Examining PAC contributions to winning Senate candidates shows comparable, although more significant, differences in the fundraising profiles of women and men (see Table 6.1).[14] Unlike in the House, where the men and women under study on average received nearly the same percentage of funds from individuals and PACs, in the Senate women received a higher percentage of funds from individuals (64.4 percent) than men (61.4 percent), whereas men quite noticeably received a higher percentage from PACs (32.1 percent) than women (20.4 percent). Similarly, in examining the source of PAC money, we see that men received more from business PACs (75.7 percent) than women (64.2 percent), but labor PACs made up a higher percentage of contributions to women (17.1 percent) than to men (9.4 percent).[15]

The relationships found in the Senate for the 2000–2004 election cycles are similar to those of the prior study covering the 1996–2000 election cycles.[16] The prior study offered one possible explanation for

Table 6.1 Average Source of Funds by Gender, Senate, 2000–2004 (in percent)

Source	Women	Men
Individuals	64.4	61.4
PACs	20.4	32.1
Business PACs	(64.2)	(75.7)
Labor PACs	(17.1)	(9.4)
Single-issue /ideological	(18.7)	(14.9)
Candidate	6.5	0.2
Other	8.7	6.3

Source: Compiled from data available at http://www.opensecrets.org.
Note: Numbers in parentheses are percentages of the PAC total.

these relationships not directly related to gender of the candidate: specifically, that the PAC contributions may reflect more the seniority of the men and women under study rather than their gender. In that study, the men were decidedly more senior than their female counterparts. In this study, though, the differences in seniority between the men and women studied have been reduced, but the relationships have not changed significantly.[17] Although the explanation for the differences in fundraising profiles between successful men and women candidates is beyond the scope of this chapter, two points should be kept in mind when considering these issues. First, a small but noticeable difference in the fundraising profiles of men and women Senate candidates does appear to exist—at least based on the limited findings of this and the previous study. Second, notwithstanding this small difference in profiles, one should not forget about the significant difference between women and men Senate candidates in terms of dollars spent during the 2000–2004 election cycles.

What all this tells us is that, at the congressional level, women have proven themselves to be successful fundraisers and able to convert their fundraising into a winning campaign. In fact, in many ways, women have done so better than men. Knowing how to raise and then effectively use campaign funds are lessons that any politician, regardless of gender, needs to learn if she or he is going to run for president. These skills are at the foundation of developing a viable campaign for the presidency. If fundraising at the congressional level is any indication, women have shown the skills necessary to compete financially at the national level.

Given this, one would expect that a woman candidate for president could establish her financial viability and overcome this fundamental threshold in establishing a viable candidacy. But, as noted above, financial viability is a necessary but not sufficient condition of viability for a truly successful run for the presidency. Viability has many tangible and intangible components, of which the ability to raise money is just one (albeit a core) factor.

The Ingredients of Viability

The concept of viability can be understood simply as the perception of a candidate's chances of winning her or his party's nomination.[18] But the simplicity of this definition belies the complexity of factors—or ingredients—that go into developing a viable presidential campaign. To understand what the term "viable" means in the presidential nomination process, we need to break down the various ingredients to understand what they are and how they affect a candidate's chances of winning the nomination.

To start, the tangible ingredients of viability represent the easiest set of ingredients to understand. These are items that candidates can affect (although not necessarily control) themselves and by which the candidate and others can more readily and perhaps more objectively test or examine. They are the building blocks to any successful campaign for the presidency:

- *Money.* As already discussed, this is a core ingredient on which many of the other ingredients of viability hinge.
- *Name recognition.* It is a fundamental proposition: voters must know who a candidate is in order to support him or her. But in what has the potential for an untenable Catch-22, a candidate needs to spend money to build name recognition but will have a difficult time raising funds unless voters recognize the candidate.
- *Network/support.* A candidate's core network and base of supporters provides additional voices to spread the candidate's message and additional resources that might absorb some of the early costs of campaigning. This ingredient includes the complex process of building funding networks that are vital to a candidate's election efforts.[19]
- *Campaign organization.* Candidates are judged by who runs their campaigns and how well they run it. A well-organized campaign helps a candidate weather the ups and downs of the campaign trail; a disorganized campaign raises questions about the candidate's ability to govern.
- *Backing of party.* At some point, even an outsider is going to have to get party regulars behind him or her; the earlier a candidate is able to do so, the better the candidate appears to be able to obtain broad-based support (financially and otherwise) even beyond the party regulars.
- *Credibility on key issues.* A candidate may be the leading expert in some particular policy area, but unless that area is of concern to the voters or of particular importance for the nation at the time, that expertise will do the candidate no good unless she or he is able to knowledgably address those key matters most affecting the nation. Thus, for example, governors need

to speak about foreign affairs; as for women candidates, they need to develop an identity based on issues other than those traditionally seen as "women's issues" (e.g., education, health).

- *Résumé.* A presidential candidate must have established a proven track record of leadership for voters to trust the person. One knock against presidential candidates like Ross Perot or Steve Forbes, or even vice-presidential candidates such as Geraldine Ferraro or Dan Quayle, was that they did not have sufficient experience in the right positions to be president.

By their nature, the intangible ingredients of viability are more difficult to identify and less readily accessible. These items are often outside a candidate's control or impact but nonetheless factor into whether a candidate is waging a viable campaign. What a candidate needs to be able to do is read the political landscape to determine what these intangible ingredients are and how they may flavor the candidate's campaign. Perhaps more importantly, a candidate must try to turn the ingredients listed below to his or her advantage to the extent possible:

- *Political timing.* Success in politics often depends at being in the right place at the right time. Remember, for example, that Ronald Reagan had twice sought the presidency before his brand of conservativism struck a chord with voters in 1980.
- *Political environment and mood.* Being able to tap into the voters' true concerns in the midst of a variety of seemingly important issues of the day—much in the way that the "It's the economy, stupid" focus of the 1992 Clinton campaign did—can prove to be an exceptionally effective way to bolster a candidate's viability.
- *Desire for change.* Whether and how strongly voters want to change the current course of affairs and policy of the nation can greatly help or hinder a candidate's viability, depending on how closely a candidate is aligned to or distinguished from that course.

The above intangible ingredients of viability apply to all potential presidential candidates, regardless of gender. But in the case of a woman running for president, other intangible ingredients would seem to affect the viability of a female candidate's campaign:

- *Gender.* By gender, I mean not so much the fact that the candidate is a woman, but more particularly the public's reaction to a woman possibly being successful at the presidential level and how the candidate addresses the "gender issue."
- *Cultural norms.* How do voters view the role of women in society, in the workplace, in politics, and as leaders? Traditional views of women may act as barriers for a woman candidate; to the extent such views are broken down, opportunities for women may abound.
- *Voting strength of women.* Since winning elections often turns on which candidate is better able to mobilize supporters to turn out and vote, the higher turnout rates of women voters may also present opportunities for a woman candidate.[20]

Although the phenomenon of a woman running for president has been rare in American politics, it is not a new one. What the nation has not seen, however, is a woman able to fully establish her viability as a candidate—to establish herself as someone who might actually win her party's nomination and then the Oval Office. For example, by the time Elizabeth Dole withdrew from her run for the presidency in October 1999, George W. Bush had raised over $57 million, Steve Forbes had over $20 million (including $16 million of his own funds), and even John McCain had received nearly twice as much money as the approximately $5 million Dole had brought in since January 1999.[21] Pat Schroeder was unable to break out of, in her words, the pigeonhole that the media placed her in as the "woman candidate."[22] Even Shirley Chisholm has stated about her run, "No one was ready to take a black woman seriously as a candidate."[23] So it would seem that the next step in moving toward electing a woman president is to establish a female candidate's viability with respect to each of the above ingredients.

The Science of Viability

There is both a science and an art to developing a viable presidential campaign. The science of viability deals with the mechanics of doing so—in other words, collecting as many of the ingredients of viability as possible. Looking to 2008, we see that a number of leading women politicians and possible presidential candidates have engaged in this science and taken steps toward building a viable campaign.

Women in Congress who were gearing up for reelection in 2006 continued their success in fundraising. Preliminary data for the 2006 election showed that the six women senators up for reelection amassed an average $17.9 million apiece, led by Hillary Clinton's $51.3 million (which many believed to be the start of a war chest for her 2008 presidential campaign).[24] Even without Clinton's numbers factored in, the remaining five women averaged over $11.3 million, which well exceeds the average $6.8 million winning male Senate candidates spent in 2004. In the other chamber of Congress, female House members up for reelection had raised an average of $1.3 million for the 2006 election, surpassing the average spent in 2004.[25]

Women in Congress also have been building networks and garnering the support of their parties. For example, a total of twenty-three current female members of Congress have established leadership PACs—that is, political action committees created by and associated with elected officials for the purpose of raising and donating money to other candidates—that have been active during the 2005–2006 election cycle, led by PACs affiliated with Representative Deborah Pryce (R-OH), Representative Nancy Pelosi (D-CA), Representative Ileana Ros-Lehtinen (R-FL), and Senator Barbara Boxer (D-CA). Although the percentage of congressional women who have active leadership PACs (27 percent) is less than the percentage affiliated with current male members of Congress (40 percent), the number of woman-affiliated PACs has nearly doubled since the 1999–2000 election cycle. Further, Representatives Pelosi and Pryce have ascended to key party leadership roles in the House. Pelosi, who first became the House Democratic minority leader in 2003 and then became Speaker of the House in 2007, is the top-ranking Democrat in the chamber, while Pryce recently served as chair of the House Republican Conference.

As noted above, any candidate must have established credibility on the key issues of the day in order to be able to build a viable campaign; for women, this means going beyond traditional "women's issues." Consider, for example, two women who were often named as potential candidates throughout 2005 and 2006. Hillary Clinton, who entered the Senate with the albatross of her failed effort to push health care reform through Congress during her husband's first term as president, secured such committee assignments as the Armed Services Committee, the Environment and Public Works Committee, and the Retirement Security and Aging Subcommittee of the Committee on Health, Education, Labor, and Pensions. These assignments allow her to address such matters as military preparedness, hurricane and flood disaster responsiveness, and issues important to elders. Similarly, Condoleezza Rice, first as national security advisor and then as secretary of state, has been placed in positions in which she is at the forefront of the nation's foreign affairs and the Bush administration's war on terrorism.

A growing number of women also are in the pipeline to take on more visible and active leadership roles in the nation's political affairs. The number of women in the House increased from fifty-eight after the 2000 election to seventy-one following the 2006 midterm election and from twelve to sixteen in the Senate. In addition, as of 2007, a total of nine governors and sixteen lieutenant governors were women. Thus, women have shown that, in the traditional proving grounds for potential presidential candidates (both at the congressional level and, with respect to the governors and lieutenant governors, at the state level), they are able to put together a viable presidential campaign. The discussion above provides just a smattering of the top cases in which women have succeeded in accumulating these ingredients—and certainly the fact that this set of examples is limited indicates that women have room to improve in these areas. Nevertheless, the examples show how women can and have knocked down what in the past might have been barriers to establishing a viable candidacy for the presidency. And as these barriers continue to fall, the easier it will be for a woman candidate for president to knock the rest of them down.

The above list focused on certain tangible ingredients—that is, things that the women could affect themselves. But what of the intangible ingredients or things that a woman cannot change herself—are barriers there being overcome as well? Much like the tangible ingredients above, evidence does point to changing perceptions that may create better opportunities for a viable woman candidacy to develop, but not without some traditional barriers remaining in place. For example, recent polling indicates that 92 percent of survey respondents would vote for a woman for president if she were qualified—compared to 91 percent in 1999, 87 percent in 1987, 73 percent in 1975, 57 percent in 1967, and 52 percent in 1955. Similarly, 55 percent of those surveyed indicated that they believe the United States is ready for a woman president—up from 48 percent in 1999.[26] However, 38 percent of respondents believe that the nation is *not* ready for a woman president, and such numbers do not differ substantially from the question of whether the United States is ready for an African American president.[27]

Along the same lines, if one makes the assumption that female voters would be more inclined to support a woman candidate, then such a candidate might have a marked advantage in generating turnout among her supporters. More women than men are registered to vote (75.6 million to 66.4 million in 2004), and women reportedly turn out to vote at higher percentages than men (60.1 percent to 56.3 percent in 2004).[28] The issue at hand, however, is whether the key assumption above is correct—will women support a woman candidate simply because she is female? Conventional wisdom among politicos is that "women hate woman candidates."[29] Further, men—not women—are more likely to think that the nation is ready for a woman president (60 percent to 51 percent, according to a CBS News/*New York Times* poll).

The discussion above shows that the foundation is in place for a woman to succeed at the science of viability. Women have already demonstrated at other levels of government that they can obtain the tangible ingredients necessary for a viable presidential campaign, and there are indications that the intangible ingredients may be in place as well. The political environment may be ripe for a qualified woman to be in the right place at the right time. Indeed, the idea of a woman president seems to be not such a novelty any more because the women discussed herein are part of the political mainstream. So what remains is how well any individual female candidate can bring all these ingredients together.

The Art of Viability

In any presidential election cycle, all the top candidates will have gathered similar ingredients. All of them will have raised sufficient money to conduct their campaign, be seen as credible on key issues, have a background they believe prepares them for the presidency, have a message that resonates at least with some portion of the populace, and so on. So how do candidates combine the ingredients they have amassed in a way to distinguish themselves and to present themselves as someone special? How do candidates use the millions of dollars they collected to emphasize their positive traits, minimize their negatives, and generally promote the image they want the voters to have of them? These questions are the nuances of campaigning; they constitute the art of viability.

There is no set answer to these questions. All the candidates must use the ingredients they have to create the proper recipe for success. But there is one ingredient that a female presidential candidate can bring to the mix that no male candidate can ever do—the fact that she is a woman. If the art of viability is to blend all the ingredients in a way to distinguish one's candidacy from all others, then a woman candidate may want to be careful not to lose the one factor that can set her apart from her male opponents, namely her gender. If a woman candidate can show that she is qualified and that she has already done and can do anything that her male opponents can do, then her gender may give her a certain perspective and voice that can rise above the cacophony of other voices fighting for dollars and votes. Her gender may be just the extra spice needed for her recipe of ingredients to become a viable and ultimately successful candidate for president.

But the art of viability is about nuances, about subtleties. In cooking, a dash of a certain spice might add a zest that accentuates all other flavors in the dish, but too much may overwhelm and ruin the meal. Likewise, a woman candidate seeking to blend the ingredient of her gender into her campaign must not push the issue too much so as to overwhelm her campaign. As Pat Schroeder's experience showed, many political observers will willingly pigeonhole a woman candidate. So overpromoting one's gender in an effort to achieve viability may simply land the woman back in the place from which she needs to escape in the first place. Thus, female presidential candidates need to undertake a careful balancing act: one in which the goal is not to be seen as a "viable woman candidate" but instead a "viable candidate for president" who happens to be a woman.

Notes

1. Chisholm became the first woman to seek the Democratic nomination and the first African American woman to run for president. She ran in eleven primaries and garnered a total of 152 votes at the Democratic convention. Margaret Chase Smith was the first woman to run for a major party's nomination in 1964, but she dropped out after the New Hampshire Republican primary. Other women who recently explored a run at a major party's nomination include Pat Schroeder in 1987, Elizabeth Dole in 1999, and Carol Moseley Braun in 2003.

2. In 2004, George W. Bush and John Kerry combined to raise over $500 million during the pre-primary and primary stages of the campaign, and then received an additional $74.6 in public funding during the general cam-

paign. The ten Democratic contenders for the 2004 nomination raised a total of $401.8 million, of which Kerry brought in $234.6 million. Combined with Bush's $269.6 million and Ralph Nader's $2.5 million raised, the total amount raised by the major party candidates and the leading independent candidate during the pre-nomination period equaled $673.9 million.

3. For discussion regarding various aspects of this phenomenon, see Farrar-Myers, "Emerging Trends"; and Farrar-Myers, "One Swift Kick."

4. See Farrar-Myers, "In the Wake of 1996," p. 149 ("Dole's fate as a candidate was directed by where the contribution dollars went").

5. For example, "Some saw [Elizabeth Dole's] inability to raise adequate funding as a gender-based obstacle facing all women candidates for high office." Watson and Gordon, "Profile: Elizabeth Dole," p. 203. Yet the authors go on to state, "Some critics asserted that it was not [Dole's] gender that caused the problem but her tendency to rarely field questions from reporters or answer tough questions on the stump and her inability to define a reason for her candidacy other than her gender."

6. The analysis herein regarding campaign financing in the 2004 elections is based on and updates a similar analysis performed by the author for the 2000 elections. See Farrar-Myers, "A War Chest Full."

7. Ideally, one also could examine the relative success of women governors vis-à-vis their male counterparts to determine how well women have been at fundraising at the state level, since holding a governorship also is a typical proving ground for presidential candidates (e.g., George W. Bush, Bill Clinton, Ronald Reagan, and Jimmy Carter in recent memory). The sporadic availability of publicly available state-level campaign finance data for gubernatorial elections makes such an examination difficult. The necessary data for examining fundraising at the congressional level, however, are available through the Federal Election Commission and Internet resources such as OpenSecrets.com, operated by the Center for Responsive Politics.

8. Figure 6.1 includes the sixty-five women who won election to the House in 2004. Two other women were subsequently elected to the House in special elections in 2005 but were not included in this analysis.

9. For purposes of the analysis herein, the late Mel Carnahan is considered as the winning candidate in the 2000 Missouri Senate election. Although Mel Carnahan died in an airplane crash about a week before the election, his name remained on the ballot and he won the election. Jean Carnahan, his widow, was appointed to fill his seat but is excluded from the analysis herein. In 2002, Jim Talent defeated Jean Carnahan in a special election in 2002 to complete Mel Carnahan's unexpired term.

10. To put Hillary Clinton's fundraising success in perspective, this amount was more than her husband, President Bill Clinton, raised in individual contributions in his 1996 reelection effort, and compares with the amounts raised by presidential candidates Al Gore, Bill Bradley, and John McCain in the 2000 presidential primary season ($33.8 million, $29.2 million, and $28.1 million, respectively).

11. See Farrar-Myers, "A War Chest Full."

12. For the purpose of Figures 6.3 and 6.4, a group of sixty-five male winning candidates from the 2004 race were randomly selected for the purpose of comparing their fundraising profiles to those of the sixty-five successful women candidates.

13. For the purposes of Figure 6.5, one woman, Stephanie Herseth (D-SD), was excluded from the analysis. Herseth was initially elected to the House during a special election in June 2004 and then was elected again in the regular election in November 2004. The most readily available data for breaking down PAC contributions to Herseth's campaigns did not distinguish between funds given for her June special election and those contributed for the November regular election.

14. As with the analysis of House members, an equal number of men were selected to be compared to women. Due to the limited number of women senators available for analysis (fourteen), men were selected based on their geographic proximity and year elected so as to match up with the women selected. Thus, for example, Mary Landrieu, elected to the Senate in 2002 from Louisiana, was matched up with Mark Pryor, elected in 2002 from Arkansas. The men selected for analysis herein were, in 2000, Burns (R-MT), Santorum (R-PA), Ensign (R-NV), Bingaman (D-NM), Jeffords (R/I-VT), and DeWine (R-OH); in 2002, Sununu (R-NH), Graham (R-SC), and Pryor (D-AR); and in 2004, Wyden (D-OR), Vitter (R-LA), Specter (R-PA), Inouye (D-HI), and Crapo (R-ID).

15. One woman, Maria Cantwell (D-WA), was excluded from the analysis regarding the source of PAC funding. Cantwell primarily self-financed her 2000 campaign, spending over $10 million of her own funds while receiving a negligible $1,990 from PACs (of which nearly $1,800 came from single-issue/ideological PAC contributions). Given (1) the small number of women in the analysis, (2) the negligible amount of PAC funding to Cantwell's election effort, and (3) the disproportionate amount of PAC money she received from single-issue/ideological PACs (approximately 90 percent), the determination was made that including Cantwell in this portion of the analysis would inappropriately skew the analysis. As an aside, if Cantwell is omitted from the analysis of women's sources of funding, the breakdown would be as follows: individuals, 68.5 percent; PACs, 22.0 percent; candidate, 0.1 percent; and other, 9.3 percent.

16. See Farrar-Myers, "A War Chest Full." Note, however, that the 2000 election cycle is found in both studies, so the fact that there are some similarities between the two studies is not surprising.

17. For the women studied, five were first elected to the Senate during the 2000–2004 election cycle, six were elected for a second term, and three were elected for their third term or more. The corresponding numbers for the men are five, four, and five.

18. Abramowitz, "Viability, Electability," p. 978.

19. For example, in both his presidential campaigns, George W. Bush gave special designations to backers who helped raise certain amounts of funds, including "Rangers" (those who in 2004 helped raise more than

$200,000), "Pioneers" (more than $100,000), and "Mavericks" (in excess of $50,000). Likewise, Howard Dean gained momentum in 2003 on the strength of the Internet-based financial contributions of his "Deaniacs."

20. As will be discussed later in the chapter, women traditionally turn out at higher percentages than men do.

21. Data based on reports for candidates' financial activity through September 30, 1999, available at http://www.fec.gov.

22. Watson and Gordon, "Profile: Pat Schroeder," p. 119.

23. Chisholm, *The Good Fight*, p. 3.

24. Maria Cantwell, Hillary Clinton, Dianne Feinstein, Kay Bailey Hutchison, Olympia Snowe, and Deborah Stabenow.

25. This amount excludes the $8.7 million raised by Katherine Harris (R-FL) for her campaign for the US Senate and the $364,000 raised by Cynthia McKinney (D-GA), who lost in the Democratic primary.

26. CBS/*New York Times* poll.

27. Diageo/Hotline, poll.

28. Center for American Women and Politics, Fact Sheet: Sex Differences in Voter Turnout, 2005.

29. A Republican political consultant quoted in Dowd, "Why Can't a Woman?" p. D15.

7

Political Parties: Advancing a Masculine Ideal

Meredith Conroy

Senator Hillary Clinton has a number of "firsts" to her name: the first and only First Lady to be elected to federal office, the first woman elected as a US senator in New York, and the first woman elected to a New York statewide office in her own right. Clinton was also the first child of Hugh and Dorothy Rodham, the first student at her high school to win the social science award, and the First Lady of Arkansas for twelve years. Today, by all accounts, Clinton has another "first" in her sights: the first female presidency. Clinton has managed to overcome many obstacles unique to female candidates to achieve political success, including difficulty raising money and the perception that women lack credibility and electability.[1] In 2006, Clinton raised over $38 million for her reelection campaign, she has high name recognition, and she has proven electability, capturing 67 percent of New York voters in the 2006 midterm election. What, then, stands between Clinton and the Oval Office? A November 2006 *US News and World Report* article summed up the barrier to a second Clinton White House in three words: "her own party."[2] Despite the widely held notion that political parties are declining in strength, the political parties as organizations still wield unmatched power, serve as a cue for an inattentive public, and exercise incredible influence over the nomination process. Overcoming the obstacles the party organization presents may be the *last* barrier to an American *first*—a woman in the White House.

In this chapter I analyze the role played by political party organizations in advancing the masculinization of the office of the president. More specifically, I uncover whether party organization recruitment is biased toward masculine candidates and analyze the effects on women seeking political nominations. Prior to addressing the heart of the analysis, I first provide an examination of general party influence in elections and the masculine bias of the presidency for context.

The Power of the Party

Some evidence suggests that the status of political parties is diminishing. The rising power of the media has bred a more candidate-centered campaign, and voters are more likely to cast split-ticket votes, lending evidence to the idea that the American public is less likely to identify with a particular political party. These factors combine to mitigate political party influence.[3] Yet despite what may appear to be a decline in political party power, E. E. Schattschneider's biting words that parties "are therefore not merely appendages of modern government; they are in the center of it and play a determinative and creative role in it," still ring true.[4]

When measuring the strength of the political parties, it is important to note that the party exists in three different locations: in government, in the electorate, and as an organization. In government the party comprises elected officeholders and officials; its power has declined as a result of an increase in media focus on individual candidates. As campaign coverage grows more candidate-centered, candidates can exercise greater influence over voters and are less dependent on their party. The reign of Newt Gingrich over the Republican Party was seen as an era of strength of party in government; Republicans were much more likely to toe the party line and vote the preference of their party. Today, there is a weakened sense of necessity for such loyalty, and candidates are more likely to vote their personal preference.

In the electorate, the party comprises the voters; it has lost power due to the waning of party identification among the public. Fewer voters identify with one party's platform and instead focus their attention on the positions of the individual candidates. We see this influence in the recent increase of split-ticket voting.

The party as an organization characterized by a small number of leaders and activists, however, has maintained relevance and influence. Both major party organizations have increased their professionalism in recent decades, putting experts in charge of endorsing and recruiting candidates, directing allocation of funds, creating professional media advertisements, and performing a myriad of other activities. In short, despite declining relevance among the electorate, political parties continue to play a crucial role in electing candidates to public office.

The principal influence that parties exercise over candidates is their endorsement. An endorsement supplies substantive evidence that a candidate is viable, and if the party is willing to recognize that the candidate is suitable, voters will give their support.[5] In a study of female congressional candidates in Pennsylvania, Raisa Derber found that candidates who received a major party organization's endorsement won more often than those who did not.[6] Although the party's endorsement does not guarantee a victory, it gives the candidate the added advantage of positive recognition from a powerful organization.

The party organization also exercises influence as a recruiter. Encouragement from political parties is one of the most important predictors of considering a candidacy. Jennifer L. Lawless and Richard L. Fox found that both men and women who were encouraged by the party to run for office were more than four times as likely to think seriously about running for office than those who were not encouraged to run:

> Comments from women and men who have been recruited reflect the political viability conveyed by gatekeepers' suggestions to run; party support brings the promise of an organization that will work on behalf of a candidate. Statements from individuals who have yet to receive political support for a candidacy demonstrate that, without encouragement, a political candidacy feels far less feasible.[7]

Women who have been encouraged by the organization are far more likely than other women to express a desire to announce their candidacy.

Even more important than recruitment is monetary support, since the party organization as a source of money is especially critical to the viability of a campaign. Money was listed as critical to a potential run for office by young men and women interviewed for the White House Project. Money from an outside source is especially critical to women because women are less likely to have strong personal and professional networks that yield access to large donations and generous donors.[8] However, if a woman locks up the party's nomination, she is guaranteed access to the *party's* money pool. This money funds get-out-the-vote drives, voter registration efforts, and mass media advertising. Women who run without the party organization's support have to fend for themselves.

Political party backing has obvious and evident advantages, and candidates fare better when they have such support. Even if their influence has declined, "Whatever else they may or may not do, *the parties must make nominations*."[9] The most influential and visible action of the party organization is to pick the candidates who will run, supplying them with the critical advantages party support provides. But before granting a candidate their resources, the leaders and activists of the party organization, like voters, have criteria their nominee must meet. Pippa Norris distinguishes between supply-side factors and demand-side factors, both of which influence the chances of a candidate being nominated. Supply-side factors determine whether the candidate comes forward; demand factors influence whether the candidate is selected. "On the demand side, eligible candidates face the problem of acceptability by the 'gatekeepers.' If willing to stand, who among the pool of eligible is seen as suitable?"[10] The party's goal is to win, and suitable candidates are those the party organizations feel have a realistic chance of victory. Male candidates have traditionally been perceived by party organizations and voters as more electable than female candidates, especially for the presidency, which explains why major party nominees for this office have exclusively been men.

The Masculine Presidency

There is considerable agreement within the psychological literature that a typical woman is seen as warm, expressive, communicative, gentle, and passive; men are expected to be tough, assertive, rational, and independent.[11] Within the realm of politics, this perceived trait distinction has had negative effects on the electability of women.[12] Leonie Huddy reports that feminine traits, such as communion, are only seen as viable under certain conditions, whereas masculine traits, such as toughness, are typically seen as relevant.[13] Moreover, masculine traits are more revered by both men and women.[14] Gordon and Miller find that voters express preference for more masculine characteristics in their leaders, especially at the higher levels of government such as the presidency.[15]

In the 2004 election, voters saw masculine trait advantages play out. Media coverage focused a disproportionate amount of attention on the masculinity (or lack thereof) of Democratic candidate John Kerry and Republican incumbent George W. Bush. A September 22, 2004, article in *USA Today* noted:

> It's macho time in the Presidential race. The best man could be the one that seems more manly. . . . The images from the 2004 campaign certainly bear that out. There's the Everyman series: Bush cutting brush, Kerry tossing a football, the pair aiming rifles and falling off their bikes. And the aristocracy series: Bush fishing in his own lake in Texas and off his father's dock in Maine, Kerry windsurfing and snowboarding near his wife's vacation retreats. And the military series: Bush with troops all over the world, Kerry with veterans all over the country, both of them with generals galore.[16]

The presidential hopefuls took turns being pictured throwing a football between campaign speeches and rallies. Bulging biceps were just as important as the candidate's positions on the issues, and the candidates' political operatives recognized that fact. Evidence suggests that George W. Bush was more successful in cultivating the masculine image; although a former cheerleader, Bush and his football were more convincing than Kerry and his buckshot.[17] As the symbol of the United States on a domestic and international scale, voters prefer a manly president, and Bush was perceived to be more manly.

Beyond sex acting as the determining factor of the traits with which males and females are associated, studies have found that the candidates' sex invokes assumptions of political expertise.[18] Huddy found that those surveyed expected women to be better at handling more "compassionate" issues, such as poverty and family policy, and worse at dealing with big business and defense issues. Women are not expected to be able to handle more masculine policy concerns, such as national security and foreign policy.[19] A 2002 Knowledge Networks survey found that two-thirds of respondents did not believe men and women were equally suited to deal with military crises. Of the two-thirds, 95 percent expressed the belief that men are better able than women to deal with military affairs.[20] The association of women with feminine policies works against their political ambitions. When asked to evaluate specific presidential duties, those responsibilities with a more masculine connotation such as being "commander in chief" were revered more than feminine duties, such as "promoting civil rights."[21]

Not just political competencies but also political offices are gendered.[22] National and executive offices, as well as those offices that deal with "masculine" policy (such as national defense or economic matters), tend to be masculinized.[23] Women are less likely to be nominated for offices that clearly deal with more masculine policies. "Feminine" offices are those primarily concerned with feminine issues, such as education and health care. Further, they are stereotypically associated with women, such as state treasurer or secretary of state (at the state level).[24] When considering the office of the president, the issues at the forefront are usually more masculine, such as foreign policy or the economy. In a climate in which domestic policies reign, it might be possible for the office to be gendered more feminine. But in its current state, the office of the president is dominated by more masculine policies and by the male gender, and the position is seen as being rightfully male, as Carol Lynn Bower explicates:

> The President's voice can hold lives in the balance, can hold nations at bay, and can hold a world in silence, waiting for a stance to be taken. The person behind that voice won the right to its discourse in the ultimate political test performance—winning a US presidential election. To triumph in the election that voice had to find a style and a strategy that would secure the favor of a sizable percentage of the voting public. To date, that voice, with only a few exceptions, has been masculine.[25]

Presidents are expected to distance themselves from femininity and uphold the ideals of masculinity, which embody strength, independence, determination, and single-mindedness.[26] In general, researchers have looked for evidence that voters distinguish between masculinity and femininity in their vote choice and are more reluctant to vote for feminine candidates.[27] But what of the political parties, specifically, the party organization? Does the party organization nominate masculine candidates more often than feminine candidates to the most desirable offices, thus severely disadvantaging women? Does the party organization perpetuate the belief that masculine traits are more viable and that men are more apt to dealing with masculine policy? In general, what responsibility do the political parties bear for propping up the masculinity of the presidency that essentially bars women from holding this position?

The Preference of the Party

Despite recent gains in female candidate viability, biased perceptions persist in the minds of voters and political parties. Robert Darcy and

Sarah Slavin Schramm examined the responses of voters toward female candidates running for the US House of Representatives from 1970 through 1974, and, controlling for incumbency, they found the electorate to be indifferent to the sex of the candidate. Female candidates fared just as well as their male counterparts.[28] More recent research on the topic confirms that women win elections at the same rate as men,[29] yet women remain vastly underrepresented at the federal level, comprising 13 percent and 14 percent of the Senate and House, respectively.[30] Darcy and Shramm concluded "that the reason why so few women were serving in Congress was due to the recruitment and nomination process."[31] Many scholars in their studies of this issue place the blame squarely on the shoulders of the political parties.

In 1984, Donald R. Matthews wrote, "the big losers in legislative recruitment everywhere have been women." In his article he details the legislative demographics of the times:

> In the United States, only 2 percent of all members of Congress (between 1917 and 1964) and only 4.5 percent of all state legislators (1920–1961) were women. As this chapter is being written there are 21 women in Congress (3.9 percent). Moreover, as Bullock and Heys (1972) remind us, 41 percent of all females who served in Congress prior to 1979 were appointed to vacancies created by the deaths of their husbands; these women usually dropped out of the institution quickly thereafter.[32]

Today, more than two decades after Matthews's analysis, Congress still does not reflect the gender makeup of the United States. Jeanne Kirkpatrick attributed the lack of women legislators to disadvantages emerging from lesser educational and occupational achievement.[33] In a similar vein, researchers point their finger at the eligibility pool. "If most political officeholders are recruited from occupations where there are few women, the selection rules, no matter how informal, will prevent women from holding office."[34] Yet in a more recent examination of eligibility and women's occupational and educational achievement, Dolan and Ford found that the demographic makeup of female candidates has shifted to younger, professional women with advanced degrees.[35] Education, career choice, and prior political experience as obstacles barring women from the nomination matter less today, but different obstacles still remain.[36] According to Richard L. Fox and Zoe M. Oxley, "The beliefs of earlier decades that women are not suited for politics have been replaced by more subtle stereotypes whereby men and women are perceived to have specific personality and policy competencies."[37] Women must now deal with the perceptions that characteristically feminine traits and feminine policy are less politically viable and that only men are capable of handling masculinized offices. These factors combine to prejudice party organization support for potential female candidates who seek the nomination for masculine races.

In formal practice, both the major political parties appear to be actively assisting female candidates through recruitment programs. Republicans and Democrats sponsor programs and workshops meant to attract politically ambitious women who could potentially run for office. The Republicans created the GOP Women's Political Action League, and Democrats have the Eleanor Roosevelt Fund to address fundraising needs for female candidates.[38] These efforts suggest that parties do, in fact, diligently labor to give women equal opportunities to run for political office. But virtuous operations executed by the party organization do not ensure equal opportunity for female candidates. Even though at first blush the parties' intentions seem noble, there is evidence to suggest that these programs make little headway in a sea of swelling party gender bias. The political parties systematically indulge biases that disadvantage women entering the political realm, including running women in unwinnable offices, recruiting men in disproportionate numbers, promoting female candidates for "feminized" offices, and supporting "masculine" women for prominent leadership positions. Each of these is addressed in turn.

One way the political parties disadvantage female candidates is by supporting them for unwinnable offices. Irwin Gertzog and M. Michele Simard examined district competitiveness to determine whether women are disproportionately nominated to "hopeless" seats, and they found that this is indeed the case.[39] Likewise, Robert A. Bernstein found that women were more likely to get challenger nominations as opposed to open seat nominations; open seat nominations overwhelmingly went to men.[40] This is important because open seats translate into a greater chance of getting elected to office than seats where incumbency effects disadvantage the challenger.[41] Additionally, women disproportionately get nominated to traditionally feminine offices.[42] Although party organizations are endorsing women at greater rates than they have in the past, the endorsements are more often for "feminized" seats and offices they have little chance of winning.

The concentration of men in party leadership positions also serves to disadvantage female candidates. David Niven found that political party organizations discriminate against women because party leaders are less likely to identify with the femininity associated with women candidates. Elites within the organization are overwhelmingly male. Niven's evidence suggests that party leaders are more likely to nominate those who are similar to them, and women generally do not fit the bill.[43]

In addition to party selection bias, the proclivity of women to run for less desirable and more feminine offices can also be traced back to the parties. In their analysis of feminine and masculine offices, Fox and Oxley found that female candidate success did not vary across office type. In the instances in which women were nominated for a masculine office race, their likelihood of winning was equal to their likelihood in a feminine office race. The paucity of women in more masculine offices thus supports both Niven's and Fox and Oxley's claims that stereotyping is more likely to occur during the selection stage, not the election stage.[44]

One of the most insidious biases against female candidates is the double bind of being properly feminine so as to not offend constituencies, yet sufficiently masculine to be seen as a legitimate leader. The political parties play a role in promoting women who are seen as overwhelmingly masculine. The classic example of a successful "masculine" woman is Janet Reno, the former US attorney general, who is caricatured as unfeminine. Although she is a woman, her political strength comes from her perceived "manliness." A *Washington Post* article captures the dilemma that is advanced when strength is identified as solely a man's characteristic:

> That's the way you bring a strong woman down—you insult her, degrade her, portray her as sexually profligate, reduce her to her own anatomy. According to others, it's equally common for women to be de-genderized: "It's a classic image, turning powerful women into powerful men," says Pippa Norris.[45]

As alluded to by Norris, the association of women and power is a difficult one to make in the political realm. The traditional view of women rejects the idea that femaleness and political power can coexist. This perpetuates a similar idea that femininity is not relevant, advancing the idea that women are not viable as political players.

A Preference for "Masculine" Female Candidates? An Analysis

Existing research has not examined whether political parties prefer masculine female candidates. To advance our knowledge of this issue, the important question to ask is, "If women are more masculine, do they then have a better shot at more desirable/masculine office nominations than women who are not?"[46] If the answer is affirmative, it indicates that the political party organizations' ideal politician is not necessarily a man, but a *masculine* candidate. Indeed, this is the case, according to an assessment of women nominated for senatorial and gubernatorial races in the 2006 midterm election. Candidates who displayed more masculine traits were more likely to be nominated to open seat races than those who displayed more feminine traits; women who were characterized as more feminine were nominated to less desirable races.

The hypothesis that political party organizations nominate women who are more masculine for open seat Senate and gubernatorial races was tested by analyzing press releases issued by the candidates' party organization and drawn from the candidates' websites. Press releases were analyzed to capture the candidates' views and personal attributes because they are a resource consistently available for all candidates running for office. In 2006, four women were nominated to run for open seat races, and seven women were nominated as challengers.[47] Those who displayed more masculine traits broke from the pack to seal up the more prestigious nominations. This same analysis also uncovered that, as candidates exude more masculinity, their vote totals go up.

These findings show that potential female presidential candidates suffer from a severe inherent disadvantage. Aware that masculine candidates are awarded more votes than more feminine candidates, political party organizations will be strategic in their candidate selection and will thus be more likely to nominate men. In those instances when party organizations do in fact nominate women, the female candidates they support are likely to be more masculine.

Conclusion

By nominating more masculine women to more desirable races, political party organizations insinuate that masculine characteristics are superior to feminine characteristics as traits of public leaders in the United States and that women who are more masculine are also more viable as political party leaders than women who are more feminine. Furthermore, their behavior suggests that feminine traits and behaviors, such as caring and collaboration, have little place in national politics. If political party organizations continue to perpetuate the idea that candidates with one gender's traits and issues are more credible and electable, then this perception will persist, and worse, it will force women to comply. Regrettably, most women conform and aim to fit the masculine political mold in order to gain electoral success. As a consequence, they reinforce masculine norms instead of seeing that they are refashioned.

Hillary Clinton is an exception, however; she is one woman who has adamantly highlighted both her masculine and feminine characteristics as a political figure. Though unsuccessful at times, Clinton has attempted to appear more masculine by rebuffing femininity: "You know, I suppose I could have stayed home and baked cookies and had teas, but what I decided to do was to fulfill my profession, which I entered before my husband was in public life."[48] In this famous rejection of traditional femininity, Clinton attempted to convey viability as a political player. Yet at times, she has also tried to nurture her more feminine, understanding side. Addressing a women's interest group, she stated: "I, for one, respect those who believe with all their heart and conscience that there are no circumstances under which abortion should be available."[49] Here, Clinton expresses sympathy. This sensitive gesture is an attempt to summon an image of femininity by a woman often seen as having too hard of an exterior, who has been criticized for not hugging her own daughter enough.

Yet this analysis finds masculinity to be associated with victory more often than femininity, which works against women and rejects the need for efforts made by Clinton to be more feminine; only those women who are more masculine are likely to be nominated for more desirable positions. Luckily for Clinton, she *is* seen as more masculine than feminine. Consequently, the femininity she is put in opposition to is her obligation to her family and home, which, in fact, may work to her detriment. But the political climate in 2008 may support Clinton's attempt to cultivate femininity *and* masculinity. The majority of the public is dismayed by several of the Bush administration's policies and may attribute insensitive policies and deplorable conditions to more masculine policy approaches, such as unilateralism and international independence. If a more bilateral approach is preferred and international collaboration is favored by the general public prior to the 2008 elections, political parties may be more likely to nominate candidates who trumpet these more feminine ideals; in this environment women's chances at more desirable office nominations may increase, and perhaps their chances at the most desirable nomination of all, a presidential nomination, will be realized.

Whether a feminine-friendly environment will be in full effect in 2008 remains to be seen, but more than likely Clinton will continue to cultivate both her masculine and feminine natures, catering to the broadest range of potential voters. If the climate is one of affinity toward feminine candidates, Clinton could be in the ideal position; her femaleness is an obvious symbol of her femininity, while her position on the Senate Armed Services Committee and experience with foreign dignitaries as a First Lady are examples of her more masculine expertise. Whether or not 2007 is ripe for a dual-gendered candidate, Clinton remains a salient example of the struggle politically ambitious women face due to their sex.

Notes

1. See Fox, *Gender Dynamics in Congressional Elections;* and Ford, *Women and Politics.*
2. Gilgoff, "Hillary's Dilemma," p. 66.
3. See Burrell, "Party Decline"; Lovinduski and Norris, *Gender and Party Politics*; and Herrnson, "The Importance of Party Campaigning."
4. Schattschneider, *Party Government,* p. 1.
5. See Herrnson, "The Importance of Party Campaigning."
6. See Derber, "The Fault, Dear Brutus"; and Bernstein, "Why Are There So Few Women in the House?"
7. Lawless and Fox, *It Takes a Candidate*, p. 93.
8. See the White House Project, www.thewhitehouseproject.com.
9. Schattschneider, *Party Government*, p. 101.
10. Norris, "Conclusion," p. 329.
11. See Broverman et al., "Sex-Role Stereotypes: A Current Appraisal"; and Eagly and Steffen, "Gender Stereotypes Stem from the Distribution of Men and Women."
12. See Huddy and Terkildsen, "Gender Stereotpyes and the Perception of Male and Female Candidates"; Leeper, "The Impact of Prejudice of Female Candidates."
13. See Huddy, "The Political Significance of Voters' Gender Stereotypes."
14. See Heith, "The Lipstick Watch"; Niven, "Party Elites and Women Candidates"; and Kinder et al., "Presidential Prototypes."
15. See Ann Gordon and Jerry Miller, "Gender, Race, and the Oval Office."
16. Keen and Lawrence, "Nominees Hope Heavy Hitters Will Help."
17. See Conroy, "Are You Man Enough?"

18. See Fox and Smith, "The Role of Candidate Sex in Voter Decision-Making"; Burrell, *A Women's Place Is in the House;* and Huddy and Terkildsen, "Gender Stereotypes and the Perception of Male and Female Candidates."

19. See Huddy, "The Political Significance of Voters' Gender Stereotypes."

20. See Lawless, "Women, War, and Winning Elections."

21. See Gordon and Miller, "Gender, Race, and the Oval Office."

22. See Fox, *Gender Dynamics in Congressional Elections;* Oxley and Fox, "Women in Executive Office"; Sanbonmatsu, "Political Parties and the Recruitment of Women"; and Niven, "Party Elites and Women Candidates."

23. See Huddy and Terkildsen, "Gender Stereotpyes and the Perception of Male and Female Candidates."

24. See Fox and Oxley, "Gender Stereotyping in State Executive Elections"; and Dolan, "Gender Differences in Support for Women Candidates."

25. Bower, "Public Discourse and Female Presidential Candidates," p. 107.

26. See Lawless, "Women, War, and Winning Elections."

27. See Conroy, "Are You Man Enough?"

28. See Darcy and Shramm, "When Women Run Against Men."

29. See Burrell, *A Women's Place Is in the House;* Dolan, "Voting for Women"; Seltzer, Newman, and Leighton, *Sex as a Political Variable.*

30. See Burrell, "Party Decline."

31. See Darcy and Shramm, "When Women Run Against Men."

32. Matthews, "Legislative Recruitment and Legislative Careers," p. 551.

33. See Kirkpatrick, *Political Women*; Welch, "The Recruitment of Women"; Merritt, "Winners and Losers"; and Dubeck, "Women and Access."

34. Darcy, Welch, and Clark, *Women, Elections, and Representation,* p. 93; see also Carroll, *Women as Candidates.*

35. See Dolan and Ford, "Change and Continuity Among Women in State Legislatures."

36. See Kelly, *The Gendered Economy.*

37. Fox and Oxley, "Gender Stereotyping in State Executive Elections," p. 847.

38. Darcy, Welch, and Clark, *Women, Elections, and Representation,* p. 158.

39. See Gertzog and Simard, "Women and the Hopeless Congressional Candidacies."

40. See Bernstein, "Why Are There So Few Women in the House?"

41. See Berch, "The 'Year of the Woman' in Context"; and Burrell, *A Women's Place Is in the House.*

42. See Fox and Oxley, "Gender Stereotyping in State Executive Elections"; and Oxley and Fox, "Women in Executive Office."

43. See Niven, "Party Elites and Women Candidates."

44. See Fox and Oxley, "Gender Stereotyping in State Executive Elections"; see also Oxley and Fox, "Women in Executive Office."

45. Mundy, "Why Janet Reno Fascinates."

46. Open seat races are more desirable than challenger seat races. Open seat races are those races in which there is not an incumbent, and thus, all things being equal, the candidates compete on a more even playing field. Challenger seats are less desired because challengers are at a severe disadvantage; incumbents are often reelected at a rate of more than 95 percent in the United States.

47. One gubernatorial challenger is excluded from the analysis; her press releases were unavailable.

48. ABC News Nightline Report, March 26, 1992.

49. Hillary Clinton, speech given to the Family Planning Advocates of New York, January 31, 2005.

8

Women as Executive Branch Leaders

Karen M. Hult

In January 2006, Michelle Bachelet became the first female president of Chile. She joined female heads of government in Finland, Germany, Jamaica, Liberia, and elsewhere. Despite the presence of women as national leaders in countries around the world, they have not yet achieved that status in the United States.[1] Moreover, while women continue to struggle for parity with men in Congress and state legislatures, they also face challenges in adding executive experience to their public resumes.[2] That said, women have occupied and are increasingly holding higher positions in US local, state, and national executive branches. To the extent that the pools from which presidential candidates emerge include those with demonstrated *executive* experience, it may be useful to probe the governmental arenas in which women participate and the nature of their involvement. Not only may doing so expand the places where the initial mentioners of possible candidates in the media, in the political parties, and among interest groups look, but it also may highlight more role models for those yet unnamed girls and women with ambitions to be called "Madam President."

In this chapter I sketch the expansive landscape of women in executive positions at varying levels of US government. While exploring the emergence, numbers, and contemporary locations of such female officials, I focus as well on the opportunities and challenges they face and the potential implications for women pursuing the presidency.

Potential "paths to power" for women presidential candidates may well wend through myriad positions, encompassing diverse tasks, at varying levels of government and in differing policy arenas and economic sectors.[3] Table 8.1 shows offices that may be relevant for developing and for showcasing capacities and qualities relevant to running for and serving as US president. Such positions also may be places to "scout" future prospects.

Elected Chief Executives

If there is a conventional "opportunity structure" for those who aspire to the presidency, it is one that includes visible high-level office.[4] Service as a governor is part of a frequent path: four of the last five presidents were governors. Governors are probably the only elected US government officials with responsibilities that are closest to the president's; *Parade* labeled them "the top training ground for the Presidency."[5] Much like presidents, governors serve as the single visible face and voice of the government, and voters typically hold them responsible for everything from the performance of the state economy to the quality of public education to responses to natural disasters.

Table 8.1 Possible Stops on a Presidential Career Path

Office	Popular Election	Appointment
Chief executive	Governor, mayor	For-profit CEO, Nonprofit CEO
Other executive office branchwide	Lieutenant governor, state attorney general	White House staffer, top gubernatorial advisor
Department/agency head	State/local agency head[a]	US cabinet secretary, state/local agency head
Senior professional/ administrator		Political appointee, career senior executive service official, state/local career official

Note: a. In many states, some agency heads stand for direct election. In 2000, there were "300 separately elected executive branch officials covering 12 major offices" (see Beyle, "The Governors," p. 210). Examples of such positions are secretary of state, state treasurer, state auditor, and superintendent of public instruction. Elected executive positions at the local level include in many jurisdictions the county sheriff, prosecutor, and treasurer.

Meanwhile, as Hurricane Katrina drove home, mayors frequently join governors as the targets of complaints and criticism. Holding such offices, then, may serve as public testing grounds for, builders of confidence in, and barriers to advancement for women who may pursue the presidency.

Governors

Only twenty-nine women have been governors throughout US history, beginning in 1925 with the elections of Miriam Ferguson (Texas: 1925–1927, 1933–1935) and Nellie Tayloe Ross (Wyoming: 1925–1927).[6] Although seventeen of these women served in the twentieth century, there were fourteen female governors in the first five years of the twenty-first century (as well as one woman appointed to be governor of the Commonwealth of Puerto Rico), with nine holding office in 2007.[7] All five of the female governors whose terms ended in 2006 sought and won reelection, a feat achieved by only five other women governors.[8] Meanwhile, eleven other women ran for governor in 2006.

Once they take office, all governors confront myriad issues and constituencies. The handful of analyses that compare contemporary female and male governors find relatively few differences. Such comparisons are complicated by the relatively low numbers of women who have held the office; by varying state political, social, and economic conditions and dynamics; and by agreed-upon evaluative dimensions.

Another frequent constraint is available data. That has led some analysts to examine gubernatorial rhetoric. Jay Barth and Margaret R. Ferguson, for instance, contend that gubernatorial "motivation . . . is most important to understand when evaluating gubernatorial leadership, because motivation focuses on what one's goals are, the ultimate differentiator of one leader from another."[9] Based on analyses of inaugural and state of the state addresses, they found that, compared with their male counterparts, female governors scored significantly higher on affiliation-intimacy and achievement motives (the interaction of which they label an "empowerment motive"). At the same time, women were "just as likely to exhibit the traditional 'power over' motive" as were men.[10] Additional multivariate work suggests that the interaction between achievement and power is "critical for governors to achieve success in the legislative arena"[11] but is not related to public approval levels.[12] Meanwhile, the achievement motive, on which women governors scored significantly higher than men governors, was negatively associated with public approval levels.[13]

Molly A. Mayhead and Brenda Devore Marshall also focus on rhetoric, examining six female governors who have served in the early twenty-first century. They observe that issues of sex and gender, though not always explicit in how the governors spoke, nonetheless surfaced in their words: these governors "have not denied their womanhood, but they have not relied on it for their campaigns or in their governing strategies. They have focused on issues traditionally associated with women, but they have transformed them into 'the people's' issues."[14] Aware of concerns about women's economic knowledge and expertise, the governors apparently used rhetoric that sought to "illuminate that women do understand state economies and the business of business."[15] Mayhead and Marshall report evidence that the governors "see themselves as the CEO and their state as a corporation" and, consistent with other work on gender and management, "promote a collaborative approach, between public and private sectors as well as across party lines."[16]

Despite these sorts of possible differences, the job of governor may be more accurately viewed as becoming transgendered. A look at 2006 reelection contests, for example, shows both female and male incumbents confronting voter concerns about state economic performance (e.g., Jennifer Granholm in Michigan, Arnold Schwarzenegger in California) and split-party government (e.g., Janet Napolitano in Arizona, Robert Ehrlich in Maryland).

Even so, transgendering has not extended to all areas. Considerable research suggests that women confront particular challenges "when speaking authoritatively on financial issues, war, military strategy, and international policy," reflecting persistent biases about women's capacity to handle a struggling economy or to respond calmly and forcefully to threats.[17] Gendered expectations mean that female governors receive special scrutiny when "crises" arise. For instance, early criticism of Louisiana governor Kathleen Babineaux Blanco's "hesitant" response to Hurricane Katrina arguably contained sexist undertones, including frequent comparisons with Mississippi governor Haley Barbour's "take charge demeanor" and "high-octane recovery commission headed by [a] former Netscape chief executive."[18] Ultimately, Blanco "emerged with what *The Times-Picayune* called a 'string of victories' from a 17-day special session of the Legislature, including tougher building codes, business tax breaks, a partial takeover of New Orleans' shaky school system and $600 million in tax cuts."[19] Still, according to a Baton Rouge pollster, "'the perception is that (Blanco) wasn't up for the job and it overwhelmed her.'"[20] Polling by the Barbara Lee Family Foundation following the September 11, 2001, terrorists attacks indicate that female governors and gubernatorial candidates are likely to continue to confront such concerns.[21]

Mayors

Becoming governor, much less reaching the presidency, almost always involves having been a candidate in other elections. Indeed, the premise of a commonly used political ambition measure "is that a governor progressing steadily up from substate to statewide elective office to the governorship will be stronger than those who start at the top as their first office."[22] Serving in a local elective office such as mayor may be such a step toward higher office. Between 1981 and 2002, for example, mayor was the "entry-level" elected office of 16 percent of governors and the penultimate position for 8 percent.[23]

Women have succeeded at being elected mayors of numerous US cities. Although New York City and Los Angeles have never elected female mayors, other large cities have, including Atlanta, Chicago, Dallas, Houston, Kansas City, Sacramento, and Scottsdale. In 2006, women were mayors of 197 of the more than 1,100 cities with populations of 30,000 or more, including twelve cities with more than 200,000 people.[24] The numbers have increased dramatically since 1999, when forty-five women were mayors of cities with populations of 30,000 or more.[25]

Female mayors have had visible successes. *Governing Magazine*, for example, named Atlanta mayor Shirley Franklin to its list of "public officials of the year," pointing to her handling of city budget problems and gaining state, county, and city support for a long-delayed court-ordered sewer modernization project. The citation also praised her restoration of public confidence in city government and her skill at revitalizing working relationships with state and county officials.[26]

More generally, as with governors, the tasks and activities of mayors appear to be moving toward transgendering. In her comparison of five pairs of female and male mayors,[27] Sue Tolleson-Rinehart found "extraordinary agreement on the characterizations of their communities and constituencies" and of their cities' most important problems.[28] They also were "very similar in their views of the essence of leadership and individual pairs were in especially close agreement."[29] All ten "used their cities' needs as the criterion for assessing political problems."[30] Of potential relevance as well, the issues that the male mayors believed were most important and those mayors' views of politics were consistent with "what the culture has come to expect of women in (legislative) office."[31]

Nonetheless, as Tolleson-Rinehart observes, the expectations of mayoral leadership are likely to continue to be gendered for the foreseeable future. Male and female mayors alike expected the public to assess the accomplishment of women mayors by comparing them against a "male standard of performance."[32] In 1983, former San Francisco mayor Dianne Feinstein convened the Women Mayor's Caucus, designed "to encourage and develop involvement and leadership potential for women mayors within the [US] Conference of Mayors."[33] Over twenty years later, female mayors complain about their lack of representation in the organization's leadership ranks. Pemberton, New Jersey, mayor Thalia Kay noted in 2002, "'Wherever you go, people will still rush to shake your husband's hand and say, 'Mayor.'"[34] Meanwhile, Jennifer L. Lawless and Richard L. Fox found that women were less likely than men (11–17 percent) to express interest in seeking a mayor's position.[35]

Other Elected State Executives

Besides the mayor's office, the path to the governorship not infrequently passes through other state-level elected positions. Thad Beyle reports, for example, that from 1900 through 2002, "three-fifths of the governors' penultimate offices . . . were other statewide elective offices, the state legislature, or law enforcement," with over one-fifth coming from statewide elective office. Since 1981, 27 percent of governors served in other statewide elective offices immediately before entering the governorship,[36] and in 2006 women held 25 percent of the 315 available positions.[37] Among the most common of these statewide positions are lieutenant governor, state attorney general, and secretary of state. Nonetheless, it also should be noted that occupying such offices scarcely guarantees a key to the governor's mansion: between 1981 and 2001, 69 percent of the lieutenant governors who ran for governor lost, as did 82 percent of the attorneys general and 70 percent of secretaries of state; also defeated in their bids were 75 percent of state auditors and 63 percent of state treasurers.[38] At the same time, the percentage of women in statewide elective office leveled off beginning in 1995 and has declined slightly since 2000.[39] Relevant as well to potential presidential candidates, "the states with the fewest women office holders are disproportionately from the South"; West Virginia, sometimes a critical state in presidential elections, has never elected a woman to a statewide office.[40]

Lieutenant Governors

Forty-two states have lieutenant governors, with a forty-third, New Jersey, scheduled to elect its first occupant of the office in 2009. In twenty-four states, these officials are elected on a team-ticket with the governor, whereas in eighteen others, lieutenant governors run for office separately.[41] According to the Center for American Women and Politics, in 2006 fifteen lieutenant governors were women, including nine Republicans and six Democrats.[42]

Although the duties of lieutenant governors vary widely, many states have been increasing their responsibilities, frequently adding tasks involving law enforcement, physical infrastructure, or homeland security to their portfolios.[43] For instance, among other tasks, Lieutenant Governor Carol Molnau of Minnesota is state transportation commissioner, and in Indiana Becky Skillman serves as secretary of agriculture, "oversees the Office of Rural Affairs and the Counterterrorism and Security Council," and is "responsible for housing, community development, tourism and energy."[44] Not surprisingly, governors are more likely to assign lieutenant governors broader and more important responsibilities when they have been elected as a team or when they are members of the same political party as the governor.[45] Such responsibilities help lieutenant governors not only to replace governors who resign or die (as has happened six times between 2003 and 2006) but also to position themselves to run for the governorship. Since many of the added jobs of lieutenant governors include tasks that are gendered masculine—such as homeland security, corrections, and energy—female lieutenant governors may be important beneficiaries. At the same time, assuming these more significant jobs also spotlight controversial or questionable actions, gender may be a bigger problem for women in these positions, who are expected to be less competent than men.

State Attorneys General

Long acknowledged as significant at the state level, state attorneys general have become more visible nationally over the past several decades.[46] The state government lawsuits against tobacco companies seeking reimbursement for smoking-related Medicaid expenses were initiated by attorneys general in Mississippi, Minnesota, Florida, and Texas. New York attorney general Eliot Spitzer has received frequent national attention for his suits against banks, insurance companies, and a host of other targets, which no doubt also helped fuel his bid for the 2006 governor's seat.

Attorneys general are elected in forty-three states and appointed by the governor in five others; in Maine, the legislature selects attorneys general by secret ballot, whereas the state Supreme Court appoints them in Tennessee.[47] Women have not been common occupants of this position. In 2006, for example, three women served in elective positions (in Illinois, New Mexico, and Wisconsin), and two others (New Hampshire, New Jersey) were gubernatorial appointees. All five were the first women to become attorney general in their states.[48]

Much like serving as lieutenant governor, being attorney general evidently can hold both promise and pitfalls for its occupants. It also is one of the few elected state government positions that slightly more women than men surveyed (11 percent versus 10 percent) expressed interest in seeking.[49]

Secretaries of State

Many Americans no doubt first learned of the state governmental position of secretary of state in the aftermath of the 2000 presidential election. That, of course, was the year that Florida secretary of state Katherine Harris presided over the disputed recounts of votes cast in several counties. All US states have similar officials. Although their duties vary, most secretaries of state handle "elections, business registration, licensing and regulation, legislative record keeping, and publishing," and some also are responsible for overseeing state lands, facilities, or warrants.[50] In thirty-nine states, these officials are elected, and in eleven others (including Florida, beginning in 2003) the governor appoints them.

Secretary of state is a more common statewide position for women to hold. In 2006, seventeen women occupied the office, reaching it through election in twelve states.[51] Less frequently does it generate the kind of visibility—and scrutiny—that Harris experienced, which in turn may make it a less useful stepping-stone to higher office. Nonetheless, between 1904 and 2004, twenty-nine secretaries of state ultimately became governors, including four women.

Two of those women, Rose Mofford and Olene Walker, however, replaced governors who had either been impeached or stepped down to assume a cabinet position. Despite some possible public perceptions of the job's feminine gendering, it has been the stepping-stone to higher office for presidential hopefuls like Jerry Brown and Mario Cuomo and for future US senators such as Mark Hatfield and John D. Rockefeller IV.[52]

Appointed Executives

Elective offices need not constitute the only path to the presidency. Voters (and financial contributors) may scrutinize potential candidates' resumes for additional evidence of policy experience, partisan work, and management capacity. Candidates also rely on experience in a variety of appointed executive positions to establish their credibility. Moreover, before running for elective office, women may be more likely than men to acquire relevant experience through government positions or political appointments.[53]

Federal Cabinet Secretaries

As Table 8.2 demonstrates, over the course of US history, twenty-one women have held twenty-four cabinet positions in twelve different departments. Since the administration of Gerald Ford, presidents have had at least one female cabinet secretary. For the most part, women have been placed in "outer cabinet" departments (in Table 8.2, all but the Justice and State Departments), and they frequently have headed departments whose responsibilities are consistent with feminine gender roles, such as education and health and human services. In other cases, women have been "gender outsiders in relation to both the policy jurisdictions and constituencies," moving into departments like energy, interior, and transportation.[54] Moreover, women secretaries may be nominated to some departments that traditionally have been led by a woman, to other departments distant from a president's agenda, and to still others in which they are expected to wield considerable power.[55] Thus, under George W. Bush, Elaine Lan Chao was named the fifth woman labor secretary, heading a department of little relevance to the president's agenda, whereas Interior Secretary Gale Norton and Secretary of State Condoleezza Rice headed departments of critical significance.

Table 8.2 Women Cabinet Secretaries

Name	Department	President	Years Served
Frances Perkins	Labor	Roosevelt	1933–1945
Oveta Culp Hobby	Health, Education and Welfare	Eisenhower	1953–1955
Carla Anderson Hills	Housing and Urban Development	Ford	1975–1977
Patricia Roberts Harris	Housing and Urban Development	Carter	1977–1979
	Health, Education, and Welfare		1979
	Health and Human Services		1979–1981
Juanita M. Kreps	Commerce	Carter	1977–1979
Shirley M. Hufstedtler	Education	Carter	1979–1981
Elizabeth Hanford Dole	Transportation	Reagan	1983–1987
	Labor	G. H. W. Bush	1989–1991
Margaret M. Heckler	Health and Human Services	Reagan	1983–1985
Ann Dore McLaughlin	Labor	Reagan	1987–1989
Lynn Martin	Labor	G. H. W. Bush	1991–1993
Barbara H. Franklin	Commerce	G. H. W. Bush	1992–1993
Donna E. Shalala	Health and Human Services	Clinton	1993–2001
Hazel R. O'Leary	Energy	Clinton	1993–1997
Janet Reno	Justice	Clinton	1993–2001
Madeleine Korbel Albright	State	Clinton	1997–2001
Alexis M. Herman	Labor	Clinton	1997–2001
Ann M. Veneman	Agriculture	G. W. Bush	2001–2005
Gale A. Norton	Interior	G. W. Bush	2001–2006
Elaine Lan Chao	Labor	G. W. Bush	2001–
Condoleezza Rice	State	G. W. Bush	2005–
Margaret Spellings	Education	G. W. Bush	2005–

Sources: Borrelli, *The President's Cabinet,* Appendix, pp. 229–231; department websites.

Recently, of course, the glass walls surrounding the inner cabinet became somewhat more porous as women were named both attorney general and secretary of state. MaryAnne Borrelli cautions, though, that Janet Reno's "career and subsequent nomination appear supportive of traditional patterns of gender politics in cabinet appointments. Like the vast majority of women secretaries, [she was] a policy generalist";[56] unlike other attorneys general, she did not have a strong relationship with the president. Even less clear is how soon similar appointments will be made, when women will be named to head the State Department at the beginning of a president's term, and when women will become secretaries of the remaining departments of the inner cabinet, Defense and the Treasury.

Although holding a cabinet position is neither a common nor a necessarily successful route to later elective office, the attention Secretary of State Rice received as a possible presidential candidate in 2008 suggests it is not unreasonable to view it in this light. Some recent female cabinet secretaries indeed have entered electoral politics. Elizabeth Hanford Dole, though she failed in her effort to secure her party's presidential nomination in 2000, did succeed at being elected US senator from North Carolina in 2002, and Janet Reno sought the Florida governorship. Perhaps at least as important for women's future presidential bids, women being named to cabinet positions and performing strongly, particularly in areas framed as "masculine" such as national security and economics, may increase public confidence in women's governing capacities. At the same time, such women—no matter what their previous experience—evidently still will struggle with assumptions about their competence.[57]

Other Senior Executives

National cabinet officers, of course, are only the tip of a single iceberg in the eligibility pool of presidential hopefuls. Hundreds of other possible candidates may be working in senior administrative and professional positions in government settings throughout the United States, which may be additional places that women ultimately seeking the White House might be found, although glass ceilings and glass walls persist.

White House staff. Since Richard Nixon, presidents have had White House office staffs of at least 400 people, fifty to seventy-five of whom are political or policy professionals. Relatively few former White House staffers have gone on to pursue visible elective office, but doing so is scarcely unprecedented. Prominent contemporary examples include Senator Elizabeth Hanford Dole, who served on the Nixon and Reagan staffs, and Vice President Richard Cheney, who worked as President Ford's chief of staff. One-time Clinton chief of staff Erskine Bowles twice ran for the US Senate in North Carolina after leaving the White House, and Mitchell Daniels, Jr., a former

Reagan staffer and George W. Bush's first director of the Office of Management and Budget, won the Indiana governorship in November 2004.

Only a relatively small number of women have occupied high-level positions on presidents' staffs. For example, no woman ever has served as chief of staff, at the top of the formal White House hierarchy. From Nixon through the first term of George W. Bush, the *US Government Manual* lists four women with the title "deputy chief of staff," three in the Clinton presidency and one under George W. Bush.[58] If one examines the overall White House hierarchy implied by the titles of staffers listed in the *US Government Manual*, one sees that women rarely occupy close to half of the positions toward the top of the hierarchy (senior advisor, assistant to the president) and are more likely to have the titles of deputy assistant to the president and special assistant to the president (see Table 8.3).[59] Nevertheless, the proportions of women in higher-level positions generally have increased over time, and they have tended to be higher in Democratic administrations. Typically, too, the last year of a presidency has been the point at which administrations report the highest percentages of women serving in the White House office.

Below the highest levels of the hierarchy, women increasingly have breached glass ceilings, serving as directors of particular White House units. Frequently, such offices involve outreach activities or those that are gender stereotyped as female; examples include the offices of public liaison, communications, and First Lady. Yet such glass walls have weakened as women also have become the national security assistant (Condoleezza Rice), assistant to the president for homeland security and counterterrorism (Frances Fragos Townsend), and White House counsel (Beth Nolan under President Bill Clinton; Harriet Miers under President George W. Bush). In all the latter cases, however, women were not the first occupants of these positions in their administrations.

Still, although women are serving more widely throughout the White House office, evidence of glass walls persists. At least according to *US Government Manual* listings from 1978 through 2004, 100 percent of the staffers in the Office of the First Lady were women in eighteen of the years.[60] Karen M. Hult and MaryAnne Borrelli report that "women also served with unusual consistency in the offices of public liaison, congressional liaison, and personnel."[61] Perhaps most important for signaling policy competence, such units rarely are central to the executive policymaking process. Indeed, "the first unequiv-

Table 8.3 Number and Percentage of Female Staffers, by Title and Year

Year	Senior Advisor	Assistant to the President	Deputy Assistant to the President	Special Assistant to the President
1969–1970	0 (0 percent)	0 (0 percent)	0 (0 percent)	1 (7 percent)
1970–1971	0 (0)	0 (0)	0 (0)	1 (5)
1971–1972	0 (0)	0 (0)	0 (0)	1 (6)
1972–1973	0 (0)	0 (0)	0 (0)	1 (6)
1973–1974	1 (25)	0 (0)	0 (0)	1 (7)
1974–1975	1 (14)	0 (0)	0 (0)	1 (5)
1975–1976	0 (0)	0 (0)	0 (0)	1 (13)
1976–1977	0 (0)	0 (0)	0 (0)	2 (20)
1977–1978	0 (0)	1 (13)	[no dep. assts.]	2 (22)
1978–1979	0 (0)	2 (20)	[no dep. assts.]	2 (29)
1979–1980	0 (0)	1 (10)	[no dep. assts.]	2 (40)
1980–1981	0 (0)	2 (22)	1 (25)	1 (14)
1981–1982	0 (0)	1 (8)	1 (7)	4 (24)
1982–1983	0 (0)	1 (7)	3 (18)	9 (23)
1983–1984	0 (0)	1 (6)	3 (21)	11 (23)
1984–1985	0 (0)	1 (7)	3 (19)	10 (20)
1985–1986	0 (0)	0 (0)	3 (14)	9 (23)
1986–1987	0 (0)	0 (0)	5 (26)	10 (22)
1987–1988	0 (0)	1 (8)	3 (20)	13 (29)
1988–1989	0 (0)	1 (8)	3 (20)	15 (33)
1989–1990	0 (0)	1 (8)	4 (18)	11 (27)
1990–1991	0 (0)	1 (7)	5 (25)	14 (30)
1991–1992	0 (0)	1 (23)	7 (37)	13 (32)
1992–1993	0 (0)	3 (39)	9 (38)	10 (29)
1993–1994	0 (0)	7 (32)	11 (46)	[no spec. assts.]
1994–1995	1 (17)	6 (32)	11 (38)	29 (46)
1995–1996	0 (0)	7 (36)	15 (50)	22 (41)
1996–1997	0 (0)	8 (38)	17 (61)	28 (57)
1997–1998	0 (0)	8 (29)	16 (59)	22 (51)
1998–1999	0 (0)	6 (32)	21 (64)	15 (50)
1999–2000	1 (33)	8 (13)	21 (66)	26 (59)
2000–2001	2 (67)	7 (29)	20 (57)	31 (72)
2001–2002	2 (40)	4 (29)	3 (12)	9 (28)
2002–2003	1 (33)	4 (27)	3 (12)	9 (33)
2003–2004	0 (0)	4 (33)	3 (12)	10 (37)
2004–2005	0 (0)	3 (23)	7 (27)	2 (100)

Source: Hult and Borrelli, "Organizational Interpretation or Objective Data?" Table 9.

Note: Table 8.3 begins with the Nixon administration, because the titles were not used with any regularity before then. Each cell contains the number of women with a specific title listed in the US Government Manual and the percentage of those with that title who were female. Percentages appear in parentheses.

ocal association of a woman with national security policy in the White House Office appeared in the 1988–89 issue of the *Government Manual*,[62] with domestic policy in 1993–1994,[63] and with economic policy and with environmental policy in 1994–1995."[64] Not until the Clinton and George W. Bush administrations have women held positions in which they could readily engage in the policy process. That both glass ceilings and glass walls have shown evidence of permeability under administrations of two different political parties, however, may suggest that the inclusion of women in a broader range of White House political and policy tasks is institutionalizing and may be altering gender expectations.[65]

Federal agencies. Women occupy senior positions throughout the national executive branch, serving as both political appointees and career civil servants. Experience in such positions may help potential presidential candidates establish their credentials as managers with experience working in the federal executive. At the same time, to the degree women's military and national security competencies are challenged, glass walls may make federal executive work less useful.

Across the departments, women make up about 27 percent of the Senior Executive Service (SES), including both career and noncareer officials.[66] President Bill Clinton appointed women to almost one-third of the available positions in the executive branch requiring Senate confirmation, and his successor, George W. Bush, also has appointed many women. Yet "the departments and agencies where women political appointees serve tend to have stereotypical female concerns," such as health, education, and social services.[67] Meanwhile, without looking at positions in departmental hierarchies, women make up more than 60 percent of the employees in the Departments of Education, Health and Human Services, Housing and Urban Development, and the Treasury; men hold more than 60 percent of the jobs in the Departments of the Air Force, Army, Navy, Defense, Energy, Homeland Security, Interior, Justice, and Transportation.[68]

Of particular concern may be the notable dearth of high-level women in national security positions, which evidently reflects and reinforces what Ole R. Holsti and James N. Rosenau called the "ignorance-apathy" and "pacifist" stereotypes of women.[69] As long as concerns about US international and domestic security are prominent and the president's role as commander in chief remains "fully masculinized," female presidential candidates likely will need to provide evidence of experience or expertise.[70] There has been some movement toward increasing the representation of women in senior positions in the State and Defense Departments. Several visible women from the two departments have received considerable attention and some mention as potential presidential or vice-presidential candidates: for example, Sheila Widnall (secretary of the navy, 1993–1997), Lieutenant General Claudia Kennedy (the first woman to achieve the rank of three-star general in the US Army), Jeanne Kirkpatrick (former US ambassador to the United Nations), former secretary of state Madeleine Korbel Albright, and Secretary of State Condoleezza Rice. In addition, in the State Department women currently occupy four of the nine undersecretary positions and nine of thirty-six assistant secretary slots;[71] in the Defense Department, one of the five undersecretaries (the comptroller/chief financial officer) is a woman, as are eight of twenty-seven deputy undersecretaries.[72]

Although the work of Nancy E. McGlen and Meredith Reid Sarkees has not been systematically updated since 2001, little suggests that the hierarchies of the State Department and especially the Defense Department have changed in ways that would make it easier for women "to break into the decision-making ranks."[73] Nor is there a good deal of evidence that the glass walls in the Defense Department, which "often segregated by the internal topography . . . to areas with limited impact on foreign policy," have broken down.[74] It seems probable as well that senior female career officials at the Defense Department would be "more hard-line" on policy issues than their male counterparts, as well as far more likely than career women at the State Department to "say their gender limits their ability to influence policy."[75] It may disturb at least some women voters and donors as well if it remains the case that, of male and female senior civil servants and political appointees in the two departments, only female career officials in the State Department have opinions that are consistent with those of women in the public.

State agencies. The numbers of women heading state departments and agencies also has been growing. Comprising roughly 2 percent of all department heads in 1964, the proportions rose to 11 percent in 1984, to more than 25 percent in 1999, and to close to 30 percent in 2005.[76] Overall, state agency heads have been "becoming younger, more representative in terms of [sex], race/ethnicity, and better educated."[77] Yet, women executives in state government continue to be concentrated in gender stereotypical agencies, such as those responsible for aging, the arts, community affairs, libraries, and human services and welfare.[78]

Looking more broadly at women administrators and professionals in state agencies, analyses of federal Equal Employment Opportunity Commission (EEOC) data from 1987 to 1997 indicate that sex segregation (glass walls) and sex-based salary inequities (glass ceilings) remained in agencies responsible for distributive or regulatory policy (e.g., corrections, highways, economic development), especially for female administrators and for nonwhite women.[79] In contrast, growing "gender balance" was more likely to be present for both administrators and professionals in departments with responsibilities for redistributive policy, such as education, employment services, and welfare.[80] Change in such conditions can be expected to be slow. Glass walls are likely to persist when "women are walled out of agencies because the agency clientele and a prevailing organizational culture interact to maintain impediments to change," as well as where "women are walled in [because] the skills necessary to perform jobs in the agency . . . are not highly valued outside the agency."[81] Even so, the "penetration of glass ceilings"—signaled by more women being appointed as heads of distributive and regulatory agencies—"may constitute an important preliminary step in helping to weaken glass walls" as well as to expand the size of candidate pools and the numbers of executive role models.[82]

Governors' offices. A final source of women leaders considered here are governors' senior staffs. As of May 2006, governors of eight states—including California and Texas—had female chiefs of staff.[83] If one also includes among "top advisors" those with other "policy influencing titles" (e.g., budget director, legal advisor), women made up over 40 percent of governors' top advisors in 2005.[84] This percentage has changed little since 1998, while the proportion of women who are chiefs of staff has declined from a reported 31 percent in 1999.[85]

Conclusion

An overview of possible steps along a presidential career path that winds through diverse executive jobs points to both opportunities and obstacles for women. Certainly, since the 1970s, more women have assumed a wider variety of positions at all levels of US government, and they wield considerable authority as governors, mayors, and agency heads. At the same time, however, evidence suggests the emergence of a "plateau effect,"[86] and many women in government continue to work under glass ceilings and within glass walls.

It is difficult to be very optimistic that a woman will soon be elected president of the United States. The bases for such a conclusion are both variegated and familiar, with factors ranging from the ambition and resources of individual women and men, to gendered expectations of office-holders and of governmental "leadership," to the structure of the US political system. Lauren Elder finds, for example, that political gender role socialization and a lack of political confidence are among the reasons that "women are significantly less likely to choose to run [for office] than men."[87] Susan J. Carroll simply notes that women are less likely to be "self-starters" in pursuing elective office.[88] Black women may face even greater challenges, as Shirley Chisholm and Carol Moseley Braun discovered in their bids for the presidency;[89] Latinas often start even further behind.[90] At the same time, gender stereotypes persist that women are not as "tough" as men and not as competent at handling security issues (especially those involving the military). Finally, it is difficult to overlook the constraints of a presidential system in which votes are cast for individuals and not for parties and in which votes are aggregated by state in the Electoral College.

Nonetheless, there is some cause for longer-term optimism. Women have breached ceilings and walls in the federal and state executives and appear poised to continue to do so. As subnational officials increasingly assume a range of "homeland security" responsibilities, more women will be in positions to show their capacity to handle security-related concerns. Ongoing efforts to encourage women to participate in government may add to both the numbers and to the visibility of female leaders; the work of the White House Project, the Women's Foreign Policy Group, the Barbara Lee Family Foundation, and the Women Under Forty Political Action Committee are illustrations. Growing numbers of women would expand and deepen the pool of possible female presidential candidates. At least as important, as more of those women become known, the "presence of visible female role models" is likely to "increase the propensity for girls to express an intention to be politically active."[91] Perhaps then, a woman in the United States will be able to take a place among female leaders of other nations.

Notes

1. For example, see Watson, "Introduction," p. 5.

2. Nor are US women faring better in the private sector. In 2005, women were approximately 17 percent of the partners at major law firms. See O'Brien, "Up the Down Staircase." In 2002, women held 7.9 percent of the "highest ranking corporate officership positions . . . with titles of chairman, vice chairman, CEO, president, COO, SEVP, and EVP"; see Catalyst, *2002 Catalyst Census.* Currently, ten of the top 500 CEOs are women; see Winik, "Is It Time?"

3. See Jalalaizi, "Women Political Leaders."

4. See Schlesinger, *Ambition in Politics.*

5. Winik, "Is It Time?" p. 2.

6. See CAWP, "History of Women Governors"; and National Governors Association, "Governors."

7. Mayhead and Marshall, *Women's Political Discourse*, p. 175.

8. Stateline.org, "State of the States," p. 8; National Governors Association, "Governors." The reelected women are Governors Jane Hull (Arizona), Ella Grasso (Connecticut), Ruth Ann Minner (Delaware), Christine Todd Whitman (New Jersey), and Miriam Ferguson (Texas); only Minner currently holds office. By comparison, there have been at least 600 two-term male governors; see National Governors Association, "Governors."

9. Barth and Ferguson, "Gender and Gubernatorial Personality," p. 66.

10. Ibid., pp. 73–76.

11. Ibid., p. 77.

12. Barth and Ferguson, "American Governors and Their Constituents."

13. Ibid.

14. Mayhead and Marshall, *Women's Political Discourse*, p. 208.

15. Ibid.

16. Ibid., p. 174.

17. Barbara Lee Family Foundation, "Speaking with Authority," p. 4.

18. Vock, "Katrina Alters Vista."

19. Ibid.

20. Ibid.

21. Barbara Lee Family Foundation, "Speaking with Authority."

22. Beyle, "The Governors," p. 206.

23. Ibid., Tables 7.1 and 7.2, p. 197.

24. CAWP, "Women Mayors in US Cities."

25. Tolleson-Rinehart, "Do Women Leaders Make a Difference?" p. 149.

26. Swope, "Spurning Spin"; see also Gurwitt, "How to Win Friends."

27. Three of the pairs were from strong mayor cities and two from weak mayor cities; three each were white and two pairs were black.

28. Tolleson-Rinehart, "Do Women Leaders Make a Difference?" p. 153.

29. Ibid., p. 155.

30. Ibid., p. 164.
31. Ibid., p. 163.
32. Ibid., p. 164.
33. US Conference of Mayors, "Women Mayors Group."
34. Fonder, "Women Mayors Pushing."
35. Lawless and Fox, *It Takes a Candidate*, p. 49.
36. In addition, the numbers of individuals moving from the US Congress to a governorship has increased from 10 percent between 1900 and 1980 to close to 16 percent between 1981 and 2003. Meanwhile, "more than half of the governors serving between 1900 and 2003 *began* their political careers either as state legislators or in law enforcement," a proportion that rose to close to 60 percent after 1950. Beyle, "The Governors," p. 196, emphasis added.
37. Women have occupied at least one-quarter of statewide elected positions since 1995, but that proportion has never risen above 28.5 percent (in 2000). See Center for American Women and Politics, "Statewide Elective Executive Women: 1969–2004" and "Women in Statewide Elective Executive Office 2006"; Carroll, "Women in State Government."
38. Beyle, "The Governors," p. 198.
39. Carroll, "Women in State Government," p. 3.
40. Schroedel and Godwin, "Prospects for Cracking," p. 265.
41. National Lieutenant Governors Association, "Projects"; Hampson, "Lieutenants Rise in Rank."
42. Center for American Women and Politics, "Women in Statewide Elective Executive Office 2006."
43. See Mosk and Wagner, "Steele Running Against History."
44. Hampson, "Lieutenants Rise in Rank."
45. In 2006, ten of the fifteen female lieutenant governors were elected as part of a team; of the remaining five, only one (Mary Fallin of Oklahoma) was of a different political party than the governor.
46. See Clayton, "Law, Politics, and the New Federalism."
47. Ibid., p. 530.
48. National Association of Attorneys General, "Full Contact List."
49. Lawless and Fox, *It Takes a Candidate*, p. 49.
50. National Association of Secretaries of State, "Additional Duties and Responsibilities."
51. Center for American Women and Politics, "Women in Statewide Elective Executive Office 2006"; National Association of Secretaries of State, "Qualifications for Secretary of State."
52. National Association of Secretaries of State, "Secretaries Who Became Governors."
53. Moore, "Religion, Race, and Gender Differences," p. 581, n. 7.
54. Borrelli, *The President's Cabinet*, p. 61.
55. Ibid.
56. Borrelli, "Gender, Politics, and Change," p. 201.
57. Ibid.

58. Even if one includes the more expansive listing in Kumar and Sullivan, *The White House World*, Appendix A, pp. 377–381, only seven women appear in the "deputy" category: six served under Bill Clinton and one in the Reagan White House.

59. As Hult and Borrelli ("Organizational Interpretation or Objective Data?") and others point out, of course, the *Manual* itself is in part a public relations document. If anything, however, that may mean that it *overstates* the numbers of women in senior positions even as it clearly understates women's presence on the White House staff. See also Tenpas, "Women on the White House Staff."

60. See Hult and Borrelli, "Organizational Interpretation," Table 8. None of the staffers listed in the Office of the First Lady were women from 1981 through 1988; in 1997, 83 percent were female.

61. Ibid., p. 22.

62. Special Assistant to the President for National Security Affairs Alison B. Fortier.

63. Assistant to the President for Domestic Policy Carol Rasco.

64. See Hult and Borrelli, "Organizational Interpretation," pp. 22–23. Council of Economic Advisors Chair Laura D'Andrea Tyson and Deputy Assistant to the President and Director, Office of Environmental Policy Kathleen A. McGinty.

65. For an argument about the relevance of stabilizing structural arrangements across presidencies of different parties for institutionalization, see, Hult and Walcott, *Empowering the White House*.

66. Noncareer SES officials may make up no more than 10 percent of the maximum number of the SES positions authorized by Congress. In 2004 (the last year for which data are available), there were 5,997 career and 674 noncareer SES positions actually filled. See Office of Personnel Management, "The Fact Book," p. 72.

67. Dolan, "Political Appointees," p. 212.

68. Figures as of September 30, 2004; OPM, "The Fact Book," p. 54.

69. "Gender and the Political Beliefs of American Opinion Leaders," p. 114.

70. Duerst-Lahti, "Gendering Presidential Functions."

71. US Department of State, "Senior Officials."

72. *US Government Manual* 2005–2006, pp. 149–151.

73. McGlen and Sarkees, "Foreign Policy Decision Makers," p. 119.

74. Ibid., p. 120.

75. Ibid., pp. 138–139.

76. Bowling and Wright, "Change and Continuity," p. 431; Palley, "Women's Policy Leadership," p. 249; Center for Women in Government and Civil Society, "Women in State Policy Leadership," p. 2.

77. Bowling and Wright, "Change and Continuity," p. 432.

78. Ibid., p. 434.

79. Reid, Kerr, and Miller, *Glass Walls and Glass Ceilings*, p. 110.

80. Ibid., p. 72.

81. Ibid., p. 23.

82. Ibid., p. 111.

83. National Governors Association, "Governors' Chiefs of Staff."

84. Center for Women in Government and Civil Society, "Women in State Policy Leadership."

85. Palley, "Women's Policy Leadership," p. 249.

86. Schroedel and Godwin, "Prospects for Cracking," p. 265.

87. Elder, "Why Women Don't Run"; see too Lawless and Fox, *It Takes a Candidate.*

88. Carroll, "Women in State Government," p. 7.

89. McClain, Carter, and Brady, *Gender and Black Presidential Politics.*

90. See Reid, Kerr, and Miller, *Glass Walls and Glass Ceilings.*

91. Campbell and Wolbrecht, "See Jane Run," p. 233.

9

Leadership Challenges in National Security

Meena Bose

> Maybe you could find one woman in ten thousand who could lead in combat, but she would be a freak and we're not running the Military Academy for freaks.
>
> —*General William Westmoreland, April 1974*[1]
> *(response to proposal to admit women to military academies)*

Any candidate for the presidency must consider the responsibilities inherent in serving as commander in chief. Military service is not a requirement for the presidency, but a presidential candidate needs to demonstrate the ability to command the respect of troops. In an era when the United States is the only global superpower, a presidential candidate must present a clear agenda for national security and combating terrorism. The terrorist attacks of September 11, 2001, painfully reinforced the fundamental importance of protecting the United States from external threats. As the war on terrorism proceeds in the coming years, future presidents will have to wrestle with how to protect the United States, and when that will entail sending US troops into combat.

For women presidential candidates, the challenges of leadership in national security and serving as commander in chief are especially great. No presidential candidate needs to have special credentials to meet these expectations—indeed, several presidents never served in uniform or in a senior defense/national security position before they entered the White House. Nevertheless, the barriers that women have encountered historically in schools, the workforce, and politics suggest that women presidential candidates will face extensive questioning on their ability to lead the defense of the United States. General Westmoreland's comment more than thirty years ago did not prevent the admission of women to the service academies, but it bluntly illustrates the hurdles that women had to overcome to integrate themselves into the military. The obstacles to leadership in the political world are similarly significant, especially to become the nation's chief executive and commander in chief.[2]

In this chapter I examine the challenges and opportunities for women presidential candidates in the twenty-first century, focusing in particular on the demands created in the post-9/11 era for protecting US national security and combating terrorism. I find that the credentials of past presidents make amply clear that many potential women presidential candidates do have the qualifications to run for office. At the same time, a woman who runs for president will face strong scrutiny about her ability to direct national defense and, subsequently, a higher threshold for gaining support. As journalists Eleanor Clift and Tom Brazaitis write, in the aftermath of the 9/11 attacks, "Women had to face the hard reality that voters may not trust them to lead the country in a time of war."[3]

To address these topics, I begin by examining the credentials of past presidents, focusing on educational background, elected office (national, state, and local), military service, and appointed positions in the executive branch. I then provide a brief summary of past women presidential and vice-presidential candidates, focusing in particular on the above credentials. Next I focus closely on the national security credentials of major party presidential candidates in the 2004 election, the first post-9/11 presidential race. Short case studies follow of two women in American politics most frequently cited as potential presidential candidates in 2008, Senator Hillary Clinton (D-NY) and Secretary of State Condoleezza Rice. (Clinton, of course, is now a declared candidate while Rice continues to insist she is not running). Senator Clinton's extensive fundraising for a virtually uncontested Senate race in 2006 suggested that she was looking toward a larger campaign.[4] And Rice's rich and varied expertise in national security affairs makes her a much-talked-about candidate for the Republican Party to pursue for the White House in 2008 or a future race.

Qualifying for the Presidency

With forty-two men having served in the office of the presidency since 1789, generalizations about US presidents are difficult to reach.

The Constitution presents only three requirements: that the president be a natural-born citizen (or citizen at the time of ratification, a provision that pertained only to the early presidents); that the president have lived in the United States for at least fourteen years; and that the president be at least thirty-five years old. These qualifications were deemed necessary to ensure the president's loyalty to the United States as well as the president's maturity to hold the nation's chief executive office.[5] Beyond these three requirements, however, some common characteristics of presidents over time become apparent.

Presidential scholars George C. Edwards III and Stephen J. Wayne identify several common features in the social and political backgrounds of presidents. As they write, "American presidents have not been typical Americans. They have been advantaged by virtue of their wealth, the professional positions they have held, and the personal contacts they have made."[6] In the twentieth century, only President Harry S. Truman lacked a college education. (Warren G. Harding earned a two-year degree.)[7] Only three twentieth-century presidents—Calvin Coolidge, Richard M. Nixon, and Ronald Reagan—experienced poverty as children. And with the rise of media technology, communication skills have become increasingly important for presidents, as evidenced most notably by former actor Ronald Reagan's political career.[8]

In their comprehensive survey of historians that ranks "presidential greatness," presidential historians Robert K. Murray and Tim H. Blessing explore these background characteristics in great detail. They find that nine presidents concluded their education with elementary or secondary school, and four of those presidents—Zachary Taylor, Millard Fillmore, Abraham Lincoln, and Andrew Johnson—never had formal schooling.[9] Nevertheless, the rise of the United States as a global power in the twentieth century, combined with the national increase in college degrees, makes an undergraduate education a practical necessity for presidents today. Harvard University has produced five presidents (John Adams, John Quincy Adams, Theodore Roosevelt, Franklin Delano Roosevelt, John F. Kennedy), William and Mary College has produced three (Thomas Jefferson, James Monroe, John Tyler), and Princeton and Yale Universities each has produced two (Princeton, James Madison and Woodrow Wilson; and Yale, George H.W. Bush and George W. Bush). Three presidents graduated from military service academies (Ulysses S. Grant and Dwight D. Eisenhower from the US Military Academy at West Point, Jimmy Carter from the US Naval Academy at Annapolis), and only three presidents completed their degrees at public schools (James Polk, University of North Carolina; Lyndon B. Johnson, Texas State University–San Marcos; Gerald Ford, University of Michigan).[10]

As for pre-presidential careers, a law degree combined with some political experience tends to describe many, though certainly not all, presidents. More than half of the presidents earned their law degree or prepared for the bar exam. Until war hero Zachary Taylor became president in 1845, all of his predecessors had been members of Congress or the Continental Congress. Sixteen presidents previously served in the US Senate, nineteen served in the US House of Representatives, and eleven served in both chambers of Congress. Seventeen presidents served as governors, and fourteen were vice presidents. In the early days of the US republic, the secretary of state position was viewed as a common stepping-stone to the presidency, but the last secretary of state to become president was James Buchanan in 1857. Several presidents also participated in local politics, including Abraham Lincoln, John Tyler, James Buchanan, Calvin Coolidge, and Andrew Johnson.[11]

As far as general credentials for the presidency, then, women would not appear to face any more significant barriers than men today. Beyond the three basic constitutional requirements, the primary expectation for presidential candidates today is education. Although this standard might have posed challenges in much of the twentieth century, as women were not granted admission to many top colleges and universities until the 1960s or later, it no longer poses a barrier today.[12] Nevertheless, women who have run for the presidency historically have faced many questions about their qualifications for the office, focusing in particular on matters of national security. A few case studies illustrate this point.

Women Who Run for President and Vice President

US history includes only a handful of women who have conducted a campaign for the presidency, and no major party has endorsed a woman candidate for the office. Publisher and banker Victoria Woodhull ran for president in 1872 as the Equal Rights Party nominee, and critics derided her as "Mrs. Satan."[13] Belva Lockwood ran for the office twice, in 1884 and 1888, on the National Equal Rights Party ticket, but neither she nor Woodhull won any Electoral College votes. The two major political parties each have had women contenders for president: Margaret Chase Smith campaigned for the

Republican nomination in 1964, and Elizabeth Dole did so in 1999, whereas Shirley Chisholm sought the Democratic nomination in 1972, Patricia Schroeder considered doing so in 1987, though she ultimately decided against it and Carol Moseley Braun ran for the Democratic nomination in 2004.[14]

Only three women in US history have run for vice president, and all three have been nominated since the second phase of the women's rights movement began in the 1960s. In 1984, the Democratic Party nominated Geraldine Ferraro to run for vice president, with Walter Mondale at the head of the ticket. The first woman to be nominated by one of the two major political parties for executive office, Ferraro mounted a strong campaign with Mondale, but the two ultimately won only Minnesota, Mondale's home state, and the District of Columbia in the election. The Green Party selected Winona La Duke as presidential candidate Ralph Nader's running mate in 2000, and the Reform Party nominated Ezola Foster to run with presidential candidate Patrick Buchanan the same year. Neither party, however, amassed a single Electoral College vote.[15] The unique presidential selection process in the United States of requiring a majority of Electoral College votes rather than of a popular vote makes a successful third-party victory highly unlikely.[16] Therefore, a closer look at the major party candidacies of women for president and vice president is most useful for evaluating future prospects.

When Margaret Chase Smith, Republican senator from Maine, announced on January 27, 1964, that she would seek the Republican nomination for president, the news made the front page of the *New York Times*.[17] Smith was the first woman to serve in both chambers of Congress (as a widow, she initially completed her husband's term in the US House of Representatives and then subsequently won election herself), as well as the first woman to seek a major party nomination for the presidency.[18] In studying press coverage of Smith's campaign, scholars Erika Falk and Kathleen Hall Jamieson have noted "less coverage, less serious coverage, and a minimization of her accomplishments."[19] For example, three newspapers in 1964 each ran approximately seven articles on Smith every month, while her closest competitor for the Republican nomination, New York governor Nelson Rockefeller, typically had twenty-five articles each month. Smith was identified as "Mrs." almost one-third of the time, whereas Rockefeller was usually identified as "Governor." And newspapers often suggested that Smith actually might be seeking the vice presidency, even though she repeatedly denied such plans.[20]

Smith's longstanding commitment to US military preparedness made her an especially compelling candidate in the presidential campaign that followed perhaps the most heated Cold War confrontation, namely, the Cuban missile crisis. A member of the Senate Armed Services Committee since 1953, Smith had vigorously and consistently advocated a strong military defense for the United States. During the Korean War, she had chaired a subcommittee that examined allegations of ammunition shortages in the conflict.[21] She had issued a "Declaration of Conscience" during Senator Joseph McCarthy's investigations about alleged communists, in which she had stoutly defended "the right to criticize; the right to hold unpopular beliefs; the right to protest, the right of independent thought,"[22] thereby clearly criticizing McCarthy's actions though never mentioning him by name. After the Bay of Pigs failure in 1961, Smith spoke of "the necessity for real firmness if we ever hope to achieve peace."[23] Despite Smith's clear interest in seeking the presidency, however, her refusal to raise campaign funds or take time from her Senate responsibilities to build a national following severely hindered her prospects.[24] Smith pursued the presidential nomination all the way to the Republican National Convention in San Francisco, but delegates ultimately selected Barry Goldwater.[25]

Eight years later, two-term US Representative Shirley Chisholm (D-NY), the first black woman to serve in Congress, campaigned to become the Democratic Party's nominee for president. Chisholm focused primarily on domestic policy, calling for cuts in defense spending to provide more resources for programs such as education.[26] Like Smith, Chisholm pursued the race up to the party convention, where she won delegate votes but ultimately lost to Senator George McGovern of South Dakota. In looking back at the race, Chisholm reflected, "The Presidency is for white males. No one was ready to take a black woman seriously as a candidate."[27] Nevertheless, when Chisholm spoke on the convention floor in 1972, she declared, "The next time a woman runs, or a black, a Jew. . . . I believe he or she will be taken seriously from the start. The door is not open yet, but it is ajar."[28]

A decade later, the Democratic Party nominated Geraldine Ferraro to become vice president of the United States. A former teacher and lawyer, Ferraro had served as assistant district attorney in Queens, New York, and she was completing her third term in the US House of Representatives when she ran for vice president in 1984.[29] As the first woman to win a major party nomination for executive office, Ferraro underwent intense public scrutiny. Media coverage focused on her clothes, makeup, and hair; after her debate with Vice President George H.W. Bush, one reporter wrote that "her manner was matched by her neutral brown suit."[30]

Ferraro addressed "women's" issues, such as abortion and the Equal Rights Amendment, but she did not hesitate to present her views on national security as well. In her October debate with Vice President George H.W. Bush, Ferraro was asked, "How can you convince the American people and the potential enemy that you would know what to do to protect this nation's security?"[31] Her reply: "The people of this country can rely upon the fact that I will be a leader. . . . I'm prepared to do whatever is necessary in order to secure this country and make sure that security is maintained."[32] But the candidates whose national security views were most important to voters were presidential incumbent Ronald Reagan and Democratic challenger Walter Mondale. Mondale lost resoundingly to Reagan, who won 59 percent of the popular vote and forty-nine states in the Electoral College contest.[33]

Although Pat Schroeder ultimately decided not to enter the 1988 presidential race, her brief consideration of a campaign in 1987 merits attention because of the reaction it received. A Colorado member of the US House of Representatives from 1973 to 1996, Schroeder joined the Armed Services Committee in her first term. The committee chairman was so furious to have a woman and a black man on his committee (Ron Dellums of California) over his express veto that he insisted the two share a chair.[34] Fifteen years later, Schroeder (who gained her own seat in the committee room two years later, when committee chairs lost their seniority-based power) contemplated a run for the presidency after Gary Hart announced he would not run. Yet Schroeder was beset by questions about her candidacy as a woman as well as about her appearance, and she soon announced that she would not enter the race. Her tearful announcement raised questions about her ability to manage the responsibilities of chief executive, particularly in national security affairs. As a Republican pollster remarked, "The number one negative for women is emotional instability."[35]

Elizabeth Dole, now a Republican senator from North Carolina, briefly ran a major-party presidential campaign in 1999. Unlike her predecessors, Dole possessed executive branch experience, having served as secretary of transportation under President Ronald Reagan and as secretary of labor under President George H.W. Bush. Dole also had experienced presidential campaigns firsthand, as her husband, former senator Bob Dole of Kansas, was the Republican candidate for president in 1996 and previously had run for president in 1988. Bob Dole also was President Gerald Ford's running mate in his unsuccessful election campaign in 1976. Elizabeth Dole commenced her candidacy in January 1999 but quickly ran into difficulties with fundraising. Dole additionally had trouble defining her agenda, earning a reputation more for asking supporters their thoughts than identifying her own priorities.[36]

In foreign policy, Dole made a strong case for US military action in Kosovo, drawing upon her extensive experience in the 1990s as president of the American Red Cross visiting refugee camps during the crisis. Yet Dole continued to face criticism for her personality traits, particularly her attention to detail. *New York Times* columnist Maureen Dowd skeptically discussed how Dole would run the Kosovo war, writing, "It's hard to imagine the woman who likes to coordinate the color of her shoes with the color of the rug on the stage where she gives a speech, dealing with any crisis that involved a lot of *variables*, a lot of unpredictable turns that she could not *control.*"[37] Yet ultimately Dole left the presidential race not because of questions about her abilities in national security but because of her inability to raise sufficient funds to compete with Republican rivals George W. Bush, John McCain, and Steve Forbes.

In looking at the presidential/vice-presidential campaigns of women in the twentieth century, then, it becomes apparent that factors other than foreign policy credentials drove these candidates out of their races. In the twenty-first century, however, expertise on national security is a natural source for discussion, particularly in the aftermath of the 9/11 attacks.

The 2004 Presidential Election: A Referendum on National Security

In many respects, the 2004 presidential race echoed election years during the Cold War, when candidates focused on a long, global struggle in which the United States played a primary role. Whereas Cold War elections engaged such issues as Korea, Vietnam, an alleged "missile gap," and defense spending, the 2004 campaign concentrated on Iraq, terrorism, and, surprisingly, candidates' military service during the Vietnam War. Ultimately, the importance of such issues for voters versus such other topics as the economy, education, health care, and values is difficult to define.[38] Nevertheless, a study of the two major candidates' agendas, public statements, and questions in presidential debates reveals the pivotal role of national security in the campaign.

As a presidential candidate in 2000, two-term Texas governor George W. Bush had focused, not surprisingly, on a domestic agenda. His campaign concentrated on tax cuts, opportunities for faith-based groups that provided community services to receive public funding, and policies that Bush declared would promote "compassionate conservatism."[39] In foreign policy, Bush promoted "the power of example" over a policy of international activism.[40] As he declared during a debate with then–Vice President Al Gore, "I don't think our troops ought to be used for what's called nation-building."[41] Bush's top foreign policy advisor, Condoleezza Rice, who would go on to become national security adviser and secretary of state, similarly noted in *Foreign Affairs* that the United States should not become "the world's '911.'"[42]

After the attacks of September 11, 2001, of course, the Bush administration's policy agenda focused foremost on national security and combating terrorism. As a *New York Times* article noted shortly after the attacks, Bush viewed his responsibility to lead the United States in this time of crisis as a God-given mission.[43] The administration's 2002 National Security Strategy declared, "We will defend the peace by fighting terrorists and tyrants. We will preserve the peace by building good relations among the great powers. We will extend the peace by encouraging free and open societies on every continent."[44] Although Bush initially enjoyed strong public support for his leadership, receiving the highest presidential approval ratings ever recorded in late September 2001, by 2004, he faced questions about the ongoing war in Iraq, the Abu Ghraib prisoner abuse scandal, and treatment of detainees in Guantanamo Bay, Cuba.[45]

John Kerry, the Democratic junior senator from Massachusetts, organized his 2004 presidential campaign largely around the issues for which Bush faced criticism. In October 2002, Kerry had voted to authorize war in Iraq, but he criticized the President for haste and a lack of postwar planning. As Kerry stated in announcing his candidacy for president, "I voted to threaten the use of force to make Saddam Hussein comply with the resolutions of the United Nations. I believe that was right—but it was wrong to rush to war without building a true international coalition—and with no plan to win the peace."[46]

Apart from the difficulties of separating his postinvasion criticism from his prewar support, Kerry also faced a number of questions about his service in the Vietnam War, focusing on allegations about the veracity of his military record as well as on Kerry's later opposition to the war.[47]

Both candidates' predominant concern with national security was evident throughout the presidential campaign. In his address to the Republican National Convention in New York City, President Bush declared, "I believe the most solemn duty of the American president is to protect the American people. . . . I'm running for President with a clear and positive plan to build a safer world, and a more hopeful America."[48] Similarly, Kerry stated at the Democratic National Convention in Boston, "This is the most important election of our lifetime. . . . We are a nation at war: a global war on terror against an enemy unlike we've ever known before."[49] During the presidential debates in the fall of 2004, both candidates returned repeatedly to homeland security, Iraq, antiterrorism policies, and defense spending. Even questions on budget deficits turned into debates about wartime spending and homeland security.[50]

Ultimately, national security may have been the decisive factor in the 2004 presidential election. The close election results—Bush won 51 percent of the popular vote and 286 Electoral College votes, whereas Kerry received 48 percent of the popular vote and 252 Electoral College votes—may not have indicated that the country supported the incumbent president's policies.[51] Nevertheless, they certainly suggested that the nation was more willing to stay the course in the war on terror than to make a change in leadership at the time. A group of pollsters who convened after the 2004 election concluded that public support for the president in a time of war and terrorism raised virtually insurmountable barriers for challengers.[52] Looking ahead to 2008, the key question for women presidential candidates, then, is whether they will be able to secure public confidence in their national security expertise and leadership abilities.

Women Presidential Candidates in 2008

After Hillary Clinton's resounding Senate victories in 2000 and 2006, pursuit of the White House is a logical progression in her career. In the Republican Party, the woman whose name crops up most frequently is Secretary of State Condoleezza Rice, even though she has declared many times that she has no interest in running for the office.[53] Nevertheless, the distinctive qualifications that both Clinton and Rice have in national security illustrate their competitiveness for the White House.

Clinton's diverse and extensive political career includes experience in both state and national government, with both executive and legislative responsibilities in the latter. A Wellesley graduate and Yale-educated lawyer, Clinton first served as a law professor in Arkansas and then became a partner in the prestigious Rose Law Firm while her husband practiced state politics. As governor, Bill Clinton frequently asked his wife to assist with his agenda as well, and she chaired statewide task forces on health care and education reform. During Bill Clinton's presidency, Hillary Clinton kept an office in the West Wing, the first First Lady ever to do so, and her agenda over eight years included health care, women's rights, and children's issues. Continuing to shatter precedent, Hillary Clinton became the first First Lady ever to be elected to Congress, and she joined the Senate in 2001. Clinton serves on the Health, Education, Labor, and Pensions Committee; the Environment and Public Works Committee; the Special Committee on Aging; and, most significantly, the Senate Armed Services Committee, the first New York senator to do so.[54]

Condoleezza Rice has spent less time in politics than Clinton, but her positions have been more consequential for foreign affairs. A Soviet expert and tenured professor of political science at Stanford University, Rice joined the National Security Council (NSC) of President George H.W. Bush in 1989 at National Security Advisor Brent Scowcroft's special invitation. For four years, she directed Soviet and East European Affairs at the NSC. Upon returning to Stanford, she was appointed provost at age thirty-eight, the youngest and first black person, as well as the first woman, to hold the number-two position at this top university. Rice reentered the world of politics with the 2000 presidential campaign, serving as then-governor George W. Bush's primary foreign policy advisor and becoming national security advisor after his election. In George W. Bush's second term, Rice became secretary of state, a position that required Senate confirmation.[55]

Both Clinton and Rice demonstrate much more experience in politics than their female predecessors who have run for president. Although Clinton's area of expertise lies primarily in domestic policy, she is steadily building a record for herself in foreign affairs through her service on the Senate Armed Services Committee and her frequent speeches about the Bush administration's policies on Iraq and terrorism. Furthermore, Clinton is respected internationally through her extensive travels as First Lady, when she honed her diplomatic skills well. No sitting member of Congress has been elected president since John F. Kennedy in 1960, but Clinton's precongressional White House experience might counter that trend.

Rice's longstanding academic and practical experience in foreign affairs are by far the most significant credentials ever in that field for a woman presidential candidate (and they present stiff competition for male presidential candidates as well). History provides no recent precedent—the last secretary of state to become president was James Buchanan—but Rice has been a highly visible proponent of the administration's agenda, serving as spokesperson as much as advisor, which enhances her political skills. Yet Rice's continuing insistence that she will not run raises questions about the feasibility of a presidential campaign. Pollster Dick Morris has proposed a grassroots movement that would position Rice well for the Republican nomination should she enter the race, but such a decentralized effort seems unlikely without some indication of Rice's support.[56]

Conclusion

The extensive political requirements for the US presidency today raise high expectations for women who run for the office. They include fundraising, proven crisis leadership, and executive experience, among others.[57] The recent presidential campaign of Elizabeth Dole illustrates the importance of these credentials, and a woman presidential candidate from either of the two major political parties would have to demonstrate skill in each area to be taken seriously. That said, some women politicians today have succeeded in at least two of those three areas—Hillary Clinton's impressive senatorial fundraising record and White House experience as First Lady give her a unique niche from which to mount a presidential run, and Condoleezza Rice's national security experience in the George W. Bush White House as well as her role in decisionmaking for the Iraq War amply illustrate her abilities in crisis leadership and executive experience.

In a presidential campaign, both Clinton and Rice would be well-prepared to address questions about her expertise in national security and combating terrorism. The key question for the 2008 presidential race, then, may not be the qualifications of women candidates, but rather, the qualifications of their competitors.[58]

Notes

1. Atkinson, *The Long Gray Line,* p. 408.

2. Of course, many other nations have elected women to their highest executive office, including such close US allies as the United Kingdom (Margaret Thatcher, 1979 to 1990) and Israel (Golda Meir, 1969 to 1974). For fascinating profiles of women chief executives worldwide, see Opfell, *Women Prime Ministers and Presidents.*

3. Clift and Brazaitis, *Madam President,* p. ix.

4. Cillizza, "Clinton Sets Bar for '08 Funds."

5. Edwards and Wayne, *Presidential Leadership,* p. 256.

6. Ibid.

7. Murray and Blessing, *Greatness in the White House,* p. 31.

8. Edwards and Wayne, *Presidential Leadership*, pp. 256–257.

9. Murray and Blessing, *Greatness in the White House*, p. 31.

10. Ibid.

11. Ibid. The Murray/Blessing study goes through Ronald Reagan, and I have updated their figures to include George H.W. Bush, William Jefferson Clinton, and George W. Bush.

12. For a history of the admissions process at three Ivy League universities—Harvard, Yale, Princeton—see Karabel, *The Chosen.*

13. Watson, "Introduction: The White House as Ultimate Prize," p. 14.

14. Ibid., p. 15.

15. Ibid., pp. 9, 15.

16. For an explanation of how the Electoral College operates and its effect on presidential elections, see Wayne, *The Road to the White House 2004.*

17. Martin, *The Presidency and Women,* p. 117.

18. Watson, "Introduction: The White House as Ultimate Prize," p. 15; and Falk and Jamieson, "Changing the Climate of Expectations," p. 48.

19. Falk and Jamieson, "Changing the Climate of Expectations," p. 48.

20. Ibid., pp. 48–49.

21. Sherman, *No Place for a Woman,* pp. 127–128.

22. Ibid., p. 110.

23. Ibid., p. 173.

24. Ibid., p. 191.

25. See biography of Margaret Chase Smith on her library website, http://www.mcslibrary.org. Accessed May 24, 2006.

26. Clift and Brazaitis, *Madam President*, p. xxii.

27. Watson and Gordon, "Profile: Shirley Chisholm, Blazing Trails," p. 55.

28. Ibid.

29. Watson and Gordon, "Profile: Geraldine Ferraro, Media Coverage of History in the Making," p. 158.

30. Heith, "The Lipstick Watch," pp. 126–127.

31. Commission on Presidential Debates, "The Bush-Ferraro Vice-Presidential Debate."

32. Ibid.

33. Pomper, "The Presidential Election," p. 60. For a discussion of Ferraro's limited influence in the race, see Keeter, "Public Opinion in 1984," pp. 105–106.

34. Watson and Gordon, "Profile: Pat Schroeder and the Campaign That Wasn't," p. 117.

35. Clift and Brazaitis, *Madam President*, p. 67.

36. Watson and Gordon, "Profile: Elizabeth Dole, Executive Leadership," pp. 201–203.

37. Clift and Brazaitis, *Madam President*, p. 100.

38. A 2004 election day poll found that voters identified "moral values" as the single most important issue in the presidential race. The survey listed "terrorism" and "Iraq" separately, however; when the two topics were considered together, they moved to the top of the list, with 19 percent of voters identifying "terrorism" as the most important issue, whereas 15 percent did so for "Iraq." See Seelye, "Moral Values Cited as a Defining Issue of the Election."

39. Greenstein, *The Presidential Difference*, p. 197.

40. Commission on Presidential Debates, "The Second Gore-Bush Presidential Debate."

41. Ibid.

42. See Rice, "Promoting the National Interest."

43. Bruni, "For President, A Mission and a Role in History." Also see Bruni, *Ambling into History,* pp. 256–258.

44. *The National Security Strategy of the United States of America.*

45. For a discussion of the short-term "rally effects" that President Bush received after 9/11, with a peak approval rating of 90 percent, see DiIulio, "Election Results, Rally Effects, and Democratic Futures," pp. 150–153.

46. See Kerry, "Announcement Speech."

47. For a recent discussion of the allegations about Kerry's military service in Vietnam, see Zernike, "Kerry Pressing Swift Boat Case Long After Loss."

48. Bush, "President's Remarks at the 2004 Republican National Convention."

49. Kerry, "Acceptance Speech."

50. Commission on Presidential Debates, 2004 Debate Transcripts.

51. Details on the 2004 presidential election results are available at http://www.cnn.com/ELECTION/2004/pages/results/.

52. Menand, "Permanent Fatal Errors: Postcard from Stanford."

53. See Goldenberg, "Clinton War Chest Adds to Rumours."

54. For background information on Clinton, see Sheehy, *Hillary's Choice*, and Clinton, *Living History*. Also see Clinton's website at http://clinton.senate.gov.

55. For background information on Rice, see Felix, *Condi: The Condoleezza Rice Story*. Also see Rice's biography on the Department of State website at http://www.state.gov/r/pa/ei/biog/41252.htm.

56. Morris and McGann, *Condi vs. Hillary,* chap. 13 passim.

57. Clift and Brazaitis, *Madam President,* pp. 315–321.

58. As of early 2007, other potential Democratic contenders for president included Al Gore, John Kerry, and John Edwards, and Barack Obama. Potential Republican contenders included John McCain, Rudolph Giuliani, George Pataki, and Mitt Romney. Of these potential candidates, Gore, Kerry, and McCain presented the strongest credentials in national security.

10

A Woman in the White House? Never Say Never

Ann Gordon

She is called the Iron Lady because of her economic policies, but also the "Mother of Liberia," or frequently "Ma Ellen." When Ellen Johnson-Sirleaf was inaugurated president of Liberia in 2006, she became the first women elected to head an African nation. Because of the fourteen years of civil war that left the country in ruins, Johnson-Sirleaf has characterized her nation as a sick child that needs the tender care only a loving mother can provide. A day before Johnson-Sirleaf's inauguration, Chile voted for Michelle Bachelet to be president, making her the first woman to be a leader of a Latin American country without following her husband. President Bachelet has promised a more inclusive cabinet and more women in top jobs. "We are going to have a new style in national politics, with more dialogue and participation," she vowed in her victory speech.[1] Just a few months prior to Johnson-Sirleaf and Bachelet taking office, Angela Merkel was elected as Germany's chancellor. Is there a global momentum for the election of women leaders? About one in twenty nations worldwide is now led by an elected woman, either as president or prime minister.

Pathways to Power

It began with Sirimavo Bandaranaike in 1960, when she was elected prime minister of Ceylon, now Sri Lanka. Known as the weeping widow, Bandaranaike was the widow of Ceylon's assassinated prime minister Solomon Bandaranaike. Succeeding a slain husband or father has been a well-traveled path for women in Asian and Latin American countries. Historically, about 30 percent of women leaders have achieved office through family ties.[2] But women have also been elected in their own right. Although women leaders have diverse backgrounds, the vast majority come to the office with years of experience, having held other national offices.[3] Having significant executive leadership experience will also be important to women who seek the US presidency. Yet, as Karen Hult thoroughly details in Chapter 8, the eligibility pool is constrained by the glass ceilings and glass walls women encounter in their careers.

Interestingly, some countries have had more than one woman leader: Bangladesh, Bermuda, Haiti, Ireland, Netherlands Antilles, New Zealand, the Philippines, and Sri Lanka. Farida Jalalzai has speculated that once a woman has broken the glass ceiling in a particular country, it is possible that the next woman seeking the office will have a better chance of attaining it.[4]

Obstacles for Women Seeking the Presidency

Around the world, most women who lead have done so in parliamentary governments. It appears to be more difficult for women to be elected in a presidential system. Historically, about 69 percent of women leaders have been prime ministers, whereas only 31 percent have been presidents.[5] As Marcia Lynn Whicker and Hedy Leonie Isaacs have observed, the US presidency is a "bastion of maleness."[6] One reason is the candidate selection process. In most presidential systems, candidates must campaign for the popular vote, whereas in parliamentary systems, it is up to the party to select the leader from within its ranks. Of course, the US system relies on the Electoral College. As Sue Thomas and Jean Reith Schroedel observe in Chapter 3, winning the Electoral College adds another impediment to a woman (or women) winning the presidency. Their analysis of voting patterns in 2004 finds evidence of an "antifemale" bias that could affect women from both the Republican and Democratic Parties.

There are many other systemic problems identified by the authors in this book. For example, Victoria Farrar-Myers details the tangible and intangible ingredients needed for viability in Chapter 6. Essential for all candidates is the ability to raise funds. Farrar-Myers provides convincing evidence that women candidates for the House and Senate are indeed successful fundraisers and expects women presidential candidates to follow suit. However, she reminds us that money is not the only tangible asset required for viability: candidates require name recognition, a solid network and base of support, a well-organized campaign, credibility on key issues, and a proven track record. She highlights the intangibles as well, pointing to the importance of timing, general mood of the country, and desire for change, as well as cultural norms and the potential for mobilizing women voters.

As the authors in this volume have carefully detailed, there are many additional barriers facing women who seek the presidency. For example, Gina Serignese Woodall and Kim L. Fridkin remind us in Chapter 4 of the persistence of gender stereotypes among voters fueled by differential press coverage of women candidates. Decades of research have shown that voters assume female and male candidates possess different personality traits. Women are thought of as honest, compassionate, and sensitive, to name a few, whereas men are seen as tough, aggressive, and better able to lead. Women and men are also assumed to have expertise over particular policy areas, with women thought to be better able to handle so-called compassion issues such as poverty and health care, whereas men are assumed to be better at foreign policy and defense. Women candidates also receive gendered press coverage. The news media pay less attention to women and are more likely to focus on the question of viability for women candidates as compared to men.

The problems women candidates face in navigating gendered expectations on the part of voters and gendered press coverage are further exacerbated by the overwhelming masculinity of presidential politics. As Meredith Conroy points out in Chapter 7, political parties can perpetuate this problem by nominating more "masculine" women to more desirable races. By drawing attention to masculinity on the campaign trail, Georgia Duerst-Lahti demonstrates in Chapter 5 how presidential elections have always been about "picking the right or best man for the job." She astutely observes that the problem for women candidates is that, "Women are expected to be feminine, but presidential candidates are judged by the quality of their masculinity."

Stereotypical beliefs about a woman's ability to deal with issues of national security and defense are particularly damaging to women who seek the presidency and have only been made more so by concerns over terrorism and national security. As Meena Bose has observed in Chapter 9, women will have to work harder to overcome these stereotypical assumptions, even if they possess ample background and experience. Indeed, Bose finds that there are many women with the necessary credentials, but women will continue to face the suspicion that they are not up to the challenge. Even before 9/11, a woman's abilities in the area of national security received extra attention. For example, during the 1984 campaign, Geraldine Ferraro was asked on *Meet the Press*, "Are you strong enough to push the button?" Have attitudes changed since Ferraro was questioned? Recent research has revealed a lack of progress on this front. One recent survey showed that respondents who were most concerned with terrorism, homeland security, and war thought that a man would make a better president than a woman.[7]

Just as attitudes about a woman's ability to serve as commander in chief did not disappear with the dawning of the twenty-first century, so too have expectations about women's roles in society persisted. As we shall see, a woman senator in 2006 has more in common with a 1950s congresswoman than one might expect.

Hillary Come Home—to the White house

Although her work included a bill that created the federal student loan program and she championed the use of farm surplus in the school lunch program as well as research into cystic fibrosis, she is best known for the phrase, "Coya Come Home."[8] It was 1954, and there were few women in Congress. Coya Knutson was elected after ousting an incumbent—no easy feat. Her 1958 reelection bid was thwarted when a letter allegedly from her husband was given to reporters, resulting in national headlines. The letter read:

> Coya,
> I want you to tell the people of the 9th District this Sunday that you are through in politics. That you want to go home and make a home for your husband and son. As your husband I compel you to do this. I'm tired of being torn apart from my family. I'm sick and tired of having you run around with other men all the time and not your husband. I love you, honey.[9]

Although it is unknown who actually wrote the letter, the damage was done, and Minnesota did not send another woman to Congress until 2000. Knutson's congressional career may have occurred in the 1950s, but women politicians in the twenty-first century must contend with the same gendered notions of women's role in society. As Caroline Heldman points out in Chapter 2, the separate spheres ideology, which presumes women belong in the private sphere and men in the public, is still a formidable obstacle. For example, Senator Hillary Clinton's marriage was analyzed in the *New York Times*, which published a front page article that said, "the former president said he had sometimes 'kicked myself' for encouraging her to run for office. There were times he wished she were not in the Senate so they could travel more, learn more, he said."[10] Bill Clinton is characterized as a neglected husband:

> Mr. Clinton is rarely without company in public, yet the company he keeps rarely includes his wife. Nights out find him zipping around Los Angeles with his bachelor buddy, Ronald W. Burkle, or hitting parties and fund-raisers in Manhattan; she is yoked to work in Washington or New York—her Senate career and political ambitions consuming her time.[11]

To underscore their difficulties, the article gave a detailed account of how much time they spend together:

> Since the start of 2005, the Clintons have been together about 14 days a month on average, according to aides who reviewed the couple's schedules. Sometimes it is a full day of relaxing at home in Chappaqua; sometimes it is meeting up late at night. At their busiest, they saw each other on a single day, Valentine's Day, in February 2005—a month when each was traveling a great deal. Last August, they saw each other at some point on 24 out of 31 days. Out of the last 73 weekends, they spent 51 together.[12]

If the article had been about a male senator, he would simply be characterized as hardworking, with no mention of the impact of his career on his marriage. But for a woman in the Senate, the story becomes that Senator Clinton's ambitions are getting in the way of her marriage. As a woman, she is expected to fulfill her obligations in the private sphere to her home and husband. That she also inhabits the public sphere appears to be an inconvenient impediment to domestic bliss.

On the other hand, concern over the role of a man potentially inhabiting the role of president's spouse has also garnered attention. As Elizabeth Dole found, when she sought the presidency, editorial cartoonists routinely drew her as the wife of former senator and Republican presidential nominee Bob Dole. She was "sexualized and domesticated" by "the (1) the settings in which she was depicted (often her home); (2) representations of her as the object of her husband's sexual revitalization by Viagra, the erectile dysfunction drug;

and (3) her nurturance of her husband Robert's insecurities concerning his possible role as 'First Husband.'"[13]

Concern over Bill Clinton as first husband has already been expressed in the media. "When the subject of Bill and Hillary Clinton comes up for many prominent Democrats these days, Topic A is the state of their marriage—and how the most dissected relationship in American life might affect Mrs. Clinton's possible bid for the presidency in 2008."[14] A Gallup poll found that 30 percent of Americans felt that preventing Bill from becoming "first husband" was a reason to vote against Senator Clinton for president, and 22 percent said it would be a reason to vote for her. Some 46 percent of Americans said it would not affect their vote.[15]

Implicit in the press coverage of Hillary Rodham Clinton's potential candidacy is a "now or never" mentality. When the news media consider the possibility of a woman president, the subject inevitably turns to Clinton, even though there are other women amply qualified for the job. Thus, women's political fortunes have been tied to Clinton's, as if she represents any or all women who would seek the oval office. However, Clinton is an individual with strengths and weaknesses all her own—whether she tries and wins or tries and fails. For example, one poll found that 64 percent thought that a woman could be "tough" enough to be president, but only 32 percent thought Clinton was "tough" enough to be president. These numbers could change over the course of a campaign, but the point is that voters are evaluating her, not just her sex. To be sure, she will be evaluated differently than a male candidate by voters (36 percent of voters were unable to imagine *any* woman tough enough to do the job) and will receive—has already received—gendered press coverage, but it should be remembered that she is also a politician with all the baggage (and then some) of any political candidate. When will there be a woman in the White House? As Senator Clinton has observed, "It depends upon the candidate, it depends upon timing, issues, message. So I can't come up with any sweeping generalizations, but I think it's obviously something that has to come to fruition."[16] Never say never.

Notes

1. Polgreen and Rohter, "Where Political Clout Demands a Maternal Touch."
2. Jalalzai, Farida, "Women Political Leaders: Past and Present," pp. 85–108.

3. Ibid.
4. Ibid.
5. Ibid.
6. Whicker and Isaacs, "The Maleness of the American Presidency."
7. Falk and Kenski, "Issue Saliency and Gender Stereotypes."
8. Gunderson, "Coya's Story."
9. Ibid.
10. Healy, "For Clintons, Delicate Dance of Married and Public Lives."
11. Ibid.
12. Ibid.
13. Gilmartin, "Still the Angel in the Household."
14. Healy, "For Clintons, Delicate Dance of Married and Public Lives."
15. Gallup poll, conducted June 26–29, 2006, surveyed 1,002 adults; margin of error +/–3% (release, July 20, 2006). Accessed at http://nationaljournal.com/members/polltrack/.
16. See http://www.usnews.com/usnews/politics/whispers/archive/september2003.htm.

Bibliography

Abramowitz, Alan I. "Viability, Electability, and Candidate Choice in a Presidential Primary Election: A Test of Competing Models." *Journal of Politics* 51 (1989): 977–992.

Acker, Joan. "Gendered Institutions: From Sex Roles to Gendered Institutions." *Contemporary Sociology* 21 (September 1992): 565–569.

Aday, Sean, and James Devitt. "Style over Substance: Newspaper Coverage of Female Candidates: Spotlight on Elizabeth Dole." The Second in the White House Project Education Fund Series: Framing Gender on the Campaign Trail. Presented at the National Press Club, Washington, DC, 2000.

Aldrich, John H. "A Dynamic Model of Presidential Nomination Campaigns." *American Political Science Review* 74 (1980): 651–669.

Alexander, D., and Kristi Andersen. "Gender as a Factor in the Attribution of Leadership Traits." *Political Research Quarterly* 46 (1993): 527–545.

Anderson, Karrin Vasby. "From Spouses to Candidates: Hillary Rodham Clinton, Elizabeth Dole, and the Gendered Office of US President." *Rhetoric and Public Affairs* 5, no. 1 (2002): 105–132.

Anderson, Margaret L. *Thinking About Women: Sociological Perspectives on Sex and Gender*. Boston: Allyn and Bacon, 1997.

Archer, D., B. Iritani, D. Kimes, and M. Barrios. "Face-ism: Five Studies of Sex Differences in Facial Prominence." *Journal of Personality and Social Psychology* 45 (1983).

Atkinson, Rick. *The Long Gray Line*. New York: Henry Holt, 1989.

Bai, Matt. "The Fallback." *New York Times Magazine,* March 12, 2006, 34.

Barbara Lee Family Foundation. "Speaking with Authority: From Economic Security to National Security," 2002, www.barbaraleefoundation.org.

Bartel, Caroline A., Steven L. Blader, and Amy Wrzesniewski, eds. *Identity and the Modern Organization*. Mahwah, NJ: Erlbaum, 2005.

Bartels, Larry M. "Candidate Choice and the Dynamics of the Presidential Nomination Process." *American Journal of Political Science* 31 (1987): 1–30.

Barth, Jay, and Margaret R. Ferguson. "American Governors and Their Constituents: The Relationship Between Gubernatorial Personality and Public Approval." *State Politics and Policy Quarterly* 2 (Fall 2002): 268–282.

———. "Gender and Gubernatorial Personality." *Women and Politics* 24, no. 1 (2002): 63–82.

Beck, Albert R. "Fundamentalists." In *Encyclopedia of Religion in American Politics,* ed. Jeffrey D. Schultz, John G. West, and Iain Maclean. Phoenix, AZ: Oryx Press, 1999.

Berch, Neil. "'The Year of the Women' in Context: A Test of Six Explanations." *American Politics Research* 24, no. 2 (1996): 169–193.

Berger, John. *Ways of Seeing*. London: BBC and Penguin, 1972.

Bernstein, Robert A. "Why Are There So Few Women in the House?" *Western Political Quarterly* 39, no. 1 (1986): 155–164.

Bevan, Tom. "Hillary's Eye on the White House May Be Shaping Her Views on War." *Chicago Sun Times*, July 21, 2006, 35.

Beyle, Thad. "The Governors." In *Politics in the American States: A Comparative Analysis*, ed. Virginia Gray and Russell L. Hanson. 8th ed. Washington, DC: Congressional Quarterly Press, 2004.

Biography of Condoleezza Rice. Department of State website. www.state.gov/r/pa/ei/biog/41252.htm, accessed June 8, 2006.

Biography of Margaret Chase Smith. www.mcslibrary.org, accessed June 8, 2006.

Borrelli, MaryAnne. "Gender, Credibility, and Politics: The Senate Hearings of Cabinet-Secretaries-Designate, 1975 to 1993." *Political Research Quarterly* 50 (March 1997): 171–197.

———. "Gender, Politics, and Change in the United States Cabinet: The Madeleine Korbel Albright and Janet Reno Appointments." In *Gender and American Politics: Women, Men, and the Political Process*, ed. Sue Tolleson-Rinehart and Jyl J. Josephson. Armonk, NY: M. E. Sharpe, 2000.

———. *The President's Cabinet: Gender, Power, and Representation.* Boulder, CO: Lynne Rienner, 2002.

Bowen, Michael A. *Hillary! How America's First Woman President Won the White House*. Boston: Branden Books, 2003.

Bower, Carol Lynn. "Public Discourse and Female Presidential Candidates." In *Anticipating Madam President*, ed. Robert P. Watson and Ann Gordon. Boulder, CO: Lynne Rienner, 2003.

Bowling, Cynthia J., and Deil S. Wright. "Change and Continuity in State Administration: Administrative Leadership Across Four Decades." *Public Administration Review* 58 (September–October 1998): 429–444.

Brady, Henry E., and Richard Johnston. "What's the Primary Message: Horserace or Issue Journalism?" In *Media and Momentum*, ed. Gary R. Orren and Nelson Polsby. Chatham, NJ: Chatham House, 1987.

Bragg, Richard. *I Am a Soldier, Too: The Jessica Lynch Story*. New York: Knopf, 2003.

Brant, Martha, and T. Trent Gegax. "Tone Deaf: Why Doesn't the Military Get It When It Comes to Sexual Assault?" *Newsweek*, February 27, 2004.

Bratton, Kathleen A., and Kerry L. Haynie. "Agenda Setting and Legislative Success in State Legislatures: The Effects of Gender and Race." *Journal of Politics* 61, no. 3 (1999): 658–679.

Broverman, Inge K., Susan R. Vogel, Donald M. Broverman, Frank E. Clarkson, and Paul S. Rosenkranz. "Sex-Role Stereotypes: A Current Appraisal." *Journal of Social Issues* 28 (1972): 59–78.

Bruni, Frank. *Ambling into History: The Unlikely Odyssey of George W. Bush.* New York: HarperCollins, 2002.

———. "For President, a Mission and a Role in History." *New York Times*, September 22, 2001, A1.

Burns, Nancy, Kay Lehman Schlozman, and Sidney Verba. *The Private Roots of Public Action.* Cambridge, MA: Harvard University Press, 2001.

Burrell, Barbara C. "Gender, Presidential Elections, and Public Policy: Making Women's Votes Matter." *Journal of Women, Politics, and Policy* 27, nos. 1–2 (2005): 31–50.

———. "Party Decline, Party Transformation, and Gender Politics: The USA." In *Gender and Party Politics*, ed. Joni Lovenduski and Pippa Norris. London: Sage, 1993.

———. "The Political Opportunity of Women Candidates for the US House of Representatives in 1984." *Women and Politics* 8, no. 1 (1988): 51–69.

———. *A Woman's Place Is in the House: Campaigning for Congress in the Feminist Era.* Ann Arbor: University of Michigan Press, 1994.

"Bush, Blair Hold Joint News Conference." May 25, 2006, www.washingtonpost.com/wp-dyn/content/article/2006/05/25/AR2006052501774.html.

Bush, George W. "President Addresses Military Families, Discusses War on Terror." August 24, 2005, www.whitehouse.gov.

———. "President's Remarks at the 2004 Republican National Convention." New York. September 2, 2004, www.whitehouse.gov/news/releases/2004/09/20040902-2.html.

Bystrom, Dianne G. "Advertising, Web Sites, and Media Coverage: Gender and Communication Along the Campaign Trail." In *Gender and Elections*, ed. Susan J. Carroll and Richard L. Fox. New York: Cambridge University Press, 2006.

———. "On the Way to the White House: Communication Strategies for Women Candidates." In *Anticipating Madam President*, ed. Robert P. Watson and Ann Gordon. Boulder, CO: Lynne Rienner, 2003.

Bystrom, Dianne G., Marcy C. Banwart, Lynda Lee Kaid, and Terry A. Robertson. *Gender and Candidate Communication: Videostyle, Webstyle, Newstyle.* New York: Routledge, 2004.

Bystrom, Dianne G., L. M. McKinnon, and C. K. Chaney. "The First Lady and the First Estate: Media Coverage of Hillary Clinton and Elizabeth Dole in the 1996 Presidential Campaign." In *The Electronic Election:*

Perspectives on the 1996 Campaign Communication, ed. Lynda Lee Kaid and Dianne G. Bystrom. Mahwah, NJ: Lawrence Erlbaum, 1999.

Calogero, Rachel M. "A Test of Objectification Theory: The Effect of the Male Gaze on Appearance Concerns in College Women." *Psychology of Women Quarterly* 28 (2004).

Campbell, David E., and Christina Wolbrecht. "See Jane Run: Women Politicians as Role Models for Adolescents." *Journal of Politics* 68 (May 2006): 233–247.

Cannon, Carl M. "You Go, Girls: Growing Support for Women Presidential Candidates." *National Journal*, July 24, 1999.

Carroll, Susan J. "Political Elites and Sex Differences in Political Ambition: A Reconsideration." *Journal of Politics* 47, no. 4 (November 1985): 1231–1243.

———. *Women as Candidates in American Politics*. Bloomington: Indiana University Press, 1994.

———. "Women in State Government: Historical Overview and Current Trends." Reprinted from the Council of State Governments, *The Book of the States*, 2004. www.cawp.rutgers.edu/Research/Reports/BookofStates.pdf, accessed May 15, 2006.

———, ed. *The Impact of Women in Public Office*. Bloomington: Indiana University Press, 2001.

Catalyst. *2002 Catalyst Census of Women Corporate Officers and Top Earners*. Cited in "Women in Business: A Snapshot." www.catalystwomen.org, accessed May 24, 2006.

CBS News. "The Quest to Become Ms. President." Online article by CBS News Sunday Morning. www.cbsnews.com/stories/2006/02/05/sunday/main1281736_page3.shtml, accessed March 1, 2006.

CBS News/*New York Times*. "Poll: A Woman for President (January 20–25, 2006)." www.cbwnews.com/stories/2006/02/03/opinion/polls/printable1281319.shtml.

CBS News Poll. "Ready for a Woman President?" *CBS News Polls*, February 5, 2006, www.cbsnews.com.

"The Ceiling of Political Ambition: A Poll Shows That Hillary Clinton Has the Biggest Mountain to Climb in the Presidential Primaries." *Pittsburgh Post-Gazette*, July 23, 2006, H3.

Center for American Women and Politics. "Fact Sheet: History of Women Governors." October 2004. www.cawp.rutgers.edu/Facts/Officeholders/govhistory.pdf, accessed February 13, 2006.

———. "Fact Sheet: Sex Differences in Voter Turnout." www.cawp.rutgers.edu. 2005.

———. "The Gender Gap: Voting Choices in Presidential Elections Fact Sheet." www.cawp.rutgers.edu/Facts/Elections/GGPresVote.pdf, accessed May 1, 2006.

———. "Statewide Elective Executive Women: 1969–2004." www.cawp.rutgers.edu/Officeholders/stwidelist.pdf, accessed May 30, 2006.

———. "Women in Elective Office 2006." www.cawp.rutgers.edu/Facts/Officeholders/elective.pdf, accessed May 19, 2006.

———. "Women in Elective Office 2007." www.cawp.rutgers.edu/Facts/Officeholders/elective.pdf, accessed January 15, 2007.

———. "Women in Presidential Cabinets." www.cawp.rutgers.edu/Facts/Officeholders/fedcab.pdf, updated 06/06.

———. "Women in Statewide Elective Executive Office 2006." www.cawp.rutgers.edu/Facts/Officeholders/stwide-current.html, accessed May 19, 2006.

———. "Women in State Legislatures 1985–2005: Fact Sheet." www.cawp.rutgers.edu/Facts/StLegHistory/stleghist.pdf, accessed May 1, 2006.

———. "Women Mayors in US Cities 2006." www.cawp.rutgers.edu/Facts/Officeholders/mayors-curr.html, accessed May 30, 2006.

Center for Women in Government and Civil Society. *Women in State Policy Leadership, 1998–2005: An Analysis of Slow and Uneven Progress.* Albany: SUNY at Albany, Winter 2006.

Chisholm, Shirley. *The Good Fight.* New York: Harper and Row, 1973.

Cillizza, Chris. "Clinton Sets Bar for '08 Funds; Senator has $20 Million for Reelection, Possible Presidential Bid." *Washington Post,* April 18, 2006, A3.

Clayton, Cornell W. "Law, Politics, and the New Federalism: State Attorneys General as National Policymakers." *Review of Politics* 56 (Summer 1994): 525–553.

Clift, Eleanor, and Tom Brazaitis. *Madam President: Shattering the Last Glass Ceiling.* New York: Scribner, 2000.

———. *Madam President: Women Blazing the Leadership Trail.* New York: Routledge, 2003.

Clinton, Hillary Rodham. *Living History.* New York: Simon and Schuster, 2003.

CNN.com. *Election 2004–US President.* www.cnn.com/ELECTION/2004/pages/results/president, accessed March 27, 2006.

Code, Lorraine. *What Can She Know? Feminist Theory and the Construction of Knowledge.* Ithaca, NY: Cornell University Press, 1991.

Commission on Presidential Debates, 2004 Debate Transcripts. www.debates.org/pages/debtrans.html.

Commission on Presidential Debates. "The Bush-Ferraro Vice-Presidential Debate, October 11, 1984." www.debates.org, accessed May 24, 2006.

———. "The Second Gore-Bush Presidential Debate," Wake Forest University, Winston-Salem, N.C., October 11, 2000. www.debates.org, accessed May 30, 2006.

Connell, R. W. *Masculinities.* Berkeley: University of California Press, 2005.

Conroy, Meredith. "Are You Man Enough? The Gender of Presidential Candidates by Print Media." Paper presented at the Western Political Science Association Annual Meeting, Las Vegas, NV, March 2007.

Cook, Elizabeth Adell. "Voter Reaction to Women Candidates." In *Women and Elective Office: Past, Present, and Future,* ed. Susan Thomas and Clyde Wilcox. New York: Oxford University Press, 1996.

Cook, Elizabeth Adell, and Clyde Wilcox. "Women Voters in the 'Year of the Woman.'" *Democracy's Feast: Elections in America,* ed. H. F. Weisberg. Chatham, NJ: Chatham House, 1995.

Cooper, Cary L., and Suzan Lewis. *Managing the New Work Force: The Challenge of Dual Income Families.* Amsterdam: Pfeiffer, 1994.

Cronin, Thomas E., and Michael A. Genovese. *The Paradoxes of the American Presidency.* New York: Oxford University Press, 1998.

Dabelko, Kirsten la Cour, and Paul S. Herrnson. "Women's and Men's Campaigns for the US House of Representatives." *Political Research Quarterly* 50 (March 1997): 121–135.

Dao, James. "After Storm, She Tries to Mend State, and Career." *New York Times*, December 29, 2005, A1, A18.

Darcy, Robert, and Sarah Slavin Schramm. "When Women Run Against Men." *Public Opinion Quarterly* 41 (1977): 1–12.

Darcy, R., Susan Welch, and Janet Clark. *Women, Elections, and Representation.* 2nd ed. Lincoln: University of Nebraska Press, 1994.

DeConde, Alexander. *Presidential Machismo: Executive Authority, Military Intervention, and Foreign Relations.* Boston: Northeastern University Press, 2000.

De Moraes, Lisa. "Steven Bochco by a Landslide." *Washington Post*, October 8, 2005, C1.

Derber, Raisa. "The Fault, Dear Brutus: Women as Congressional Candidates in Pennsylvania." *Journal of Politics* 44 (May 1982): 463–479.

Devitt, James. 1999. "Framing Gender on the Campaign Trail: Women's Executive Leadership and the Press." Washington, DC: A report for the Women's Leadership Fund, 1999.

Diageo/Hotline. "Poll Conducted by Financial Dynamics, Feb. 16–19, 2006." www.pollingreport.com/politics.htm.

DiIulio, John J. "Election Results, Rally Effects, and Democratic Futures." In *Classic Ideas and Current Issues in American Government,* ed. Meena Bose and John J. DiIulio, Jr. Boston: Houghton Mifflin, 2007. Originally published in *Crossroads: The Future of American Politics*, ed. Andrew Cuomo. Random House, 2003, 94–100.

Dodson, Debra L. "Acting for Women: Is What Legislators Say, What They Do?" In *The Impact of Women in Public Office*, ed. Susan J. Carroll. Bloomington: University of Indiana Press, 2001.

———. "Representing Women's Interests in the US House of Representatives." *In Women and Elective Office: Past, Present, and Future*, ed. Sue Thomas and Clyde Wilcox. New York: Oxford University Press, 1998.

Dodson, Debra L., and Susan J. Carroll. *Reshaping the Agenda: Women in State Legislatures.* New Brunswick, NJ: Center for the American Woman and Politics, 1991.

Dolan, Julie. "Gender Equity: Illusion or Reality for Women in the Federal Executive Service?" *Public Administration Review* 64 (May 2004): 299–308.

———. "Political Appointees in the United States: Does Gender Make a Difference?" *PS: Political Science and Politics* 34 (June 2001): 212–216.

———. "Support for Women's Interests in the 103rd Congress: The Distinct Impact of Congressional Women." *Women and Politics* 18 (1997): 81–94.

Dolan, Kathleen A. "Gender Differences in Support for Women Candidates: Is There a Glass Ceiling in American Politics?" *Women and Politics* 17 (1997): 27–41.

———. "How the Public Views Women Candidates." In *Women and Elective Office: Past, Present, and Future,* ed. Sue Thomas and Clyde Wilcox. 2nd ed. New York: Oxford University Press, 2005.

———. *Voting for Women: How the Public Evaluates Women Candidates.* Boulder, CO: Westview, 2004.

———. "Voting for Women in the 'Year of the Woman.'" *American Journal of Political Science* 42, no. 1 (1998): 272–293.

Dolan, Kathleen A., and Lynne E. Ford. "Change and Continuity Among Women State Legislators: Evidence from Three Decades." *Political Research Quarterly* 50 (1997): 137–151.

———. "Are All Women State Legislators Alike?" In *Women and Elective Office: Past, Present, and Future*, ed. Sue Thomas and Clyde Wilcox. New York: Oxford University Press, 1998.

Dowd, Maureen. "Why Can't a Woman?" *New York Times*, October 24, 1999, D15.

Dubeck, Paula. "Women and Access to Political Office: A Comparison of Female and Male State Legislators." *Sociology Quarterly* 17 (1976): 42–52.

Duerst-Lahti, Georgia. "Gendering Presidential Functions." Poster prepared for the annual meeting of the American Political Science Association, Washington, DC, September 2005.

———. "Governing Institutions, Ideologies, and Gender: Toward the Possibility of Equal Political Representation." *Sex Roles: A Journal of Research* 47 (2002): 371–388.

———. "Institutional Gendering: Theoretical Insights into the Environment of Women Officeholders." In *Women and Elective Office: Past, Present, and Future*, ed. Sue Thomas and Clyde Wilcox. 2nd ed. New York: Oxford University Press, 2005.

———. "Knowing Congress as a Gendered Institution: Manliness and the Implications of Women in Congress." In *Women Transforming Congress*, ed. Cindy Simon Rosenthal. Norman: University of Oklahoma Press, 2002.

———. "Presidential Elections: Gendered Space and the Case of 2004." In *Gender and Elections: Shaping the Future of American Politics*, ed. Susan J. Carroll and Richard L. Fox. New York: Cambridge University Press, 2006.

———. "Reconceiving Theories of Power: Consequences of Masculinism in the Executive Branch." In *The Other Elites*, ed. MaryAnne Borrelli and Janet M. Martin. Boulder, CO: Lynne Rienner, 1997.

Duerst-Lahti, Georgia, and Rita Mae Kelly, eds. *Gender Power, Leadership, and Governance*. Ann Arbor: University of Michigan Press, 1995.

Dworkin, Andrea. *Pornography: Men Possessing Women.* New York: E. P. Dutton, 1989.

Eagly, Alice H., and Valerie J. Steffen. "Gender Stereotypes Stem from the Distribution of Men and Women into Social Roles." *Journal of Personality and Social Psychology* 46 (1984): 991–1004.

Edwards, George C., III, and Stephen J. Wayne. *Presidential Leadership: Politics and Policy Making*. 7th ed. New York: Thomson Wadsworth, 2006.

"8 for '08: The White House Project and Parade Announce Eight Female Candidates for 2008 Presidency." www.thewhitehouseproject.org/v2/press/2006/February/20060216-8for08pressrel.html, accessed July 24, 2006.

Elder, Laurel. "Why Women Don't Run: Explaining Women's Underrepresentation in America's Political Institutions." *Women and Politics* 26, no. 2 (2004): 27–56.

Estrich, Susan. *The Case for Hillary Clinton*. New York: Regan Books, 2005.

Falk, Erika, and Kate Kenski. "Issue Saliency and Gender Stereotypes: Support for Women as Presidents in Times of War and Terrorism." *Social Science Quarterly* 87, no. 1 (2006): 1–18.

Falk, Erika, and Kathleen Hall Jamieson. "Changing the Climate of Expectations." In *Anticipating Madam President*, ed. Robert P. Watson and Ann Gordon. Boulder, CO: Lynne Rienner, 2003.

Faludi, Susan. *Stiffed: The Betrayal of the American Man*. New York: Harper Perennial, 1999.

Farrar-Myers, Victoria A. "Emerging Trends in Presidential Campaign Finance: Early Lessons from the 2004 Campaign." Paper presented at the Annual Meeting of the American Political Science Association, Chicago, 2004.

———. "In the Wake of 1996: Clinton's Legacy for Presidential Campaign Finance." In *The Presidency and the Law: The Clinton Legacy*, ed. David Gray Adler and Michael A. Genovese. Lawrence: University Press of Kansas, 2002.

———. "One Swift Kick: The Role and Impact of 527 Groups in the 2004 Presidential Election." Paper presented at the Annual Meeting of the American Political Science Association, Washington, DC, 2005.

———. "A War Chest Full of Susan B. Anthony Dollars: Fund-Raising Issues for Female Presidential Candidates." In *Anticipating Madam President*, ed. Robert P. Watson and Ann Gordon. Boulder, CO: Lynne Rienner, 2003.

Farrell, John Aloysius. "Hillary Sticking to Guns." *Denver Post*, June 18, 2006, E1.

Federal Election Commission. *Distribution of Electoral Votes.* www.fec.gov/pages/elecvote.htm, accessed March 27, 2006.

Felix, Antonia. *Condi: The Condoleezza Rice Story.* Updated ed. New York: Newmarket Press, 2005.

Feminist Daily News Wire. February 9, 2006. "Nearly 100 Percent of Americans Would Vote for a Woman President." www.feminist.org/news/newsbyte/printnews.asp?id=9513, accessed March 25, 2006.

Ferguson, Kathy E. *The Feminist Case Against Bureaucracy.* Philadelphia: Temple University Press, 1984.

Fonder, Melanie. "Women Mayors Pushing for More Power Among Peers." Women's E-News. June 24, 2002. http://womensenews.org/article.cfm/dyn/aid/950, accessed May 26, 2006.

Ford, Lynne E. *Women and Politics: The Pursuit of Equality.* 2nd ed. Boston: Houghton Mifflin, 2006.

Fox, Richard L. *Gender Dynamics in Congressional Elections.* Thousand Oaks, CA: Sage, 1997.

Fox, Richard L., and Jennifer L. Lawless. "Entering the Arena? Gender and the Decision to Run for Office." *American Journal of Political Science* 48, no. 2 (April 2004): 264–280.

———. "Family Structure, Sex Role Socialization, and the Decision to Run for Office." *Women and Politics* 24 (2003): 19–48.

Fox, Richard L, and Zoe M. Oxley. "Gender Stereotyping in State Executive Elections: Candidate Selection and Success." *Journal of Politics* 65, no. 3 (2003): 833–850.

Fox, Richard, and Eric R.A.N. Smith. "The Role of Candidate Sex in Voter Decision-Making." *Political Psychology* 19 (1998): 405–419.

Fredrickson, Barbara L., and Kristen Harrison. "Throwing Like a Girl: Self-Objectification Predicts Adolescent Girls' Motor Performance." *Journal of Sports and Social Issues* 29, no. 1 (2005): 79–101.

Fredrickson, Barbara L., and T. A. Roberts. "Objectification Theory: Toward Understanding Women's Lived Experiences and Mental Health Risks." *Psychology of Women Quarterly* 21 (1997).

Frutkin, A. J. "The Politics of Programming: Rod Lurie Is Betting that a Female, and Independent, President Will Resonate with Politically Divided Viewers." *Mediaweek*, July 11, 2005, 16–19.

Gapinski, Katherine D., Kelly D. Brownell, and Marianne LaFrance. "Body Objectification and 'Fat Talk': Effects on Emotion, Motivation, and Cognitive Performance." *Sex Roles: A Journal of Research* (May 2003).

Gertzog, Irwin, and M. Michele Simard. "Women and the Hopeless Congressional Candidacies: Nomination Frequency, 1916–1978." *American Politics Quarterly* 9 (1981): 449–466.

Gilgoff, Dan. "Hillary's Dilemma." *US News and World Report,* November 20, 2006, 62–66.

Gilmartin, Patricia. "Still the Angel in the Household: Political Cartoons of Elizabeth Dole's Presidential Campaign." *Women and Politics* 22, no. 4 (2001): 51–67.

Givhan, Robin. "In the Oval Office, Pumps and Circumstance." *Washington Post*, May 5, 2006, C1.

———. "Something Up Their Sleeves: Gesture Is the Epitome of 'Candidate Casual.'" *Washington Post*, December 5, 2003.

Goldenberg, Suzanne. "Clinton War Chest Adds to Rumours of 2008 White House Bid." *The Guardian,* April 19, 2006, 15.

Goodman, Ellen. "TV Series May Hurry History." *Spokesman Review*, June 8, 2006.

Goodman, Tim. "Fall TV Preview: Addicted to Fall TV." *San Francisco Chronicle*, September 11, 2005, 20.

Gordon, Ann. "From the Guest Editor. A Woman President: Is America Ready?" *White House Studies* 1 (Summer, 2001).

Gordon, Ann, and Jerry Miller. "Does the Oval Office Have a Glass Ceiling? Gender Stereotypes and Perceptions of Candidate Viability." *White House Studies* 1, no. 3 (2001): 325–333.

———. "Gender, Race, and the Oval Office." In *Anticipating Madam President*, ed. Robert P. Watson and Ann Gordon. Boulder, CO: Lynne Rienner, 2003.

Greenberg, Anna. "Race, Religiosity, and the Women's Vote." *Women and Politics* 22, no. 3 (2001): 59–82.

Greenstein, Fred I. *The Presidential Difference: Leadership Style from FDR to George W. Bush.* 2nd ed. Princeton, NJ: Princeton University Press, 2004.

Gunderson, Dan. "Coya's Story." Minnesota Public Radio, http://news.minnesota.publicradio.org/features/2004/05/16_gundersond_coya/, accessed August 1, 2006.

Gurwitt, Rob. "How to Win Friends and Repair a City." *Governing*, April 2004, 22–27.

Hampson, Rick. "Lieutenants Rise in Rank." *USA Today*, July 24, 2005. www.usatoday.com/news/nation/2005-07-24-lt-governors_xx.htm, accessed May 26, 2006.

Han, Lori Cox. "Presidential Leadership: Governance from a Woman's Perspective." In *Anticipating Madam President*, ed. Robert P. Watson and Ann Gordon. Boulder, CO: Lynne Rienner, 2003.

———. *Women and American Politics: The Challenges of Political Leadership*. Boston: McGraw-Hill, 2007.

Healy, Patrick. "For Clintons, Delicate Dance of Married and Public Lives." *New York Times,* May 23, 2006, D1.

Heith, Diane J. "Footwear, Lipstick, and an Orthodox Sabbath: Media Coverage of Nontraditional Candidates." *White House Studies* 1, no. 3 (2001): 335–348.

———. "The Lipstick Watch: Media Coverage, Gender, and Presidential Campaigns." In *Anticipating Madam President*, ed. Robert P. Watson and Ann Gordon. Boulder, CO: Lynne Rienner, 2003.

Heldman, Caroline. "The Political Consequences of Female Objectification." Unpublished essay, 2006.

Heldman, Caroline, Susan J. Carroll, and Stephanie Olson. "'She Brought Only a Skirt': Print Media Coverage of Elizabeth Dole's Bid for the Republican Nomination." *Political Communication* 22 (2005): 315–335.

Heldman, Caroline, and Jennifer Holmes. "Consumer Culture and the Gaze." Paper presented at the annual meeting of the Western Political Science Association, March 2005, Oakland, Calif.

Herrnson, Paul S. "Do Parties Make a Difference? The Role of Party Organizations in Congressional Elections." *Journal of Politics* 48, no. 3 (1986): 589–615.

———. *Playing Hardball: Campaigning for the US Congress.* Upper Saddle River, NJ: Prentice Hall, 2001.

———. "The Importance of Party Campaigning." *Polity* 20, no. 4 (1988): 714–719.

Hochschild, Arlie Russell, with Anne Machung. *The Second Shift: Working Parents and the Revolutions at Home*. New York: Viking, 1989.

Hogg, Michael A. "Organizational Orthodoxy and Corporate Autocrats: Some Nasty Consequences of Organizational Identification in Uncertain Times." In *Identity and the Modern Organization,* ed. Caroline A. Bartel, Steven L. Blader, and Amy Wrzesniewski. Mahwah, NJ: Erlbaum, 2005.

———. "Uncertainty, Social Identity, and Ideology." In *Advances in Group Processes,* ed. Shaun R. Thye and Edward J. Lawler. Vol. 22. San Diego: Elsevier, 2005, 203–229.

Holsti, Ole R., and James N. Rosenau. "Gender and the Political Beliefs of American Opinion Leaders." In *Women in World Politics*, ed. Francine D'Amico and Peter R. Beckman. Westport, CT: Bergin and Garvey, 1995.

Holtzman, Elizabeth, and Shirley Williams. "Women in the Political World: Observations." *Daedalus* 116 (1987): 199–210.

Huddy, Leonie. "The Political Significance of Voters' Gender Stereotypes." In *Research in Micropolitics: New Directions in Political Psychology.* Greenwich, CT: JAI Press, 1994.

Huddy, Leonie, and Nayda Terkildsen. "The Consequences of Gender Stereotypes for Women Candidates at Different Levels and Types of Office." *Political Research Quarterly* 46 (1993): 503–525.

———. "Gender Stereotypes and the Perception of Male and Female Candidates." *American Journal of Political Science* 37 (1993): 119–147.

Htun, Mala. "What It Means to Study Gender and the State." *Politics and Gender* 1 (March 2005): 157–166.

Hult, Karen M., and MaryAnne Borrelli. "Organizational Interpretation or Objective Data? Examining the US Presidency through the *Government Manual*." Paper presented at the annual meeting of the American Political Science Association, Washington, DC, September 2005.

Hult, Karen M., and Charles E. Walcott. *Empowering the White House: Governance Under Nixon, Ford, and Carter*. Lawrence: University Press of Kansas, 2004.

Institute for Women's Policy Research. *The Status of Women in the States.* Washington, DC: Institute for Women's Policy Research, 2001.

Iyengar, Shanto, and Donald R. Kinder. *News That Matters: Television and Public Opinion.* Chicago: University of Chicago Press, 1987.

Iyengar, Shanto, Nicholas A. Valentino, Stephen Ansolabehere, and Adam F. Simon. "Running as a Woman: Gender Stereotyping in Women's Campaigns." In *Women, Media, and Politics,* ed. Pippa Norris. New York: Oxford University Press, 1997.

Jacobson, Gary C. *The Politics of Congressional Elections.* 4th ed. New York: Longman, 1997.

Jalalzai, Farida. "Women Political Leaders: Past and Present." *Women and Politics* 26, nos. 3–4 (2004): 85–108.

Jamieson, Kathleen Hall. *Beyond the Double Bind: Woman and Leadership.* New York: Oxford University Press, 1995.

Johnson, Cathy Marie, Georgia Duerst-Lahti, and Noelle H. Norton. *Creating Gender: The Sexual Politics of Welfare Policy.* Boulder, CO: Lynne Rienner, 2007.

Kahn, Kim Fridkin. "The Distorted Mirror: Press Coverage of Women Candidates for Statewide Office." *Journal of Politics* 54 (1994): 497–517.

———. "Does Being Male Help? An Investigation of the Effects of Candidate Gender and Campaign Coverage on Evaluations of US Senate Candidates." *Journal of Politics* 54, no. 2 (1992): 497–517.

———. "Does Gender Make a Difference? An Experimental Examination of Sex Stereotypes and Press Patterns in Statewide Campaigns." *American Journal of Political Science* 38 (1994): 162–195.

———. "Gender Differences in Campaign Messages: The Political Advertisements of Men and Women Candidates for US Senate." *Political Research Quarterly* 46 (1993): 481–502.

———. *The Political Consequences of Being a Woman: How Stereotypes Influence the Conduct and Consequences of Political Campaigns.* New York: Columbia University Press, 1996.

Kahn, Kim Fridkin, and Edie N. Goldenberg. "Women Candidates in the News: An Examination of Gender Differences in US Senate Campaign Coverage." *Public Opinion Quarterly* 55 (1991): 190–199.

Kahn, Kim Fridkin, and Patrick J. Kenney. "Do Negative Campaigns Mobilize or Suppress Turnout? Clarifying the Relationship Between Negativity and Participation." *American Political Science Review* 93, no. 4 (1999): 877–889.

Kahn, Kim Fridkin, and Ann Gordon. "How Women Campaign for the US Senate." In *Women, Media, and Politics,* ed. Pippa Norris. New York: Oxford University Press, 1997.

Kann, Mark E. *A Republic of Men: The American Founders, Gendered Languages, and Patriarchal Politics.* New York: New York University Press, 1998.

Karabel, Jerome. *The Chosen: The Hidden History of Admission and*

Exclusion at Harvard, Yale, and Princeton. Boston: Houghton Mifflin, 2005.

Kathlene, Lyn. "In a Different Voice: Women and the Policy Process." In *Women and Elective Office: Past, Present, and Future*, ed. Sue Thomas and Clyde Wilcox. New York: Oxford University Press, 1998.

———. "Power and Influence in State Legislative Policymaking: The Interaction of Gender and Position in Committee Hearing Debates." *American Political Science Review* 88 (1994): 560–576.

Kaufman, Karen M. "The Partisan Paradox: Religious Commitment and the Gender Gap in Party Identification." *Public Opinion Quarterly* 68, no. 4 (2004): 491–512.

Kedrowski, Karen, and Marilyn Stine Sarow. "The Gendering of Cancer Policy: Media Advocacy and Congressional Policy Attention," In *Women Transforming Congress*, ed. Cindy Simon Rosenthal. Norman: University of Oklahoma Press, 2002.

Keen, Judy, and Jill Lawrence. "Nominees Hope Heavy Hitters Will Help." *USA Today,* October 21, 2004.

Keeter, Scott. "Public Opinion in 1984." In *The Election of 1984*, ed. Gerald M. Pomper. New York: Chatham House, 1985.

Kelly, Rita Mae. *The Gendered Economy: Work, Careers, and Success.* Thousand Oaks, CA: Sage, 1991.

Kennedy, Carole. "Is America Ready for a Woman President? Is the Pope Protestant? Does a Bear Live in the City?" *White House Studies* 1, no. 3 (Summer 2001).

Kenney, Sally J. "Field Essay: New Research on Gendered Political Institutions." *Political Research Quarterly* 49 (1996): 445–466.

Kenski, Kate, and Erika Falk. "Of What Is the Glass Ceiling Made? A Study of Attitudes About Women and the Oval Office." *Women and Politics* 26, no. 2 (November 2004).

Kerry, John. "Acceptance Speech at the Democratic National Convention." Boston, 29 July 2004. www.washingtonpost.com/wp-dyn/articles/A25678-2004Jul29.html.

———. "Announcement Speech," Patriot's Point, South Carolina, September 2, 2003. www.4president.org/speeches/johnkerry2004announcement.htm, accessed May 31, 2006.

Kilbourne, Jean. "Still Killing Us Softly: Advertising and the Obsession with Thinness." In *Feminist Perspectives on Eating Disorders,* ed. P. Fallon, M. A. Katzman, and S. C. Wooley. New York: Guilford Press, 1994.

Kinder, D. R., Mark D. Peters, Robert P. Abelson, and Susan T. Fiske. "Presidential Prototypes." *Political Behavior* 2, no. 4 (1980): 315–337.

King, Cheryl Simrell. "Sex Role Identity and Decision Styles: How Gender Helps Explain the Paucity of Women at the Top." In *Gender Power, Leadership, and Governance,* ed. Georgia Duerst-Lahti and Rita Mae Kelly. Ann Arbor: University of Michigan Press, 2005.

King, David C., and Richard E. Matland. "Sex and the Grand Old Party: An Experimental Investigation of the Effect of Candidate Sex on Support for a Republican Candidate." *American Politics Research* 31, no. 6 (2003): 595–612.

Kirkpatrick, Jeanne. *Political Women.* New York: Basic Books, 1974.

Klatch, Rebecca. "Women of the New Right in the United States: Family, Feminism, and Politics." *Identity Politics and Women.* Boulder: Westview, 1994.

Koch, Jeffrey. "Candidate Gender and Assessments of Senate Candidates." *Social Science Quarterly* 80 (1999): 84–96.

———. "Do Citizens Apply Gender Stereotypes to Infer Candidates' Ideological Orientations?" *Journal of Politics* 62 (2000): 414–429.

———. "Gender Stereotypes and Citizens' Impressions of House Candidates Ideological Orientations." *American Journal of Political Science* 46 (2002): 453–462.

Krasno, Jonathan S. *Challengers, Competition, and Reelection: Comparing Senate and House Elections.* New Haven: Yale University Press, 1994.

Kropf, Martha, and John A. Boiney. "The Electoral Glass Ceiling? Gender, Viability, and the News in US Senate Campaigns." *Women and Politics* 23 (2001): 79–103.

Kumar, Martha Joynt, and Terry Sullivan, eds. *The White House World: Transitions, Organization, and Office Operations.* College Station: Texas A&M University Press, 2003.

Kurtz, Howard. "Jeff Gannon Admits Past 'Mistakes,' Berates Critics." *Washington Post*, February 19, 2005, C1.

Larson, Stephanie Greco. "'Running as Women'? A Comparison of Female and Male Pennsylvania Assembly Candidates' Campaign Brochures." *Women and Politics* 22, no. 2 (2001): 107–124.

Lawless, Jennifer L. "Women, War, and Winning Elections: Gender Stereotyping in the Post–September 11th Era." *Political Research Quarterly* 57, no. 3 (2004): 479–490.

Lawless, Jennifer L., and Richard L. Fox. *It Takes a Candidate: Why Women Don't Run for Office.* New York: Cambridge University Press, 2005.

———. "Why Don't Women Run for Political Office?" Brown Policy Report. Taubman Center for Public Policy, Brown University, 2004.

Leeper, Mark S. "The Impact of Prejudice on Female Candidates: An Experimental Look at Voter Inference." *American Politics Quarterly* 19 (1991): 248–261.

Levy, Ariel. *Female Chauvinist Pigs: Women and the Rise of Raunch Culture.* New York: Free Press, 2005.

Levy, Dena, Charles Tien, and Rachell Aved. "Do Differences Matter? Women Members of Congress and the Hyde Amendment." *Women and Politics* 23 (2001): 105–128.

Lieberman, Michelle, and Linda Mooney. "Southern Attitudes Toward Working Women." Southern Sociological Society, 2001.

Lottes, Ilsa L., and Peter J. Kuriloff. "The Effects of Gender, Race, Religion, and Political Orientation on the Sex Role Attitudes of College Freshmen." *Adolescence* 27, no. 107 (1992): 675–688.

Lovinduski, Joni, and Pippa Norris. *Gender and Party Politics*. London: Sage, 1993.

Mandel, Ruth B. *In the Running: The New Woman Candidate*. New York: Ticknor and Fields, 1981.

Martin, Janet M. *The Presidency and Women: Promise, Performance, and Illusion.* College Station: Texas A&M University Press, 2003.

Masci, David. *CQ Researcher: Religion and Politics*. Washington, DC: Congressional Quarterly Press, 2004.

Matschiner, Melannie, and Sarah K. Murnen. "Hyperfemininity and Influence." *Psychology of Women Quarterly* 23, no. 3 (1999): 631–642.

Matthews, Donald R. "Legislative Recruitment and Legislative Careers." *Legislative Studies Quarterly* 9, no. 4 (1984): 547–585.

Mayhead, Molly A., and Brenda Devore Marshall. *Women's Political Discourse: A Twenty-First Century Perspective*. Lanham, MD: Rowman and Littlefield, 2005.

McClain, Paula D., Niambi M. Carter, and Michael C. Brady. "Gender and Black Presidential Politics: From Chisholm to Moseley Braun." In *Gendering Politics and Policy: Recent Developments in Europe, Latin America, and the United States*, ed. Heidi Hartmann. Binghamton, NY: Haworth Political Press, 2006.

McClain, Paula D., Niambi M. Carter, and Michael C. Brady. "Gender and Black Presidential Politics: From Chisholm to Moseley Braun." *Journal of Women, Politics and Policy* 27, nos. 1–2 (2005): 51–68.

McDermott, Monika. "Voting Cues in Low-information Elections: Candidate Gender as a Social Information Variable in Contemporary United States Elections." *American Journal of Political Science* 41, no. 1: 270–283.

McDonald, Forrest. *The American Presidency: An Intellectual History*. Lawrence: University Press of Kansas, 1994.

McDonnell, Patrick J., and Eva Vergara. "Chile's First Female President Sworn In." *Los Angeles Times*, March 12, 2006, A3.

McGlen, Nancy E., and Meredith Reid Sarkees. "Foreign Policy Decision Makers: The Impact of Gender." In *The Impact of Women in Public Office*, edited by Susan J. Carroll. Bloomington: Indiana University Press, 2001.

McKee, J. P., and A. C. Sherriffs. "The Differential Evaluation of Males and Females." *Journal of Personality* 25 (1957): 356–371.

McKinnon, Catherine. *Feminism Unmodified*. Cambridge, MA: Harvard University Press, 1987.

Mead, Frank S., and Samuel S. Hill. *Handbook of Denominations in the United States*. 11th ed. Nashville, TN: Abingdon Press, 2001.

Media Matters for America. "Cameron's Fake Kerry Story Capped FOX Commentators' Manicure Fixation." www.mediamatters.org, October 4, 2004.

Menand, Louis. "Permanent Fatal Errors: Postcard from Stanford." *New Yorker*, December 6, 2004.

Merolla, Jennifer, Jean Reith Schroedel, and Mirya Holman. "The Paradox of Protestantism and Women in Elected Office in the United States." Claremont Graduate University, Working Paper, 2005.

Merritt, Sharyne. "Winners and Losers: Sex Differences in Municipal Elections." *American Journal of Political Science* 21 (1977): 731–743.

Mezey, Susan Gluck. "Does Sex Make a Difference? A Case Study of Women in Politics." *Western Political Quarterly* 31 (1978): 492–501.

Miller, Pat. "From Paradigm to Parody: War and the Shifting Sands of American Manhood." *West Virginia University Philological Papers* 1 (Fall 2004): 117–123.

"Month-by-Month." Infoplease, Pearson Education, July 29, 2006. www.infoplease.com/ipa/A0878626.html.

Morin, Richard, and Megan Rosenfeld. "With More Equity, More Sweat." *Washington Post*, March 22, 1998, A1.

Moore, Robert G. "Religion, Race, and Gender Differences in Political Ambition." *Politics and Gender* 1 (December 2005): 577–596.

Morris, Dick, and Eileen McGann. *Condi vs. Hillary: The Next Great Presidential Race*. New York: Regan Books, 2005.

———. *Rewriting History*. New York: Regan Books, 2004.

Mosk, Matthew, and John Wagner. "Steele Running Against History: Lt. Governors' Little Luck in Md." *Washington Post*, August 7, 2005, C1.

Muehlenkamp, Jennifer J., and Renee Saris-Baglama. "Self-Objectification and Its Psychological Outcomes for College Women." *Psychology of Women Quarterly* 26 (2002).

Mueller, C. "Nurturance and Mastery: Competing Qualifications for Women's Access to High Public Office?" *Research in Politics and Society* 2 (1986): 211–232.

Mundy, Liza. "Why Janet Reno Fascinates, Confounds, and Even Terrifies America." *Washington Post*, January 25, 1998, W6.

Murnen, Sarah K., Linda Smolak, J. Andrew Mills, and Lindsey Good. "Thin, Sexy Women and Strong, Muscular Men: Grade-School Children's Responses to Objectified Images of Women and Men." *Sex Roles: A Journal of Research* 49 (November 2003).

Murray, Robert K., and Tim H. Blessing. *Greatness in the White House: Rating the Presidents from George Washington Through Ronald Reagan.* 2nd ed. University Park: Pennsylvania State University Press: 1994.

Naff, Katherine C. *To Look Like America: Dismantling Barriers for Women and Minorities in Government.* Boulder, CO: Westview, 2001.

National Association of Attorneys General. "Full Contact List for the Attorneys General." www.naas.org/ag/full_ag_table.php, accessed May 26, 2006.

National Association of Secretaries of State. "The Office of the Secretary of State." www.nass.org, accessed May 19, 2006.

———. "Patterns of Public Service." www.nass.org, accessed May 19, 2006.

———. "Qualifications for Secretary of State" and "Additional Duties and Responsibilities." www.nass.org, accessed May 19, 2006.

———. "Secretaries Who Became Governors." www.nass.org, accessed May 19, 2006.

National Governors Association. "Governors." www.nga.org, accessed March through May 2006.

———. "Governors' Chiefs of Staff." www.nga.org, accessed May 25, 2006.

National Lieutenant Governors Association. "Projects: Team Election Data." www.nlga.us/Projects/Team percent20Election percent20Data.htm, accessed May 26, 2006.

National Security Strategy of the United States of America, September 2002. www.whitehouse.gov/nsc/nss.pdf, accessed May 31, 2006.

Niven, David. "Party Elites and Women Candidates: The Shape of Bias." *Women and Politics* 19 (1998): 57–80.

Noll, Stephanie M., and Barbara Fredrickson. "A Mediated Model Linking Self-Objectification, Body Shame, and Disordered Eating." *Psychology of Women Quarterly*, no. 4 (December 22, 1998).

Norlinger, Jay. "Political Virility: Real Men Vote Republican." *WSJ.com Opinion Journal.* September 17, 2003, www.opinionjournal.com, accessed March 8, 2005.

Norris, Pippa. "Conclusions: Comparing Legislative Recruitment." In *Gender and Party Politics*, ed. Joni Lovenduski and Pippa Norris. London: Sage, 1993.

Norton, Noelle H. "Transforming Policy from the Inside: Participation in Committee." In *Women Transforming Congress*, ed. Cindy Simon Rosenthal. Norman: University of Oklahoma Press, 2002.

Norton, Noelle, and Barbara Norris. "Feminist Organizational Structure in the White House: The Office of the Women's Initiative and Outreach." *Political Research Quarterly* 56, no. 4 (December 2003): 477–487.

O'Brien, Timothy L. "Up the Down Staircase: Why Do So Few Women Reach the Top of Big Law Firms?" *New York Times,* March 19, 2006, C4.

Opfell, Olga S. *Women Prime Ministers and Presidents.* Jefferson, NC: McFarland and Company, 1993.

O'Regan, Valeria. *Gender Matters: Female Policymakers' Influence in Industrialized Nations.* Westport, CT: Praeger, 2000.

Oxley, Zoe M., and Richard L. Fox. "Women in Executive Office: Variation Across American States," *Public Research Quarterly* 57, no. 1 (2004).

Paletz, David L. *The Media in American Politics: Contents and Consequences.* New York: Longman, 2002.

Palley, Marion Lief. "Women's Policy Leadership in the United States." *PS: Political Science and Politics* 34 (June 2001): 247–250.

Parsons, T., and R. F. Bales. *Family Socialization and Interaction Process.* New York: Free Press, 1955.

Patterson, Thomas E. "Doing Well and Doing Good: How Soft News and Critical Journalism Are Shrinking the News Audience and Weakening Democracy—and What News Outlets Can Do About It." Joan Shorenstein Center for Press, Politics, and Public Policy, John F. Kennedy School of Government, Harvard University, 2000.

———. *The Mass Media Election.* New York: Praeger, 1980.

———. *Out of Order*. New York: Vintage Books, 1994.

Peek, Charles W., and Sharon Brown. "Sex Prejudice Among White Protestants: Like or Unlike Ethnic Prejudice?" *Social Forces* 59 (1980): 169–185.

Pew Research Center for the People and the Press. "Abortion and Rights of Terror Suspects Top Court Issues." August 3, 2005. http://people-press.org/reports/display.php3?ReportID=253, accessed May 1, 2006.

———. "Race Tightens Again, Kerry's Image Improves: Democrats, Blacks Less Confident in Accurate Vote Count." October 20, 2004. http://people-press.org/reports/display.php3?ReportID=229.

———. "Religion and the Presidential Vote: Bush Gains Broad-Based." December 6, 2004. http://people-press.org/commentary/display.php3?AnalysisID=103, accessed May 1, 2006.

Podhoretz, John. *Can She Be Stopped? Hillary Clinton Will Be the Next President of the United States Unless . . .* New York: Crown Forum, 2006.

Polgreen, Lydia, and Larry Rohter. "Where Political Clout Demands a Maternal Touch." *New York Times*, January 22, 2006, D4.

"Poll: Majority Ready for Woman President." *USA Today*, February 22, 2005.

Pomper, Gerald M. "The Presidential Election." In *The Election of 1984*, ed. Gerald M. Pomper. New York: Chatham House, 1985.

Poniewoznik, James. "Hail to the She: TVs Woman President Has Stature, but Can She Surmount the Double Standards?" *Time*, September 26, 2005, 90.

Powell, Stewart M. "Poll Finds Readiness for Female President." *Houston Chronicle*, February 20, 2006, A1.

Quintanilla, Michael. "Premiere Vision: The First Spring-Summer Collection of the Millennium." *Los Angeles Times*, March 26, 1999.

Rainey, James. "Who's the Man? They Are; George Bush and John Kerry State Shoulder to Shoulder in One Respect: Macho Is Good. Very Good. It's Been That Way Since Jefferson's Day." *Los Angeles Times*, March 18, 2004.

Ranney, Austin. "Parties in State Politics." In *Politics in the American States,* ed. Herbert Jacob and Kenneth N. Vines. 2nd edition. Boston: Little, Brown, 1971.

Rashotte, Lisa Slattery, and Murray Webster, Jr. "Gender Status Beliefs." *Social Science Research* 34 (2005): 618–633.

Rasmussen Reports. "72% Say They're Willing to Vote for Woman President: Just 49% Think Most of Their Friends Would Do the Same." www.rasumssenreports.com, 2005.

Reid, Margaret F., Brinck Kerr, and Will Miller. *Glass Walls and Glass Ceilings: Women's Representation in State and Municipal Bureaucracies*. Westport, CT: Praeger, 2003.

Rhode, Deborah L. *Speaking of Sex: The Denial of Gender Inequality.* Cambridge, MA: Harvard University Press, 1997.

Rice, Condoleezza. "Promoting the National Interest." *Foreign Affairs* (January–February 2000).

"Rice Rules Out '08 Presidential Run." *Chicago Tribune*, January 17, 2006, 8.

Rich, Frank. "How Kerry Became a Girlie-Man." *New York Times*, September 5, 2004, sec 2, 1.

Riggle, Ellen, Penny Miller, Todd G. Shields, and Mitzi Johnson. "Gender Stereotypes and Decision Context in the Evaluation of Political Candidates." *Women and Politics* 17 (1997).

Roberts, Tomi-Ann. "Female Trouble: The Menstrual Self-Evaluation Scale and Women's Self-Objection." *Psychology of Women Quarterly* 28 (March 2004).

Romano, Lois. "Beyond the Poll Numbers, Voter Doubts About Clinton." *Washington Post*, July 13, 2006, A1.

Rosenwasser, Shirley M., and Norma Dean. "Gender Role and Political Office: Effects of Perceived Masculinity/Femininity of Candidate and Political Office." *Psychology of Women Quarterly* 13 (1989): 77–85.

Rosenwasser, Shirley M., and Jana Seale. "Attitudes Toward a Hypothetical Male or Female Candidate—a Research Note." *Political Psychology* 9 (1988): 591–599.

Rowat, Alison. "There's a Female President on TV: So Can There Be One in the White House by 2008? It's About Time the World Found Out." *Glasgow Herald*, May 12, 2006, 2.

Ruben, Ann Moliver. "Someday a Woman Will Be President! (Commentary)." *White House Studies* 2, no. 3 (Summer 2002): 331–338.

Ryan, Suzanne. "All Hail the Chief." *Boston Globe*, September 27, 2005, 4.

Sabato, Larry J. *Feeding Frenzy: Attack Journalism and American Politics*. Baltimore: Lanahan Publishers, 2000.

Saidel, Judith R., and Karyn Lococco. "Agency Leaders, Gendered Institutions, and Representative Bureaucracy." *Public Administration Review* 65 (March–April 2005): 158–170.

Saint-Germain, Michelle A. "Does Their Difference Make a Difference? The Impact of Women on Public Policy in the Arizona Legislature." *Social Science Quarterly* 70 (1989): 956–968.

Sanbonmatsu, Kira. "The Legislative Party and Candidate Recruitment in the American States." *Party Politics* 12, no. 2 (2006): 233–256.

———. "Political Knowledge and Gender Stereotypes." *American Politics Research* 31, no. 6 (2003): 575–594.

———. "Political Parties and the Recruitment of Women to State Legislatures." *Journal of Politics* 64, no. 3 (2002).

Sapiro, Virginia. "If US Senator Baker Were a Woman: An Experimental Study of Candidate Images." *Political Psychology* 3 (Spring–Summer 1981–1982): 161–183.

———. "Private Costs of Public Commitments or Public Costs of Private Commitments? Family Roles Versus Political Ambition." *American Journal of Political Science* 26, no. 2 (May 1982): 265–279.

———. *The Political Integration of Women.* Urbana: University of Illinois Press, 1983.

Schattschneider, E. E. *Party Government.* New York: Holt, Rinehart, and Winston, 1942.

Schlesinger, Joseph A. *Ambition and Politics.* Chicago: Rand McNally, 1966.

Schroedel, Jean Reith, Jennifer Merolla, and Pamela Foerstel. "Women's Relative Lack of Electoral Success in the United States." *Human Rights Global Focus* 2, no. 3 (2005): 5–13.

Schroedel, Jean Reith, and Marcia L. Godwin. "Prospects for Cracking the Political Glass Ceiling: The Future of Women Officeholders in the Twenty-First Century." In *Women and Elective Office: Past, Present, and Future*, edited by Sue Thomas and Clyde Wilcox. 2nd ed. New York: Oxford University Press, 2005.

Schultz, Jeffrey D., John G. West, and Iain Maclean. *Encyclopedia of Religion in American Politics.* Phoenix, AZ: Oryx Press, 1999.

Sciolino, Elaine. "Is France Ready to Elect a Woman? This Woman Seems to Think So, and Men Agree." *New York Times,* April 7, 2006, A12.

Sears, David O., Colette van Laar, Mary Carillo, and Rick Kosterman. "Is It Really Racism? The Origins of White Americans' Opposition to Race-Targeted Policies." Center for Research in Society and Politics, February 1997.

Seelye, Katharine Q. "Moral Values Cited as a Defining Issue of the Election." *New York Times*, November 4, 2004, P4.

Seltzer, Richard A., Jody Newman, and Melissa Voorhees Leighton. *Sex as a Political Variable: Women as Candidates and Voters in US Elections.* Boulder, CO: Lynne Rienner, 1997.

Shales, Tom. "Geena Davis Sweeps Up the Oval Office." *Washington Post*, Tuesday, September 27, 2005, C1.

Sheehy, Gail. *Hillary's Choice.* New York: Random House, 1999.

Sherkat, Darren E. "'That They Be Keepers of the Home': The Effect of Conservative Religion on Early and Late Transitions into Housewifery." *Review of Religious Research* 41 (March 2000): 344–358.

Sherman, Janaan. *No Place for a Woman: A Life of Senator Margaret Chase Smith.* New Brunswick, NJ: Rutgers University Press, 2000.

Sherriffs, A. C., and J. P. McKee. "Qualitative Aspects of Beliefs About Men and Women." *Journal of Personality* 25 (1957): 451–464.

Sigelman, Lee, Carol K. Sigelman, and Christopher Fowler. "A Bird of a Different Feather? An Experimental Investigation of Physical Attractiveness and the Electability of Female Candidates." *Social Psychology Quarterly* 50, no. 1 (March 1987): 32–43.

Simon, Stephanie. "Abortion Ban Foes Petition for a Choice." *Los Angeles Times*, April 9, 2006, A1 and A15.

Slater, Amy, and Marika Tiggeman. "A Test of Objectification Theory in Adolescent Girls." *Sex Roles: A Journal of Research* (May 2002).

Smith, Dan. "Voters Think US Ready for Woman as President." *Sacramento Bee,* March 10, 2006, A5.

Smith, R. Jeffrey. "Sexual Assaults in Army on Rise: Report Blames Poor Oversight and Training." *Washington Post,* June 3, 2004, A1.

Snyder, Claire. *Citizen-Soldiers and Manly Warriors: Military Service and Gender in the Civic Republican Tradition*. Lanham, MD: Rowman and Littlefield, 1999.

Stacey, Judith. "The Rhetoric and Politics of 'Family Values' Discourse in the USA." International Sociological Association, 1994.

Stammer, Larry B. "A Wife's Role Is 'to Submit,' Baptists Declare." *Los Angeles Times*, June 10, 1998, A1, A26, and A27.

Stateline.org. *State of the States: A Stateline.org Report—2006 State Policy Developments and Trends*. Washington, DC: Stateline.org, 2006.

Stephens, D. L., R. P. Hill, and C. Hanson. "The Beauty Myth and Female Consumers: The Controversial Role of Advertising." *Journal of Consumer Affairs* 28 (1994).

Strambough, Stephen J., and Valeria O'Regan. "A Novelty No More: The Changing Politics of Female Gubernatorial Candidates." Paper presented at the annual meeting of the Western Political Science Association, Albuquerque, NM, March 16–18, 2006.

Swatos, William H. "The Politics of Gender and the 'Two-party' Thesis in American Protestantism." *Social Compass* 44, no. 1 (1997): 23–35.

Swers, Michelle L. *The Difference Women Make: The Policy Impact of Women in Congress*. Chicago: University of Chicago Press, 2002.

Swope, Christopher. "Spurning Spin: Atlanta's Mayor Leads with Candor and Can-Do-Ism." *Governing*. November 2004. www.governing.com/poy/2004/franklin.htm, accessed May 30, 2006.

Tamerius, Karin L. "Sex, Gender, and Leadership in the Representation of Women." In *Gender Power, Leadership, and Governance*, ed. Georgia Duerst-Lahti and Rita Mae Kelly. Ann Arbor: University of Michigan Press, 1995.

Tenpas, Katherine Dunn. "Women on the White House Staff: A Longitudinal Analysis, 1939–1994." In *The Other Elites: Women, Politics, and Power in the Executive Branch*, ed. MaryAnne Borrelli and Janet M. Martin. Boulder, CO: Lynne Rienner, 1997.

Thomas, Sue. *How Women Legislate*. New York: Oxford University Press, 1994.

———. "Introduction: Women and Elective Office: Past, Present, and Future." In *Women and Elective Office,* ed. Sue Thomas and Clyde Wilcox. New York: Oxford University Press, 1998.

———. "The Personal Is Political: Antecedents of Gendered Choices of Elected Representatives." *Sex Roles: A Journal of Research* (2002): 343–353.

Thomas, Sue, and Clyde Wilcox, eds. *Women and Elective Office: Past, Present, and Future*. 2nd ed. New York: Oxford University Press, 2005.

Tolleson-Rinehart, Sue. "Do Women Leaders Make a Difference? Substance, Style, and Perceptions." In *The Impact of Women in Public Office*, ed. Susan J. Carroll. Bloomington: Indiana University Press, 2001.

Tyrrell, R. Emmett, Jr., with Mark W. Davis. *Madame Hillary: The Dark Road to the White House*. Washington, DC: Regnery Publishing, 2004.

US Conference of Mayors. "Women's Mayors' Group." www.usmayors.org/uscm/about/affiliate_organizations/elected_a.., accessed May 26, 2006.

US Department of Labor, Bureau of Labor Statistics. "Labor Force Statistics from the Current Population Survey." www.bls.gov/cps/wlf-databook2005.htm, accessed February 24, 2006.

US Department of State. "Senior Officials," available at www.state.gov.

US Government Manual, available at http://www.gpoaccess.gov/gmanual/index.html.

US Office of Personnel Management. "The Fact Book," available at www.opm.gov.

Vega, Arturo, and Juanita M. Firestone. "The Effects of Gender on Congressional Behavior and Substantive Representation of Women." *Legislative Studies Quarterly* 20 (1995): 213–222.

Vock, Daniel C. "Katrina Alters Vista for Barbour, Blanco." Stateline.org, January 2, 2006. www.stateline.org/live/ViewPage.action?siteNodeld=137andlanguageld=1..., accessed January 9, 2006.

Walsh, Katherine Cramer. "Enlarging Representation: Women Bringing Marginalized Perspectives to Floor Debate in the House of Representatives." In *Women Transforming Congress,* ed. Cindy Simon Rosenthal. Norman: University of Oklahoma Press, 2002.

Watson, Robert P. "Introduction: The White House as Ultimate Prize." In *Anticipating Madam President*, ed. Robert P. Watson and Ann Gordon. Boulder, CO: Lynne Rienner, 2003.

Watson, Robert P., and Ann Gordon. "Profile: Elizabeth Dole, Executive Leadership." In *Anticipating Madam President*, ed. Robert P. Watson and Ann Gordon. Boulder, CO: Lynne Rienner, 2003.

———. "Profile: Geraldine Ferraro, Media Coverage of History in the Making." In *Anticipating Madam President*, ed. Robert P. Watson and Ann Gordon. Boulder, CO: Lynne Rienner, 2003.

———. "Profile: Pat Schroeder and the Campaign That Wasn't." In *Anticipating Madam President,* ed. Robert P. Watson and Ann Gordon. Boulder, CO: Lynne Rienner, 2003.

———. "Profile: Shirley Chisholm, Blazing Trails." In *Anticipating Madam President*, ed. Robert P. Watson and Ann Gordon. Boulder, CO: Lynne Rienner, 2003.

Wayne, Stephen J. *The Road to the White House 2004: The Politics of Presidential Elections.* New York: Thompson Wadsworth, 2004.

Wegner, David. "The Impact of Feminists: An Interview with World Magazine Editor, Marvin Olasky." *Journal for Biblical Manhood and Womanhood* 3, no. 4 (1998): 1–5.

Welch, Susan. "The Recruitment of Women to Public Office." *Western Political Quarterly* 31 (September 1978): 464–475.

Westlye, Mark C. *Senate Elections and Campaign Intensity.* Baltimore: Johns Hopkins University Press, 1991.

Whicker, Marcia Lynn, and Hedy Leonie Isaacs. "The Maleness of the American Presidency." In *Women in Politics: Outsiders or Insiders?* ed. Lois Duke Whitaker. Upper Saddle River, NJ: Prentice-Hall Press, 1999.

Whistler, Donald E., and Gary D. Wekkin. "Religion and Politics Among Southern High School Seniors: A Gender and Race Analysis." *Journal of Southern Religion* 6 (October 2003): 1–36.

White House Project. http://www.thewhitehouseproject.org/, accessed May 1, 2006.

———. "Making Ms. President a Reality." http://www.thewhitehouseproject.org/v2/programs/perception/CIC/index.html, accessed 4/2006.

Wilcox, Clyde. "The Christian Right in Twentieth Century America: Continuity and Change." *Review of Politics* 50 (1988): 659–681.

Williams, Leonard. "Gender, Political Advertising, and the Air Wars." In *Women and Elective Office: Past, Present, and Future,* ed. Sue Thomas and Clyde Wilcox. New York: Oxford University Press, 1998.

Wilson, Marie C. *Closing the Leadership Gap: How Women Can and Must Help Run the World.* New York: Viking Penguin, 2004.

———. "Is America Ready for a Woman President? (National Affairs)." *USA Today (Magazine)*, November 1, 2002, 140.

Winik, Lyric Wallwork. "Is It Time for a Woman President?" *Parade.* April 30, 2006. www.parade.com/articles/edition_04-30-2006..., accessed May 22, 2006.

Winsky Mattei, Laura R. "Gender and Power in American Legislative Discourse." *Journal of Politics* 60, no. 2 (May 1998): 440–461.

Witt, Linda, Karen M. Paget, and Glenna Matthews. *Running as a Woman: Gender and Power in American Politics.* New York: Free Press, 1994.

WNBC/Marist Poll. "National Poll: Campaign 2008, Is America Ready for a Woman President?" October 21, 2005.

Yahoo News, Entertainment. "Madonna: 'America Not Ready for a Female President.'" Monday, March 27, 2006.

Zernike, Kate. "Kerry Pressing Swift Boat Case Long After Loss." *New York Times*, May 28, 2006.

The Contributors

Meena Bose is Peter S. Kalikow Chair in Presidential Studies at Hofstra University. She is the author of *Shaping and Signaling Presidential Policy: The National Security Decision Making of Eisenhower and Kennedy* (1998); coeditor of *From Cold War to New World Order: The Foreign Policy of George H.W. Bush* (with Rosanna Perotti, 2002); and coeditor of *The Uses and Abuses of Presidential Ratings* (with Mark Landis, 2003). Her current research focuses on the changing role of the United Nations in US foreign policy.

Meredith Conroy is a doctoral student in the Department of Political Science at Purdue University. Her research interests include the presidency, gender and politics, and mass media and politics.

Georgia Duerst-Lahti is professor of political science and faculty of the Women's and Gender Studies program at Beloit College. During her time there, she has chaired both departments and served as associate dean. Her research concentrates on gendered institutions and political campaigns, with a particular focus on masculinity and masculinism. She is currently researching changing gender and leadership in public organizations. Her most recent coauthored book, *Creating Gender: The Sexual Politics of Welfare Policy*, published by Lynne Rienner (2006), develops a framework for compound gender ideology.

Victoria Farrar-Myers is associate professor of political science at the University of Texas at Arlington. She specializes in the US presidency, presidential-congressional relations, separation of powers, and campaign finance reform. Among her numerous publications, Farrar-Myers is the author of *Scripted for Change: The Institutionalization of the American Presidency* (forthcoming) and coauthor of *Legislative Labyrinth: Congress and Campaign Finance Reform* (with Diana Dwyre, 2001).

Kim L. Fridkin is professor of political science at Arizona State University. She is the author of *The Political Consequences of Being a Woman* (1996) and coauthor of *No-Holds Barred: Negative Campaigning in US Senator Campaigns* (with Patrick J. Kenney, 2003) and *The Spectacle of US Senate Campaigns* (with Patrick J. Kenney, 1999). Her current research interests include women and politics and political communication.

Ann Gordon is associate professor of political science at Chapman University in Orange, California. She is the coauthor of *When Stereotypes Collide: Race/Ethnicity, Gender, and Videostyle in Congressional Campaigns* (2005), author of *Playing Politics: An Active Learning Approach to US Government* (2004), and coeditor of *Anticipating Madam President* (2003). Her research interests include gender, race and ethnicity in politics, voting behavior, campaigns and elections, and political communication.

Lori Cox Han is professor and chair of political science at Chapman University in Orange, California. She is the author of *Governing from Center Stage: White House Communication Strategies During the Television Age of Politics* (2001), coeditor of *In the Public Domain: Presidents and the Challenge of Public Leadership* (with Diane J. Heith, 2005), author of *Women and American Politics: The Challenge of Political Leadership* (2006), and coeditor of *The Presidency and the Challenge of Democracy* (with Michael A. Genovese, 2006). Han's research focuses on the US presidency, mass media and politics, and women and politics.

Caroline Heldman is assistant professor of political science at Occidental College in Los Angeles. She specializes in gender, race, and presidential politics. Her work has appeared in the *American Political Science Review*, the *Journal of Politics*, and *Political Communications*. She has previously worked as a congressional staffer and professional pollster. She is currently working on a book examining presidential power and persuasion through the media.

Karen M. Hult is professor of political science at Virginia Polytechnic Institute and State University. She is the author of four books: *Empowering the White House: Governance Under Nixon, Ford, and Carter* (with Charles E. Walcott, 2004), *Governing the White House: From Hoover through LBJ* (with Charles E. Walcott, 1995), *Governing Public Organizations: Politics, Structures, and Institutional Design* (with Charles E. Walcott, 1990), and *Agency Merger and Bureaucratic Redesign* (1987). Her current research includes projects on the organization of speechwriting in the Reagan White House, the public presentation of the White House staff (with MaryAnne Borrelli), and a revision of *Governing Public Organizations*.

Jean Reith Schroedel is professor of politics and policy and applied women's studies program at the Claremont Graduate University. Her primary research and teaching interests are fetal policymaking, gender politics, and congressional politics. Schroedel has written numerous articles and several books. In 2001, she was awarded the American Political Science Association's prestigious Victoria Schuck Award for her most recent book, *Is the Fetus a Person? A Comparison of Policies Across the Fifty States* (2000).

Sue Thomas is senior policy researcher at the Pacific Institute for Research and Evaluation. She is formerly associate professor of government and director of women's studies at Georgetown University. Among her publications are *How Women Legislate* (1994) and *Women and Elective Office: Past, Present, and Future* (2005).

Gina Serignese Woodall is faculty associate and academic advisor in the Department of Political Science at Arizona State University. She has coauthored (with Kim Fridkin) additional research on gender, campaigns, and the media in other edited volumes.

Index

Abortion, 44, 51, 59, 62, 66, 101, 102, 143, 175
Abu Ghraib (prisoner abuse scandal), 110, 177
Adams, John, 171
Adams, John Quincy, 171
Air Force One, 9, 32
Albright, Madeleine Korbel, 156, 161
Alien, 27
Allen, George, 109
Allen, Joan, 32
Allen, Mackenzie (president on *Commander in Chief*), 1–2, 34–38, 83
Allen, Woody, 23
The American President, 32

Bachelet, Michelle, 8, 43, 82, 147, 185
Bandaranaike, Sirimavo, 185–186
Bandaranaike, Soloman, 185
Barbara Lee Family Foundation, 151, 163
Barbour, Haley, 109, 150
Bartlet, Josiah "Jed" (president on *The West Wing*), 33–35
Battlestar Galactica, 33, 36
Bauer, Gary, 78
Bayh, Evan, 109
Bay of Pigs crisis (1961), 174
Bauty culture, 28–29, 36
Bergen, Polly, 32
Biden, Joe, 109
Bingaman, Jeff, 130
Blagojevich, Rod, 109
Blair, Tony, 110
Blanco, Kathleen Babineaux, 69, 150, 151
Bochco, Steven, 34, 35
Bowles, Erskine, 157
Boxer, Barbara, 116, 125
Bradley, Bill, 129
The Brady Bunch Movie, 32
Braun, Carol Moseley, 108, 128, 163, 173
Bresden, Phil, 109
Brown, Jerry, 155
Brownback, Sam, 109
Buchanan, James, 172
Buchanan, Patrick, 173
Burns, Conrad, 130
Business PACs, 117, 120
Bush, George H.W., 22, 91, 156, 171, 175, 179, 181
Bush, George W., 7, 10, 11, 22, 23–24, 26, 50, 51, 52, 53, 55, 56, 65, 78, 79, 80, 86, 87, 88, 99, 107, 110, 124, 126, 128, 129, 130, 137, 143, 155, 156, 158, 160, 171, 176, 177, 178, 179, 180, 181, 182
Bush, Laura, 11

Candidate-centered campaigns, 134
Candidate emergence phase, 8, 107–108
Cantwell, Maria, 116, 130, 131
Carnahan, Jean, 129
Carnahan, Mel, 129
Carter, Jimmy, 7, 10, 56, 129, 156, 171
Center for American Women and Politics, 93
Chao, Elaine Lan, 155, 156
Cheney, Richard "Dick", 157,
Childrearing, 7
Child care, 44, 57, 62, 70
Chisholm, Shirley, 18, 113, 124, 128, 163, 173, 174
Citizen-soldier, 20, 24–26, 38, 39
Clark, Wesley, 107
Clinton, Bill, 7, 10, 22, 33, 56, 91, 123, 129, 156, 158, 160, 166, 179, 181, 189–190
Clinton, Hillary Rodham, 3, 4, 6, 9–11, 12, 17, 21, 29, 34, 43, 61, 76, 88, 93, 108, 109, 111, 115, 116, 125, 129, 131, 133, 143, 144, 170, 178–180, 189–190
Close, Glenn, 32
Cold War, the, 81, 174, 176
Collins, Susan, 9, 62, 67, 116, 117
Commander in Chief (ABC TV show), 1–3, 18, 33–38, 39, 43, 83
Commander in chief , 18, 21, 22, 24, 78, 81, 100, 103, 107, 137, 160, 169–170, 188
The Contender, 32, 34
Coolidge, Calvin, 171, 172
Co-verbal behaviors, coworkers, 90
Crapo, Mike, 130
Cuban Missile Crisis (1962), 174
Cuomo, Mario, 155

Daniels, Mitchell Jr., 157–158
Daschle, Tom, 109
Dave, 32
Dean, Howard, 109, 131
Debates, presidential, 23–24, 105, 107, 177, 178
Dellums, Ron, 175
De Niro, Robert, 32
DeWine, Mike, 130
Dole, Elizabeth Hanford, 4, 9, 18, 29, 37, 38, 78–81, 86, 114, 116, 124, 128, 129, 156, 157, 173, 175–176, 180, 189
Dole, Robert, 22, 176, 189
Double bind, 29, 46, 70, 91, 141
Double standard, 56–57
Douglas, Michael, 32
Dowd, Maureen, 80, 176
Dukakis, Michael, 9, 22, 23

Easley, Michael, 109
Eastwood, Clint, 32
Edwards, John, 109, 183
Ehrlich, Robert, 150
Eisenhower, Dwight D., 171
Eleanor Roosevelt Fund, 140
Electoral College, 52–55, 60, 64, 163, 172, 173, 175, 178, 181, 186
Ensign, John, 130
Equal Employment Opportunity Commission (EEOC), 12, 162
Equal Rights Amendment (ERA), 2, 35, 62, 175
Estrich, Susan, 4, 9
Evangelical Christians, 50–51, 53, 59, 63–64
"Exceptional woman," 13, 44, 46

Fallin, Mary, 165
Family values, 51, 52
Faulkner, Shannon, 25
Federal agencies, women in, 160–161
Federal Election Commission (FEC), 115–116, 129
Feingold, Russ, 109
Feinstein, Dianne, 9, 116, 131, 152
Female objectification, 20, 28–31, 37, 38, 39
Feminalism, 90, 91, 111
Femininity, 26, 29, 88, 89–93, 98, 99, 138, 140, 141, 143, 144

Feminism, 20, 27, 30, 34, 35, 44, 62, 66, 99
Feminization of candidates, 20, 22, 24
"Feminine" offices, 138, 140, 141
Ferguson, Miriam, 7, 149, 164
Ferraro, Geraldine, 6, 18, 60, 123, 173, 174, 175, 182, 188
Fillmore, Millard, 171
First Gentleman/Husband, 32, 35, 38, 190
First Lady, 34, 69, 133, 158, 166, 179, 180
Fleischer, Ari, 80
Forbes, Steve, 78, 79, 86, 123, 124, 176
Ford, Gerald, 155, 156, 157, 172, 176
Ford, Harrison, 9, 32
Fortier, Alison B., 166
Foster, Ezola, 173
Framing (by news media), 23, 57–61, 66, 79, 86, 100, 102–103, 111
Franklin, Barbara H., 156
Franklin, Shirley, 9, 151
Frist, Bill, 109
Frontloading, 113
Funding networks, 122, 125
Fundraising, 5, 13, 78, 114–121, 125, 129, 130, 140, 170, 176, 180

Gender, 90–91, 124
Gender barriers (to elected office), 2, 124
Gender bias in campaigns, 24, 26, 88–89, 140
Gender bias in media coverage (press), 8, 13, 20, 22, 36–39, 75–81, 86, 89–96, 98, 108, 136–137, 173, 175, 187, 190
Gender dualism, 91, 98
Gendered institutions, 20–21, 26, 44, 47–52, 56–57, 61, 89, 91–93, 96–98, 100, 111, 160
Gendered language, 21–22, 24, 36, 37, 88, 97, 100
Gender equality, 45, 50, 111
Gender gap, 58, 101
Gender ideology, 90, 101
Gender power, 93
Gender role identity, 22
Gender stereotype, 6, 13, 18, 31, 35, 36, 46, 49, 58, 60–61, 70–75, 76–78, 80–83, 98–99, 139, 158, 160, 163, 187
Gender, social and cultural aspects of, 13, 18, 20, 24–25, 27, 31, 35, 39, 44, 47, 50, 90–92, 124, 187
Gender socialization, 22
Gender transformation, 92–93, 96, 99, 101–102, 111
Gingrich, Newt, 23, 109, 134
Giuliani, Rudolph, 69, 109, 183
Glass ceiling, 17, 18, 157, 158, 160, 162–163, 186
Glass wall, 156, 157, 158, 160–161, 162, 163, 186
Golden Globe Awards (Best Actress in a Drama Series in 2006), 1, 34
Goldwater, Barry, 174
Goodman, Ellen, 36
GOP Women's Political Action League, 140
Gore, Al, 78, 87, 129, 177, 183
Governors, women, 7, 9, 56, 62, 65, 69, 108, 109, 126, 129, 149–151, 164
Governor's offices, women in, 162
Graham, Lindsey, 130
Granholm, Jennifer, 150
Grant, Ulysses S., 171
Grasso, Ella, 164
Great-man model of the presidency, 8, 98
Gregoire, Christine, 76
Guantanamo Bay, Cuba, 177

Hagel, Chuck, 109
Harding, Warren G., 171
Harris, Katherine, 29, 131, 154
Harris, Patricia Roberts, 156
Hart, Gary, 175
Hatfield, Mark, 155
Haysbert, Dennis, 1

Health care, 4, 10, 44, 46, 57, 70, 74, 77, 81, 100, 125, 138, 177, 179, 187
Heckler, Margaret M., 156
Herman, Alexis M., 156
"Heroic man," 97–98
Herseth, Stephanie, 130
Hills, Carla Anderson, 156
Hobby, Oveta Culp, 156
Hoffman, Dustin, 32
Horserace coverage, 78
Huckabee, Mike, 109
Hufstedtler, Shirley M., 156
Hull, Jane, 164
Hurricane Katrina, 26, 69, 110, 149, 150
Hussein, Saddam, 177
Hutchison, Kay Bailey, 9, 62, 116, 117, 131
Hypermasculinity, 20, 21, 24, 32

Ideological PACs, 120, 130
Incumbency, 7, 20, 49, 75, 81, 96, 97, 139, 140, 146, 150
Independence Day, 32
Inouye, Daniel, 130
Institutional gendering, 47–57
Internet, 4
In the Line of Fire, 32
Invisible primary, 10, 111, 114
Iraq War, 10, 11, 23, 81, 100, 103, 110, 176, 177, 178, 180, 182

Jane Austen's Mafia! 2
Jefferson, Thomas, 97, 171
Jeffords, Jim, 130
Johnson, Andrew, 171, 172
Johnson, Lyndon B., 172
Johnson-Sirleaf, Ellen, 43, 82, 185

Kay, Thalia, 152
Kennedy, Lt. Gen. Claudia, 161
Kennedy, John F., 89, 171, 180
Kerry, John, 23–24, 54, 87–88, 91, 102, 107, 109, 128, 129, 137, 177–178, 183
Keyes, Alan, 78
Kirkpatrick, Jeanne, 139, 161
Kisses for My President, 32
Kline, Kevin, 32
Knutson, Coya, 188
Korean War, 174
Kosovo, US intervention in, 176
Kreps, Juanita M., 156
Kucinich, Dennis, 108

Labor PACs, 117, 120
La Duke, Winona, 173
Landrieu, Mary, 116, 130
Lazio, Rick, 88
Leadership PACs, 125
Leadership, styles of, 5, 8, 21, 26, 31, 32–33, 46–47, 70, 72, 77
Lieutenant governors, women, 126, 153, 165
Lincoln, Abraham, 171, 172
Lockwood, Belva, 18, 172
Lurie, Rod, 34, 38
Lynch, Jessica, 25–26

MacMurray, Fred, 32
Madison, James, 171
Madonna, 17
Male/female issues, 4–5, 20, 43–44, 46, 48, 57–58, 60–61, 66, 70–71, 76–77, 81–82, 91, 100, 123, 137–138, 150, 163, 175, 187
Male gaze, 28, 30–31
Male/subject–female/object split, 28
Malkovich, John, 32
The Manchurian Candidate, 32–33
Martin, Lynn, 156
Masculinism, 90, 91, 95–96, 111
Masculinity, 13, 20–24, 26, 29, 31, 37, 38, 87–89, 90–93, 96–99, 101–103, 105, 108–109, 111, 137, 138, 142–143, 187
Masculinity and the presidency, 20–21, 79, 88, 96, 98, 138, 187
Mayors, women, 151–152
McCain, John, 78, 79, 109, 124, 129, 176, 183

McCarthy, Joseph, 174
McGinty, Kathleen A., 166
McGovern, George, 19, 174
McGrory, Mary, 80
McKinney, Cynthia, 131
McLaughlin, Ann Dore, 156
Media coverage of woman candidates, 8, 13, 20, 22, 29, 75–81, 85, 86, 88–89, 173, 175, 187
Meir, Golda, 181
Merkel, Angela, 43, 82, 185
Miers, Harriet, 158
Mind/body dichotomy, 29, 30
Minner, Ruth Ann, 164
Mofford, Rose, 155
Molnau, Carol, 153
Mondale, Walter, 6, 18, 173, 175
Monroe, James, 171
Morris, Dick, 4, 9, 11, 180
Murray, Patty, 116

Nader, Ralph, 129, 173
Napolitano, Janet, 9, 62, 67, 108, 109, 150
National Association of Evangelicals (NAE), 51–55, 64–65
National security, 4–5, 13, 26, 83, 137, 157, 160, 169–170, 172, 175–180, 183, 187–188
National Security Strategy (2002), 177
9/11, 5, 26, 47, 58, 69, 81, 82, 100, 111, 170, 176, 188
9/11 Commission, 101, 102
Nixon, Richard M., 19, 157, 158, 159, 171
Nolan, Beth, 158
NYPD Blue, 1

Obama, Barack, 3, 10–11, 183
O'Leary, Hazel R., 156
O'Reilly, Bill, 23
Othering, 22, 25, 27

Palmer, David (president on *24*), 1
Party support (for women candidates), 5, 134–136
Pataki, George, 109, 183
Pawlenty, Tim, 109
Pelosi, Nancy, 7, 29, 83, 125
Perkins, Frances, 92, 156
Perot, H. Ross, 123
Personality traits (male/female), 45–46, 77, 136, 139, 187
PI: Post Impact, 32
Podhoretz, Jon, 12
Political action committees (PACs), 117, 120–121, 125, 130
Political parties, 13, 59, 90, 133–136, 138–143, 187
Political parties, decline of, 133–134
Polk, James, 172
Pop culture, presidential portrayals in, 31–38
Pre-primary campaign, 78, 80, 114, 128
Presidential machismo, 8
Priming, 103, 107
Pryce, Deborah, 125
Pryor, Mark, 130
Public financing, 113
Public/private spheres, 20, 26–27, 34, 35, 39, 45–47, 48, 61, 188–189. *See also* Separate spheres ideology
Pullman, Bill, 32

Quayle, Dan, 123

Racial barriers (to elected office), 2
Rasco, Carol, 166
Reagan, Ronald, 7, 18, 51, 56, 91, 123, 129, 156, 157, 158, 166, 171, 175, 181
Religion in politics, 50–55
Reno, Janet, 141, 156, 157
Reproductive rights, 59–61
Rice, Condoleezza, 3, 4, 9, 11, 12, 17, 21, 43, 83, 93, 108, 109, 126, 155, 156, 157, 158, 161, 170, 177, 178–180
Richards, Ann, 7
Richardson, Bill, 109
Rockefeller, John D. IV, 155

Rockefeller, Nelson, 173
Roe v. Wade (1973), 51, 59
Romney, Mitt, 109, 183
Roosevelt, Franklin D., 156, 171
Roosevelt, Theodore, 171
Ros-Lehtinen, Ileana, 125
Ross, Nellie Tayloe, 149
Rove, Karl, 102,
Royal, Segolene, 83

Santorum, Rick, 130
Santos, Matt (president on *The West Wing*), 1
Sapiro, Virginia, 71–72
Schroeder, Patricia, 124, 128, 173, 175
Schwarzenegger, Arnold, 150
Scowcroft, Brent, 179
Sebelius, Kathleen, 9
Secretaries of state, women, 154–155
Self-objectify, 31
Senior Executive Service (SES), 148, 160, 166
Separate spheres ideology, 26–27, 31, 39, 52, 92, 188–189
Sex difference, 89
Sex role, 62, 70
Shalala, Donna E., 156
Shales, Tom, 36
Sheen, Martin, 33–34, 37
Siena College Research Institute, 3, 4, 94
Single issue PACs, 120, 130
Skillman, Becky, 153
Smith, Margaret Chase, 18, 128, 173–174
Smith, Will, 32
Smits, Jimmy, 1
Snowe, Olympia, 9, 116, 117, 131
Social conservatives, 52
Societal gendering, 44–47
Soft news, 6
Southern Baptists, 50
Specter, Arlen, 130
Spellings, Margaret, 156
Spitzer, Eliot, 154
Split-party government, 150
Split-ticket voting, 134
Stabenow, Deborah, 116, 131
State agencies, women in, 161–162
State attorneys general, women, 153–154
State-level elected office, women in, 152–155
Stereotypes, gender, 70–75, 78, 81, 83, 85
Stereotypes, negative, 6, 8
Streep, Meryl, 32–33
Structural barriers to elected office, 20
Subject/object dichotomy, 28, 31
Sununu, John E., 130
Sutherland, Donald, 36
Swift Boat Veterans for Truth, 107

Tailhook scandal (1991), 25
Talent, Jim, 129
Taylor, Zachary, 171, 172
Thatcher, Margaret, 46, 79, 181
Townsend, Frances Fragos, 158
Trudeau, Gary, 80
Truman, Harry S., 171
24 (Fox TV show), 1
Tyler, John, 171, 172
Tyson, Laura D'Andrea, 166

US Capitol (building), 29
USS *Abraham Lincoln*, 23, 26

Veneman, Ann M., 156
Vietnam War, 87, 176, 178
Vilsack, Tom, 109
Vitter, David, 130
Voter turnout, 66, 124, 127

Wag the Dog, 32
Walker, Olene, 155
Warner, Mark, 109
War on terror, 4, 5, 13, 27, 44, 46, 47, 58, 81, 101, 103, 126, 169–170, 178
Washington, Denzel, 32
Weaver, Sigourney, 32
Westmoreland, Gen. William, 169, 170

The West Wing, 1, 33–35, 37
White House Project, the, 9, 61, 73, 74, 83, 85, 94, 135, 163
White House staff, women on, 157–160
Whitman, Christine Todd, 164
Widnall, Sheila, 161
Wilson, Marie C., 74
Wilson, Woodrow, 171
Women as voters, 60, 66, 88–90, 124, 127, 161, 187
Women's Foreign Policy Group, 163
Women's issues (see also male/female issues), 5, 44, 70–71, 81–82, 187
Women Under Forty Political Action Committee, 163
Woodhull, Victoria, 18, 172
Wyden, Ron, 130

"Year of the woman" (1992), 100

About the Book

From the political rumor mill to pop culture, all signs suggest that the United States is finally ready for a woman in the White House. But is the vision of an imminent Madam President truly in line with today's political reality?

Rethinking Madam President offers a critical assessment of the inroads made by female candidates into the previously male bastion of electoral success—exploring whether they actually apply to the presidency. The authors tackle a range of provocative issues: the conflation of the presidency with masculinity, particularly when it comes to security and military concerns; media coverage focusing, even today, on the novelty of a female candidate; public support for women that often evaporates in the voting booth; and more. Although Madam President is *not* an impossibility, they conclude, it would be a mistake to ignore the very significant hurdles that women still face on the path to the Oval Office.

Lori Cox Han is professor of political science at Chapman University. Her publications include *Women and American Politics* and *Governing from Center Stage*. **Caroline Heldman** is assistant professor of political science at Occidental College.